高等院校英语系列教材

英国文学选读教程

主编 ◎ 邵建宇　　副主编 ◎ 李烨辉

A Coursebook of Selected Readings in
British Literature

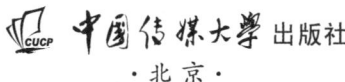
·北京·

前 言 PREFACE

本书编著者考察了当今国内众多高校英国文学课的教学计划与课程体系，以《普通高等学校本科外国语言文学类专业教学指南（上）—英语类专业教学指南》对英语专业学生的素质要求、知识要求及能力要求为依托，结合自己英国文学课二十余年的讲授经验，对本教材的体量大小、涵盖内容、衔接顺序、章节框架以及详略轻重等进行了深入的思考和缜密的设计，力求实现"作者尽心、读者友好"的目标。

本书与同类文学选读教材相较创新如下：

第一，服务教学、体量精准。教材体量、章节编排直接对标高校每学期的计划教学周次。编著者对各大高校的教学计划考察后发现，每学期除去复习周与考试周（某些高校的读书周等），实际授课周次多为16周，故本着服务教学的宗旨，章节数应设定为16章。依照英国文学的发展脉络，每章选取一位某阶段最具代表性的作家及其最经典的作品的两篇选段，供学生沉浸式阅读与全方位练习（详见创新三、四）。教师可直接按照本教材的编排顺序制定教学计划，一个教学周对应一章学习内容；教师也可根据课程的学时数（2学时/周或4学时/周）以及学生的文学基础，把握教学节奏，例如可选取每章的 Text A 作为必读、必讲、必练内容，而将 Text B 供选读、自修所用。这样，保证学生在有限的课时内，对英国文学有一个相对完整、详略得当的掌握，同时避免教材设置与教学需求脱节的状况。

第二，删繁就简、普及经典。本教材以英国文学史为经，以各时期最具代表性的名家名篇为纬，力图编织一幅美丽有序的英国文学的画卷。编著者基于二十余年的英国文学教学讲授经验，经过反复比照，在精彩纷呈的英国文学大花园中优中选优，选出自15世纪以来，16位不容错过的名家及其名篇选段，其中包括杰弗雷·乔叟（Geoffrey Chaucer）的《坎特伯雷故事集》(*The Canterbury Tales*)、埃德蒙·斯宾塞（Edmund Spenser）的《仙后》(*The Faerie Queene*)、弗朗西斯·培根（Francis Bacon）的《论学习》(*Of Studies*)、威廉·莎士比亚(William Shakespeare)的《哈姆雷特》(*Hamlet*)、约翰·弥尔顿(John Milton)的《失乐园》(*Paradise Lost*)、丹尼尔·笛福(Daniel Defoe)的《鲁滨逊漂流记》(*Robinson Crusoe*)、威廉·华兹华斯(William Wordsworth)的《我孤独地漫游,像一朵云》(*I Wandered Lonely as a Cloud*)、简·奥斯汀(Jane Austen)的《傲慢与偏见》(*Pride and Prejudice*)、珀西·比希·雪莱(Percy Bysshe Shelley)的《西风颂》(*Ode to the West Wind*)、查尔斯·狄更斯(Charles Dickens)的《大卫·科波菲尔德》(*David Copperfield*)与《雾都孤儿》(*Oliver Twist*)、夏洛蒂·勃朗特(Charlotte Brontë)的《简·爱》(*Jane Eyre*)等。这些极具代表性的选篇涵盖诗歌、散文、小说、戏剧等主要文学体裁,可以在潜移默化中帮助读者提升语言应用能力及文学素养。

第三,经典精读、全面提升。本教材各章节均包含作家生平、选篇释义、课后练习与提升推介四部分,而编著者尽心打造的课后演练部分,涵盖听、说、读、写、译等全方位的技能精炼,与市面上众多英国文学选读教材相比,优势立现。

练习一:重点词汇精练题,精选文段中的典句,引导学生根据所给近义词辨析句中高频词汇的词义,旨在帮助学生循序渐进地掌握英语专业的核心词汇,同时培养学生通过精读文本细节,联系上下文来揣摩词义的能力;

练习二:经典语句赏析题,选取本章节作家作品中最脍炙人口的警句妙语,鼓励学生进行填词、英译汉等练习,便于读者在品味至理名言中感受作家的思想精髓与语言风格;

练习三:文学名词应用题,尝试选取语篇中出现的文学手法或修辞手法,旨在以宏观视角切入文本,教师可引导学生根据选篇内容,开展研究性学习,以期为学生文学素养的提高奠定理论基础;

练习四:文本细节理解题,请学生依照问题提示再读文本,引导学生聚焦关键部分,有的放矢地在文本中寻找答案,增强学生对作者写作手法、情节设置和行文逻辑的掌握;

练习五:课堂讨论题,引导学生经由自我阅读、自我思考、小组讨论、个人展示以及团队合作等环节对选段中的情节、人物或语句发表个人见解,聆听伙伴声音,在交流共享中提升听说能力、思辨能力与交际能力;

练习六:思辨类写作,针对选段中涉及的现象,要求学生将其与自身所处的社会现实相联系,在理解文本的基础上进行相关性联想、批判性思考与开放性写作。当文学照进现实,读者对文学作品的理解会更鞭辟入里,同时也会思考文学的社会意义以及担负

前 言

的社会责任。

本教材的课后演练遵照循序渐进、深入浅出的原则，处处力求贴合作家风格与选段特色，以期达到"任课教师随讲随用，学生读者随读随练"的效果。

第四，应注尽注、各取所需。编著者严格参照专业大纲的要求，基于二十余年一线教学经验，结合文学教材的市场现状调查，秉承"读者友好"的初衷，尽量照顾大多英语专业高年级学生的语言水平及需求，做到"应注尽注、各取所需"。直接注释词汇在文中的具体含义而不赘述其他词义，尽量避免学生因生词障碍而影响阅读连贯性，防止因注释冗长而打乱学生阅读节奏，力求成为学生文学阅读的润滑剂，原著积累的助推器。

本书主要服务于高等院校英语专业高年级学生的英国文学选读等课程，故教学内容可根据课程设置（选修还是必修）、课时、教学目的以及学生基础等加以调整与取舍。本书同样适合广大英语爱好者自学之用。

由于编著者水平有限，教学章节所囿，本书难概英国文学之全貌，也必有诸多不足之处，敬请读者批评指正。

编者

2023 年 11 月

目 录 CONTENTS

Unit 1　Geoffrey Chaucer (1343–1400) ································· 001
　　Life and Works ··· 001
　　Text A　The Canterbury Tales The General Prologue (An Excerpt) ················ 002
　　Text B　The Canterbury Tales The Miller's Prologue and Tale (An Excerpt) ········ 008

Unit 2　Edmund Spenser (1552–1599) ································· 016
　　Life and Works ··· 016
　　Text A　The Faerie Queene Book I, Canto I (An Exerpt) ···················· 017
　　Text B　Amoretti ·· 020

Unit 3　Francis Bacon (1561–1626) ··································· 023
　　Life and Works ··· 023
　　Text A　Of Studies ·· 024
　　Text B　Of Marriage and Single Life ···································· 027

Unit 4　William Shakespeare (1564–1616) ···························· 030
　　Life and Works ··· 030
　　Text A　HamletAct III, Scene 1, Lines 1–102 ···························· 031
　　Text B　Sonnet 18 ··· 038

Unit 5　John Milton (1608–1674) ····································· 041
　　Life and Works ··· 041
　　Text A　Paradise LostAn Excerpt of Book 1 (1674 version) ············· 042

Text B　When I Consider How My Light Is Spent ········· 047

Unit 6　Daniel Defoe (1660–1731) ········· 050
Life and Works ········· 050
Text A　Robinson Crusoe Chapter IX　A Boat ········· 051
Text B　Robinson Crusoe An Excerpt from Chapter XIV ········· 067

Unit 7　Jonathan Swift (1667–1745) ········· 078
Life and Works ········· 078
Text A　Gulliver's Travels Part I　A Voyage to Lilliput Chapter I ········· 079
Text B　Gulliver's Travels Part Four: A Voyage to the Country of the Houyhnhnms Chapter VII ········· 089

Unit 8　William Blake (1757–1827) ········· 098
Life and Works ········· 098
Text A　London ········· 099
Text B　The Tyger ········· 101

Unit 9　William Wordsworth (1770–1850) ········· 104
Life and Works ········· 104
Text A　I Wandered Lonely as a Cloud ········· 105
Text B　The Solitary Reaper ········· 107

Unit 10　Jane Austen (1775–1817) ········· 111
Life and Works ········· 111
Text A　Pride and Prejudice Chapter I ········· 112
Text B　Sense and Sensibility Chapter I ········· 120

Unit 11　Percy Bysshe Shelley (1792–1822) ········· 126
Life and Works ········· 126
Text A　Ode to the West Wind Ⅰ ········· 127
Text B　To a Skylark ········· 133

目 录

Unit 12　John Keats (1795–1821) ·············· 139
　　Life and Works ·············· 139
　　Text A　Ode to a Nightingale ·············· 140
　　Text B　Ode on a Grecian Urn ·············· 145

Unit 13　Charles Dickens (1812–1870) ·············· 150
　　Life and Works ·············· 150
　　Text A　David Copperfield Chapter I I am Born ·············· 151
　　Text B　Oliver Twist or The Parish Boy's Progress Chapter I ·············· 163

Unit 14　Charlotte Brontë (1816–1855) ·············· 168
　　Life and Works ·············· 168
　　Text A　Jane Eyre An Autobiography Chapter I ·············· 169
　　Text B　Jane Eyre An Autobiography Chapter XXIII ·············· 177

Unit 15　Thomas Hardy (1840–1928) ·············· 189
　　Life and Works ·············· 189
　　Text A　Tess of the d'Urbervilles A Pure Woman Chapter V ·············· 190
　　Text B　Tess of the d'Urbervilles A Pure Woman Chapter LVIII ·············· 201

Unit 16　Oscar Wilde (1854–1900) ·············· 210
　　Life and Works ·············· 210
　　Text A　The Importance of Being Earnest A Trivial Comedy for Serious People Act I (Excerpts) ·············· 211
　　Text B　The Importance of Being Earnest A Trivial Comedy for Serious People Act I (Excerpt) ·············· 223

Unit 1　Geoffrey Chaucer (1343−1400)

Life and Works

Geoffrey Chaucer (1343-1400), acclaimed as the Father of English Literature, was the greatest English poet of the Middle Ages. Chaucer was the son of John Chaucer, a well-off London wine-seller and deputy to the king's butler. Chaucer was introduced to court life as page to Elisabeth de Burgh, Countess of Ulster in 1356 and three years later, he was a participant in the English military expedition to France during the Hundred Years' War. In 1366, Chaucer was married to Philipa de Roet, a lady-in-waiting to Edward III's wife and subsequently went abroad frequently on diplomatic missions, having the access to the works of Dante, Boccaccio and Petrarch. Chaucer held a range of high posts such as Justice of the Peace, Clerk of the King's Works, and Deputy Forester of the Royal Forest in his last decade. Chaucer died on October 25, 1400 and was buried in the Westminster Abbey.

Chaucer's first major poem, The Book of the Duchess, was written in 1369 to commemorate the death of Blanche of Lancaster, mother of King Henry IV. Chaucer managed to find time to complete the writing of The House of Fame, The Parliament of Fowls, and Troilus and Criseyde even after he was appointed controller of the customs house of London in 1374. Chaucer's

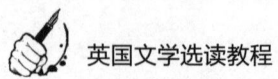

uncompleted masterpiece, The Canterbury Tales, was written between the years 1388 and 1400 with a general prologue and twenty-four tales, depicting the pilgrims from all classes of the English feudal society.

Text A

The Canterbury① Tales
The General Prologue
(An Excerpt)

When April with his showers sweet with fruit
The drought of March has pierced unto the root
And bathed each vein with liquor that has power
To generate therein and sire the flower;
When **Zephyr**② also has, with his sweet breath,
Quickened again, in every holt and heath,
The tender shoots and buds, and the young sun
Into the **Ram**③ one half his course has run,
And many little birds make melody
That sleep through all the night with open eye
(So Nature pricks them on to ramp and rage)
Then do folk long to go on pilgrimage,
And **palmers**④ to go seeking out strange strands,
To distant shrines well known in sundry lands.
And specially from every shire's end
Of England they to Canterbury wend,
The holy blessed martyrs there to seek
Who helped them when they lay so ill and weak.

Befell that, in that season, on a day

---

① **Canterbury**: England's ecclesiastical center, the site of **Canterbury** Cathedral and the Archbishop of **Canterbury**.
② **Zephyr**: the Greek god of the west wind.
③ **the Ram**: the first of twelve signs of the zodiac with the symbol of a **ram**.
④ **palmers**: persons wearing two crossed palm leaves as a sign of a pilgrimage made to the Holy Land.

Unit 1 Geoffrey Chaucer (1343–1400)

In **Southwark**①, at the Tabard, as I lay
Ready to start upon my pilgrimage
To Canterbury, full of devout homage,
There came at nightfall to that hostelry
Some nine and twenty in a company
Of sundry persons who had chanced to fall
In fellowship, and pilgrims were they all
That toward Canterbury town would ride.
The rooms and stables spacious were and wide,
And well we there were eased, and of the best.
And briefly, when the sun had gone to rest,
So had I spoken with them, every one,
That I was of their fellowship anon,
And made agreement that we'd early rise
To take the road, as you I will apprise.

But none the less, whilst I have time and space,
Before yet farther in this tale I pace,
It seems to me accordant with reason
To inform you of the state of every one
Of all of these, as it appeared to me,
And who they were, and what was their degree,
And even how arrayed there at the inn;
And with a knight thus will I first begin.

Aknight there was, and he a worthy man,
Who, from the moment that he first began
To ride about the world, loved chivalry,
Truth, honour, freedom and all courtesy.
Full worthy was he in his liege-lord's war,
And therein had he ridden (none more far)
As well in Christendom as heathenesse,
And honoured everywhere for worthiness.
At **Alexandria**②, he, when it was won;

---

① **Southwark**: borough of southern London.
② **Alexandria**: city and port between Lake Mareotis and the Mediterranean Sea in northern Egypt.

Full oft the table's roster he'd begun
Above all nations' knights in **Prussia**①.
In **Latvia**② raided he, and Russia,
No christened man so oft of his degree.
In far **Granada**③ at the siege was he
Of **Algeciras**④, and in Belmarie.
At Ayas was he and at Satalye
When they were won; and on the Middle Sea
At many a noble meeting chanced to be.
Of mortal battles he had fought fifteen,
And he'd fought for our faith at Tramissene
Three times in lists, and each time slain his foe.
This self-same worthy knight had been also
At one time with the lord of Palatye
Against another heathen in Turkey:
And always won he sovereign fame for prize.
Though so illustrious, he was very wise
And bore himself as meekly as a maid.
He never yet had any vileness said,
In all his life, to whatsoever **wight**⑤.
He was a truly perfect, gentle knight.
But now, to tell you all of his array,
His steeds were good, but yet he was not gay.
Of simple fustian wore he a **jupon**⑥

Sadly discoloured by his **habergeon**⑦;
For he had lately come from his voyage
And now was going on this pilgrimage.
  （Modern Version）

Whan that April with his shoures soote

---

① **Prussia**: historical region of northern Germany bordering on the Baltic Sea.
② **Latvia**: independent country in north central Europe bordering on the Baltic Sea and indented by the Gulf of Riga.
③ **Granada**: medieval Moorish kingdom of southern Spain.
④ **Algeciras**: city and port on the Bay of **Algeciras** west of Gibraltar in southwestern Spain.
⑤ **wight**: a living being.
⑥ **jupon**: a tight-fitting garment like a shirt often padded and quilted and worn under medieval armor.
⑦ **Habergeon**: a medieval jacket of mail shorter than a hauberk.

Unit 1　Geoffrey Chaucer (1343–1400)

The droghte of March hath perced to the roote,
And bathed every veyne in swich licour
Of which vertu engendred is the flour,
Whan Zephirus eek with his sweete breeth
Inspired hath in every holt and heeth
The tendre croppes, and the yonge sonne
Hath in the Ram his halve cours yronne,
And smale foweles maken melodye,
That slepen al the nyght with open ye
(so priketh hem Nature in hir corages),
Thanne longen folk to goon on pilgrimages,
And palmeres for to seken straunge strondes,
To ferne halwes, kowthe in sondry londes;
And specially from every shires ende
Of Engelond to Caunterbury they wende,
The hooly blisful martir for to seke,
That hem hath holpen whan that they were seeke.

Bifil that in that seson on a day,
In Southwerk at the Tabard as I lay
Redy to wenden on my pilgrymage
To Caunterbury with ful devout corage,
At nyght was come into that hostelrye
Wel nyne and twenty in a compaignye,
Of sondry folk, by aventure yfalle
In felaweshipe, and pilgrimes were they alle,
That toward Caunterbury wolden ryde.
The chambres and the stables weren wyde,
And wel we weren esed atte beste.
And shortly, whan the sonne was to reste,
So hadde I spoken with hem everichon
That I was of hir felaweshipe anon,
And made forward erly for to ryse,
To take oure wey ther as I yow devyse.

But nathelees, whil I have tyme and space,
Er that I ferther in this tale pace,

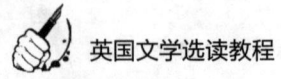

Me thynketh it acordaunt to resoun
To telle yow al the condicioun
Of ech of hem, so as it semed me,
And whiche they weren, and of what degree,
And eek in what array that they were inne;
And at a knyght than wol I first bigynne.

Aknyght ther was, and that a worthy man,
That fro the tyme that he first bigan
To riden out, he loved chivalrie,
Trouthe and honour, fredom and curteisie.
Ful worthy was he in his lordes werre,
And therto hadde he riden, no man ferre,
As wel in cristendom as in hethenesse,
And evere honoured for his worthyness.
At Alisaundre he was whan it was wonne.
Ful ofte tyme he hadde the bord bigonne
Aboven alle nacions in Pruce;
In Lettow hadde he reysed and in Ruce,
No cristen man so ofte of his degree.
In Gernade at the seege eek hadde he be
Of Algezir, and riden in Belmarye.
At Lyeys was he and at Satalye,
Whan they were wonne; and in the Grete See
At many a noble armee hadde he be.
At mortal batailles hadde he been fiftene,
And foughten for oure feith at Tramyssene
In lystes thries, and ay slayn his foo.
This ilke worthy knyght hadde been also
Somtyme with the lord of Palatye
Agayn another hethen in Turkye.
And everemoore he hadde a sovereyn prys;
And though that he were worthy, he was wys,
And of his port as meeke as is a mayde.
He nevere yet no vileynye ne sayde
In al his lyf unto no maner wight.
He was a verray, parfit gentil knyght.

But, for to tellen yow of his array,

His hors were goode, but he was nat gay.

Of fustian he wered a gypon

Al bismotered with his habergeon,

For he was late ycome from his viage,

And wente for to doon his pilgrymage.

(Chaucer's Version)

Exercise

I. Word Matching

Directions: Please choose the most appropriate ones from the given words to explain the original boldfaced words in the following lines.

A. **blockade**   B. **various**   C. **evil**   D. **pious**   E. **eminent**

1. In far Granada at the **siege** was he

Of Algeciras, and in Belmarie.

2. Though so **illustrious**, he was very wise

And bore himself as meekly as a maid.

3. To distant shrines well known in **sundry** lands.

4. To Canterbury, full of **devout** homage,

There came at nightfall to that hostelry.

5. He never yet had any **vileness** said,

In all his life, to whatsoever wight.

II. Blank Filling

Directions: Please fill in the following blanks with words or expressions that best express the contextual meaning of the classic dicta.

1. When April with his _____ sweet with fruit

The drought of March has pierced unto the root

And bathed each _____ with liquor that has power

To generate therein and sire the flower.

　　　　　　　　　　　　　　　　　　—*The Canterbury Tales*

2. The fields have eyes, and the woods have _____.

　　　　　　　　　　　　　　　　　　—*The Canterbury Tales*

3. And she was _____ as is the rose in May.

　　　　　　　　　　　　　　　　　　—*The Legend of Good Women*

4. Many a _____ word is spoken in jest.

　　　　　　　　　　　　　　　　　　—*The Canterbury Tales*

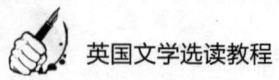

5. The guilty think all talk is of _____ .

—*The Canterbury Tales*

III. Term Defining

Directions: *Please explain the following literary terms based on The Canterbury Tales.*

1. frame narrative
2. prologue
3. pilgrimage

IV. Content-Based Questions

Directions: *Please give a concise and adequate answer to the following questions.*

1. What season is described in the opening passage of *The Canterbury Tales*?
2. Why did everyone go on a pilgrimage to Canterbury?
3. What company did I chance to meet at the Tabard Inn that night?
4. What agreement did they make when the sun had gone to rest?
5. What aspects of each member of the company did I seem to inform the readers of?

V. Discussion Question

Directions: *Please discuss the following question in pairs or groups.*

Please discuss the tales with your partner(s) and conceive compelling reasons for a certain palmer of the company to go on the shrine.

VI. Essay Question

The Canterbury Tales impresses its readers with its diversity of the palmers. Please write a 200-word essay to illustrate the reasons why they manage to find the common ground in spite of their actual differences.

Text B

The Canterbury Tales
The Miller's Prologue and Tale
(An Excerpt)

Here follow the words between the Host and the Miller

When the Knight had thus told his tale,
In all the company there was no one young nor old
Who did not say it was a noble story

Unit 1　Geoffrey Chaucer (1343–1400)

And worthy to draw into memory,
And especially the gentlefolk every one.
Our Host laughed and swore, As I may move about (I swear),
This goes well; the bag is opened.
Let's see now who shall tell another tale;
For truly the game is well begun.
Now tell you, sir Monk, if you can,
Something to equal the Knight's tale.
The Miller, who for drunkenness was all pale,
So that he hardly sat upon his horse,
He would not **doff**① neither hood nor hat,
Nor give preference to any man out of courtesy,
But in **Pilate**②'s voice he began to cry,
And swore, By (Christ's) arms, and by blood and bones,
I know a noble tale for this occasion,
With which I will now requite the Knight's tale.
Our Host saw that he was drunk on ale,
And said, Wait, Robin, my dear brother;
Some better man shall first tell us another.
Wait, and let us act properly.
By God's soul, said he, that will not I;
For I will speak or else go my way.
Our Host answered, Tell on, in the devil's name!
Thou art a fool; thy wit is overcome.
Now listen, said the Miller, everyone!
But first I make a protestation
That I am drunk; I know it by my sound.
And therefore if that I misspeak or say (amiss),
Blame it on ale of Southwerk, I you pray.
For I will tell a legend and a life
Both of a carpenter and of his wife,
How a clerk has set the carpenter's cap (fooled him).

Here begins The Miller's Tale.

---

① **doff**: take off (the hat) in greeting or as a sign of respect.
② **Pilate**: Pontius, Roman procurator of Judea (c. 26–c. 36), who is remembered for presiding at the trial of Jesus Christ and authorizing his crucifixion.

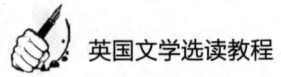

There was once dwelling at Oxford
A rich churl, who took in boarders,
And of his craft he was a carpenter.
With him there was dwelling a poor scholar,
Who had learned the arts curriculum, but all his desire
Was turned to learning astrology,
And he knew a certain (number of) of astronomical operations,
To determine by scientific calculations,
If men asked him, in specific (astronomical) hours
When men should have drought or else showers,

Or if people asked him what should happen
Concerning every thing; I can not reckon them all.

This clerk was called clever Nicholas.
Of secret love he knew and of its satisfaction;
And moreover he was sly and very discreet,
And like a maiden meek in appearance.
A room had he in that hostelry
Alone, without any company,
Very elegantly strewn with sweet-smelling herbs;
And he himself as sweet as is the root
Of **licorice**① or any zedoary (a ginger-like herb).
His **Almagest**②, and books large and small,
His **astrolabe**③, belonging to his art (of astronomy),
His counting stones (for his abacus) lie neatly apart,
Arranged on shelves at his bed's head;
His linen press covered with a red woolen cloth;
And all above there lay a fine **psaltery**④,
On which at night he made melody
So sweetly that all the room rang;

---

① **licorice**: the dried root of a European leguminous plant.
② **Almagest**: any of several early medieval treatises on a branch of knowledge.
③ **astrolabe**: a compact instrument used to observe and calculate the position of celestial bodies before the invention of the sextant.
④ **psaltery**: an ancient musical instrument resembling the zither.

Unit 1 Geoffrey Chaucer (1343-1400)

And The Angel to the Virgin he sang;
And after that he sang the King's Tune.
Very often his merry throat was blessed.
And thus this sweet clerk spent his time
Living on his friends' support and his (own) income.

This carpenter had recently wedded a wife,
Whom he loved more than his life;
She was eighteen years of age.
Jealous he was, and held her narrowly in confinement,
For she was wild and young, and he was old
And believed himself likely to be a cuckold.
He knew not **Cato**[①], for his wit was rude,
Who advised that man should wed his equal.
Men should wed according to their status in life,
For youth and old age are often in conflict.
But since he was fallen in the snare,
He must endure, like other folk, his troubles.

    (Modern Version)

Heere folwen the wordes betwene the Hoost and the Millere

Whan that the Knyght had thus his tale ytoold,
In al the route nas ther yong ne oold
That he ne seyde it was a noble storie
And worthy for to drawen to memorie,
And namely the gentils everichon.
Oure Hooste lough and swoor, So moot I gon,

This gooth aright; unbokeled is the male.
Lat se now who shal telle another tale;
For trewely the game is wel bigonne.
Now telleth ye, sir Monk, if that ye konne,
Somwhat to quite with the Knyghtes tale.
The Millere, that for dronken was al pale,

---

① **Cato**: Marcus Porcius **Cato**, **Cato** The Censor, or **Cato** The Elder; (234-149 b.c.); Roman statesman and orator.

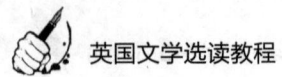

So that unnethe upon his hors he sat,
He nolde avalen neither hood ne hat,
Ne abyde no man for his curteisie,
But in Pilates voys he gan to crie,
And swoor, By armes, and by blood and bones,

I kan a noble tale for the nones,
With which I wol now quite the Knyghtes tale.
Oure Hooste saugh that he was dronke of ale,
And seyde, Abyd, Robyn, my leeve brother;
Som bettre man shal telle us first another.
Abyd, and lat us werken thriftily.
By Goddes soule, quod he, that wol nat I;
For I wol speke or elles go my wey.
Oure Hoost answerde, Tel on, a devel wey!
Thou art a fool; thy wit is overcome.
Now herkneth, quod the Millere, alle and some!
But first I make a protestacioun
That I am dronke; I knowe it by my soun.
And therfore if that I mysspeke or seye,
Wyte it the ale of Southwerk, I you preye.
For I wol telle a legende and a lyf
Bothe of a carpenter and of his wyf,
How that a clerk hath set the wrightes cappe.

Heere bigynneth the Millere his tale.

Whilom ther was dwellynge at Oxenford
A riche gnof, that gestes heeld to bord,
And of his craft he was a carpenter.
With hym ther was dwellynge a poure scoler,
Hadde lerned art, but al his fantasye

Was turned for to lerne astrologye,
And koude a certeyn of conclusiouns,

To demen by interrogaciouns,

Unit 1　Geoffrey Chaucer (1343–1400)

If that men asked hym, in certein houres
Whan that men sholde have droghte or elles shoures,
Or if men asked hym what sholde bifalle
Of every thyng; I may nat rekene hem alle.

This clerk was cleped hende Nicholas.
Of deerne love he koude and of solas;
And therto he was sleigh and ful privee,
And lyk a mayden meke for to see.
A chambre hadde he in that hostelrye
Allone, withouten any compaignye,
Ful fetisly ydight with herbes swoote;
And he hymself as sweete as is the roote
Of lycorys or any cetewale.
His Almageste, and bookes grete and smale,
His astrelabie, longynge for his art,

His augrym stones layen faire apart,
On shelves couched at his beddes heed;
His presse ycovered with a faldyng reed;
And al above ther lay a gay sautrie,
On which he made a-nyghtes melodie
So swetely that all the chambre rong;
And Angelus ad virginem he song;
And after that he song the Kynges Noote.
Ful often blessed was his myrie throte.
And thus this sweete clerk his tyme spente
After his freendes fyndyng and his rente.

This carpenter hadde wedded newe a wyf,
Which that he lovede more than his lyf;
Of eighteteene yeer she was of age.
Jalous he was, and heeld hire narwe in cage,

For she was wylde and yong, and he was old
And demed hymself been lik a cokewold.
He knew nat Catoun, for his wit was rude,

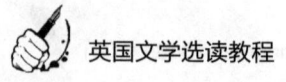

>   That bad man sholde wedde his simylitude.
>   Men sholde wedden after hire estaat,
>   For youthe and elde is often at debaat.
>   But sith that he was fallen in the snare,
>   He moste endure, as oother folk, his care.
>   (Chaucer's Version)

Exercise

I. Word Matching

Directions: Please choose the most appropriate ones from the given words to explain the original boldfaced words in the following lines.

A. **clever**　　B. **boor**　　C. **custody**　　D. **declaration**　　E. **return**

1. I know a noble tale for this occasion,
   With which I will now **requite** the Knight's tale.
2. But first I make a **protestation**
   That I am drunk; I know it by my sound.
3. There was once dwelling at Oxford
   A rich **churl**, who took in boarders.
4. And moreover he was **sly** and very discreet,
   And like a maiden meek in appearance.
5. She was eighteen years of age.
   Jealous he was, and held her narrowly in **confinement**.

II. Blank Filling

Directions: Please fill in the following blanks with words or expressions that best express the contextual meaning of the classic dicta.

1. Men should wed according to their status in life,
   For youth and old age are often in _____.

   　　　　　　　　　　　　　　　　　—*The Canterbury Tales*

2. There's no workman, whatsoever he be, That may both work well and _____.

   　　　　　　　　　　　　　　　　　—*The Canterbury Tales*

3. The _____ so short, the craft so long to lerne.

   　　　　　　　　　　　　　　　　　—*The Parliament of Fowls*

4. People can _____ of mere imagination.

   　　　　　　　　　　　　　　　　　—*The Canterbury Tales*

5. He who accepts his _____ unhurt I'd say is rich although he lacked a shirt. But truly poor are they who whine and fret and covet what they cannot hope to get.

—*The Canterbury Tales*

III. Term-Defining

Directions: Please explain the following literary terms based on The Canterbury Tales.

1. fabliau
2. alliteration
3. fable

IV. Content-Based Questions

Directions: Please give a concise and adequate answer to the following questions.

1. How did all the company evaluate the tale told by the knight?
2. Whom did the host intend to invite to tell another tale?
3. For what reason would the miller requite the Knight's tale according to I?
4. Whose legend and life was the miller inclined to tell?

V. Discussion Questions

Directions: Please discuss the following questions in pairs or in groups.

Please discuss with your partner(s) based on the miller's prologue and his tale whether the noble tale told by the miller was the life of a saint. Why or why not?

VI. Essay Questions

Women play the roles of narrators or characters of almost all the tales in *The Canterbury Tales*. Please write a 200-word essay on the real treatment of women in the age of Chaucer after your close reading of women's representation in them.

Self-Improving Reading

The Knight's Tale in *The Canterbury Tales* by Geoffrey Chaucer

The Wife of Bath's Tale in *The Canterbury Tales* by Geoffrey Chaucer

Unit 2　Edmund Spenser (1552–1599)

Life and Works

Edmund Spenser, the Poet's Poet, was born into a London family probably related with the Lancashire branch of the old family of Le Despensers in 1552. Spenser was first educated in the Merchant Taylors' grammar school, where he had the privilege to meet his headmaster, Richard Mulcaster, who had a reputation for his humanist ideals and enlightened views on education. At the age of seventeen, Spenser entered the University of Cambridge as a sizar, where he studied the Greek and Latin classics, the philosophy of Plato and Aristotle, the Virgil's pastoral poetry and the Italian epics, and received his M.A. degree with twists and turns in 1576. Spenser was sent to Ireland, serving under Lord Grey with Walter Raleigh during the Elizabethan reconquest of the country and resided there for almost his following years. He was driven from his home by Irish rebels during the Nine Years War in 1598 and died a year later, interred in Westminster Abbey adjacent to Geoffrey Chaucer.

Spenser's *The Shepheardes Calender*, a collection of eclogues, was published in 1595, which, consisting of twelve pastoral poems, was dedicated to Sir Philip Sidney. In the same year, Spenser published his best sonnet sequence, *Amoretti* to commemorate the wooing of his second wife, Elizabeth Boyle. Spenser's long allegorical poem, *The Faerie Queene*, one of the

Unit 2 Edmund Spenser (1552–1599)

greatest in the English language was written in the Spenserian stanza in the 1590s, but he only managed over half of his planned twelve books, with each one specifying a specific Christian virtue in its main figure, before his death in 1599.

Text A

The Faerie Queene
Book I, Canto I
(An Exerpt)

A Gentle Knight was pricking on the plaine,
Ycladd in mightie armes and silver shielde,
Wherein old dints of deepe wounds did remaine,
The cruell markes of many a bloudy fielde;
Yet armes till that time did he never wield:
His angry steede did chide his foming bitt,
As much disdayning to the curbe to yield:
Full jolly knight he seemd, and faire did sitt,
As one for knightly **giusts**[①] and fierce encounters fitt.

But on his brest a bloudie Crosse he bore,
The deare remembrance of his dying Lord,
For whose sweete sake that glorious badge he wore,
And dead as living ever him ador'd:
Upon his shield the like was also scor'd,
For soveraine hope, which in his helpe he had:
Right faithfull true he was in deede and word,
But of his cheere did seeme too solemne sad;
Yet nothing did he dread, but ever was ydrad.

Upon a great adventure he was bond,
That greatest Gloriana to him gave,
That greatest Glorious Queene of Faerie lond,

---

① **Giust**: archaic variant of joust (fight on horseback as a knight or man-at-arms).

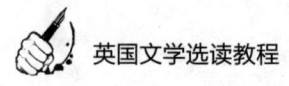

To winne him worship, and her grace to have,
Which of all earthly things he most did crave;
And ever as he rode, his hart did earne
To prove his **puissance**① in battell brave
Upon his foe, and his new force to learne;
Upon his foe, a Dragon horrible and stearne.

A lovely Ladie rode him faire beside,
Upon a lowly Asse more white then snow,
Yet she much whiter, but the same did hide
Under a vele, that wimpled was full low,
And over all a blacke **stole**② she did throw,
As one that inly mournd: so was she sad,
And heavie sat upon her **palfrey**③ slow;
Seemed in heart some hidden care she had,
And by her in a line a milke white lambe she lad.

 Exercise

I. Word Matching

Directions: Please choose the most appropriate ones from the given words to explain the original boldfaced words in the following lines.

A. **cover**   B. **scorn**   C. **insignia**   D. **desire**   E. **carry**

1. His angry steede did chide his foming bitt,
   As much **disdayn**ing to the curbe to yield
2. For whose sweete sake that glorious **badge** he wore.
3. To winne him worship, and her grace to have,
   Which of all earthly things he most did **crave**.
4. Under a vele, that **wimpled** was full low,
   And over all a blacke stole she did throw.
5. The cruell markes of many a bloudy fielde;
   Yet armes till that time did he never **wield**.

II. Blank Filling

Directions: Please fill in the following blanks with words or expressions that best express the contextual meaning of the classic dicta.

---

① **Puissance**: strength or power.
② **stole**: a long wide scarf or similar covering worn by women usually across the shoulders.
③ **palfrey**: (archaic) a saddle horse other than a warhorse.

1. A Gentle _____ was pricking on the plaine,
   Ycladd in mightie armes and silver shielde,
   Wherein old dints of deepe wounds did remaine,
   The cruell markes of many a bloudy fielde.

   —The Faerie Queene

2. One day I wrote her _____ upon the strand, But came the waves and washèd it away: Again I wrote it with a second hand, But came the tide and mademy pains his prey.

   —The Faerie Queene

3. For since mine eyes your joyous sight did miss, my cheerful day is turned to cheerless _____ .

   —The Faerie Queene

4. Fresh spring the herald of love's mighty _____ .

   —Amoretti

5. All _____ doth frailty breed!

   —Poetical Works

III. Term Defining

Directions: *Please explain the following literary terms based on The Faerie Queene.*

1. Spenserian stanza
2. Alexandrine
3. canto

IV. Content-Based Questions

Directions: *Please give a concise and adequate answer to the following questions.*

1. What specific tasks did the Faerie Queene assign to the gentle knight?
2. What does the Faerie Queene represent in the verse?
3. Who was riding beside the knight on the whole adventure?
4. What other figures were there in the same scene and what did they represent respectively?

V. Discussion Question

Directions: *Please discuss the following question in pairs or groups.*

Please discuss this canto of *The Faerie Queene* with your partner(s) and recount the exact scene unfolded before the readers' eyes, which involved the figures in the above Content-Based Questions.

VI. Essay Question

The true worth of a race must be measured by the character of its womanhood. Please write a 200-word essay on the view of women depicted in the adventures of Edmund Spenser's *The Faerie Queene*.

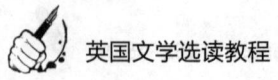

Text B

Amoretti

Sonnet 34

Like as a ship, that through the ocean wide,
By conduct of some star, doth make her way,
When as a storm hath dimmed her trusty guide,
Out of her course doth wander far astray:
So I, whose star, that **wont**① with her bright ray
Me to direct, with clouds is overcast,
Do wander now, in darkness and dismay,
Through hidden perils round about me placed;
Yet hope I well that, when this storm is past,
My **Helice**②, the **loadstar**③ of my life,
Will shine again, and look on me at last,
With lovely light to clear my cloudy grief.
Till then I wander careful, comfortless,
In secret sorrow, and sad pensiveness.

Sonnet 75

One day I wrote her name upon the strand,
But came the waves and washed it away:
Again I wrote it with a second hand,
But came the tide, and made my pains his prey.
'Vain man,' said she, 'that dost in vain assay,
A mortal thing so to immortalize;
For I myself shall like to this decay,
And **eke**④ my name be wiped out likewise.'
'Not so,' (quod I); 'let baser things devise
To die in dust, but you shall live by fame:
My verse your vertues rare shall eternize,

---

① **wont**: accustomed, used.
② **Helice**: the Big Dipper.
③ **loadstar**: (archaic) a star that leads or guides; the North Star.
④ **eke**: (archaic) also.

Unit 2 Edmund Spenser (1552–1599)

And in the heavens write your glorious name:
Where whenas death shall all the world subdue,
Our love shall live, and later life renew.'

Exercise

I. Word Matching

Directions: Please choose the most appropriate ones from the given words to explain the original boldfaced words in the following lines.

A. **risk**　　　　B. **immortalize**　　　　C. **darken**　　　　D. **shore**

1. Like as a ship, that through the ocean wide,
   By conduct of some star, doth make her way,
   Whenas a storm hath **dim**med her trusty guide,
   Out of her course doth wander far astray.
2. Do wander now, in darkness and dismay,
   Through hidden **peril**s round about me placed.
3. One day I wrote her name upon the **strand**.
4. My verse your vertues rare shall **eternize**.

II. Blank Filling

Directions: Please fill in the following blanks with words or expressions that best express the contextual meaning of the classic dicta.

1. Man's wretched state, That floures so fresh at morne, and fades at _____ late.
   　　　　　　　　　　　　　　　　　　　　　　　—*The Works of Edmund Spense*
2. Gold all is _____ that doth golden seem.
   　　　　　　　　　　　　　　　　　　　　　　　—*The Faerie Queene*
3. Each goodly thing is hardest to _____ .
   　　　　　　　　　　　　　　　　　　　　—*The Works of the British Poets*
4. How many perils doe enfold The righteous man to make him daily _____ .
   　　　　　　　　　　　　　　　　　　　　　　　—*The Works of Edmund Spenser*
5. One day you will ask me which is more important? My life or yours? I will say mine and you will walk away not knowing that you are my _____ .
   　　　　　　　　　　　　　　　　　　　　　　　　　　　　　—*Khalil Gibran*

III. Term Defining

Directions: Please explain the following literary terms based on Amoretti.

1. sonnet
2. Spenserian sonnet
3. personification

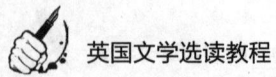

IV. Content-Based Questions

Directions: *Please give a concise and adequate answer to the following questions.*

1. What does the speaker compare himself to in Sonnet 34?
2. What happened to the star that used to direct me with her bright ray in Sonnet 34?
3. Whose name did I write upon the strand again and again in Sonnet 75?

V. Discussion Question

Directions: *Please discuss the following question in pairs or groups.*

Please discuss Sonnets 34 and 75 with your partner(s) and generalize the respective conclusions of the speaker's ways of expressing love to the beloved in the two poems.

VI. Essay Question

I want the deepest, darkest, sickest parts of you that you are afraid to share with anyone because I love you that much. There are endless and characteristic ways of expressing love. Please work out a micro-writing of your inner voice to your beloved.

Self-Improving Reading

The Shepheardes Calendar by Edmund Spenser

Sonnet 1 in *Amoretti* by Edmund Spenser

Unit 3　Francis Bacon (1561–1626)

Life and Works

　　Francis Bacon, a universal genius, was born in London on January 22, 1561, the son of Sir Nicolas Bacon, Lord Keeper of the Seal and Lady Anne Cooke Bacon, the sister-in-law of Lord Burghley. Bacon began his two-year study at Trinity College, Cambridge at the age of 12 and entered the Honorable Society of Gray's Inn to study law in 1576. Bacon had been straining every nerve to work his way up the legal and political positions, appointed solicitor general in 1607, attorney general in 1613, Lord Keeper of the Seal four years later and finally Lord Chancellor in 1618. Bacon was impeached by the Parliament somehow due to corruption and was fined 40,000 pounds and sentenced to the Tower of London in 1621, but was released after an imprisonment for four days. Bacon died of pneumonia after performing a series of experiments with ice on April 9, 1626.

　　Francis Bacon, generally credited as the father of scientific method and the father of modern essays, made consequential contributions in a variety of fields. He illustrated the nature of science and the significance of generating inductive hypotheses out of the masses of data gathered from observation and experimentation with works such as *The Advancement of*

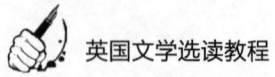

Learning in 1603 *and Novum Organum* in 1620. Bacon's *Essays*, the precious gem of English prose, mainly reflected human characters, nature and intentions, covering many household topics such as truth, love, beauty, friendship, marriage, religion, education, health and death, and including over 50 essays beginning with Of in the titles such as *Of Studies*, *Of Truth*, *Of Marriage and Single Life* and *Of Discourse*.

Text A

Of Studies

  Studies serve for delight, for ornament, and for ability. Their chief use for delight, is in privateness and retiring; for ornament, is in discourse; and for ability, is in the judgment, and disposition of business. For expert men can execute, and perhaps judge of particulars, one by one; but the general **counsels**①, and the plots and **marshalling**② of affairs, come best, from those that are learned. To spend too much time in studies is sloth; to use them too much for ornament, is affectation; to make judgment wholly by their rules, is the humor of a scholar. They perfect nature, and are perfected by experience: for natural abilities are like natural plants, that need **proyning**③ by study; and studies themselves, do give forth directions too much at large, except they be bounded in by experience. Crafty men contemn studies, simple men admire them, and wise men use them; for they teach not their own use; but that is a wisdom without them, and above them, won by observation. Read not to contradict and **confute**④; nor to believe and take for granted; nor to find talk and discourse; but to weigh and consider. Some books are to be tasted, others to be swallowed, and some few to be chewed and digested; that is, some books are to be read only in parts; others to be read, but not curiously; and some few to be read wholly, and with diligence and attention. Some books also may be read by deputy, and extracts made of them by others; but that would be only in the less important arguments, and the meaner sort of books, else distilled books are like common distilled waters, flashy things. Reading maketh a full man; conference a ready man; and writing an exact man. And therefore, if a man write little, he had need have a great memory; if he confer little, he had need have a present wit: and if he read little, he had need have much cunning, to seem to know, that he

---

① **counsels**: advice, especially given by older people or experts.
② **marshaling**: bringing together and ordering in an appropriate or effective way.
③ **proyning**: pruning; cutting off or cutting back parts of for better shape or more fruitful growth.
④ **confute**: overwhelm in argument.

doth not. Histories make men wise; poets witty; the mathematics **subtile**①; natural philosophy deep; moral grave; logic and rhetoric able to contend. **Abeunt studia in mores**②. Nay, there is no **stond**③ or impediment in the wit, but may be wrought out by fit studies; like as diseases of the body, may have appropriate exercises. Bowling is good for the stone and reins; shooting for the lungs and breast; gentle walking for the stomach; riding for the head; and the like. So if a man's wit be wandering, let him study the mathematics; for in demonstrations, if his wit be called away never so little, he must begin again. If his wit be not apt to distinguish or find differences, let him study the schoolmen; for they are cymini **sectores**④. If he be not apt to beat over matters, and to call up one thing to prove and illustrate another, let him study the lawyers' cases. So every defect of the mind may have a special receipt.

Exercise

I. Word Matching

Directions: Please choose the most appropriate ones from the given words to explain the original boldfaced words in the following sentences.

A. **idleness**   B. **likely**   C. **industry**   D. **desire**   E. **oppose**

1. Their chief use for delight, is in privateness and retiring; for ornament, is in discourse; and for ability, is in the judgment, and **disposition** of business.

2. To spend too much time in studies is **sloth**.

3. Read not to contradict and **confute**.

4. Some books are to be read only in parts; others to be read, but not curiously; and some few to be read wholly, and with **diligence** and attention.

5. If his wit be not **apt** to distinguish or find differences, let him study the schoolmen.

II. Blank Filling

Directions: Please fill in the following blanks with words or expressions that best express the contextual meaning of the classic dicta.

1. Studies serve for delight, for _____ , and for ability.

—*Essays*

2. Some books are to be tasted, others to be swallowed, and some few to be chewed and _____ .

—*Essays*

---

① **subtile**: (archaic) **subtle**.
② **Abeunt studia in mores**: (Latin) studies pass on into character.
③ **stond**: dialectal English variant of stand; a halt for defense or resistance.
④ **cymini sectores**: (Latin) literally, a carver of cumin seed; splitters of hairs; one that makes excessively fine distinctions in reasoning.

3. Reading maketh a full man, conference a ready man, and writing an _____ man.

—*Essays*

4. It is a miserable state of mind to have few things to desire, and many things to _____.

—*Essays*

5. Children sweeten labours, but they make misfortunes more _____.

—*Essays*

III. Term Defining

Directions: *Please explain the following literary terms based on Of Studies.*

1. aphorism
2. allusion
3. hypothesis

IV. Content-Based Questions

Directions: *Please give a concise and adequate answer to the following questions related to Text A.*

1. How many uses of studies does Francis Bacon enumerate in this essay? Please name and interpret them in your characteristic way.

2. Who are experts in marshalling of affairs in Bacon's mind? Why?

3. What are the limitations of studies mentioned in the text?

V. Discussion Question

Directions: *Please discuss the following question in pairs or groups.*

Please discuss this concept that Histories make men wise; poets witty; the mathematics subtile; natural philosophy deep; moral grave; logic and rhetoric able to contend with your partner(s) and choose your favorite one from the above disciplines and give an account of its subtle influence on the formation of your character.

VI. Essay Question

Some books are to be tasted, others to be swallowed, and some few to be chewed and digested. Please write a 200-word essay to introduce your corresponding methods of reading different types of books.

Unit 3 Francis Bacon (1561-1626)

Text B

Of Marriage and Single Life

He that hath wife and children hath given hostages to fortune; for they are impediments to great enterprises, either of virtue or mischief. Certainly the best works, and of greatest merit for the public, have proceeded from the unmarried or childless men; which both in affection and means, have married and endowed the public. Yet it were great reason that those that have children, should have greatest care of future times; unto which they know they must transmit their dearest pledges. Some there are, who though they lead a single life, yet their thoughts do end with themselves, and account future times impertinences. Nay, there are some other, that account wife and children, but as bills of charges. Nay more, there are some foolish rich covetous men, that take a pride, in having no children, because they may be thought so much the richer. For perhaps they have heard some talk, Such an one is a great rich man, and another except to it, Yea, but he hath a great charge of children; as if it were an abatement to his riches. But the most ordinary cause of a single life, is liberty, especially in certain self-pleasing and humorous minds, which are so sensible of every restraint, as they will go near to think their **girdles**① and **garters**②, to be bonds and shackles. Unmarried men are best friends, best masters, best servants; but not always best subjects; for they are light to run away; and almost all fugitives, are of that condition. A single life doth well with churchmen; for charity will hardly water the ground, where it must first fill a pool. It is indifferent for judges and magistrates; for if they be facile and corrupt, you shall have a servant, five times worse than a wife. For soldiers, I find the generals commonly in their **hortatives**③, put men in mind of their wives and children; and I think the despising of marriage amongst the Turks, maketh the vulgar soldier more base. Certainly wife and children are a kind of discipline of humanity; and single men, though they may be many times more charitable, because their means are less exhaust, yet, on the other side, they are more cruel and hardhearted (good to make severe inquisitors), because their tenderness is not so oft called upon. Grave natures, led by custom, and therefore constant, are commonly loving husbands, as was said of Ulysses, **vetulam suam praetulit immortalitati**④. Chaste women are often proud and **froward**⑤, as presuming upon the merit of their chastity. It

---

① **girdles**: a woman's close-fitting undergarments often boned and usually elasticized that extends from the waist to below the hips
② **garters**: straps hanging from a girdle or corset to support a stocking
③ **hortatives**: strong encouragement.
④ **vetulam suam praetulit immortalitati**: (Latin) he preferred his old wife to immortality.
⑤ **forward**: habitually disposed to disobedience and opposition.

is one of the best bonds, both of chastity and obedience, in the wife, if she think her husband wise; which she will never do, if she find him jealous. Wives are young men's mistresses; companions for middle age; and old men's nurses. So as a man may have a quarrel to marry, when he will. But yet he was reputed one of the wise men, that made answer to the question, when a man should marry: A young man not yet, an elder man not at all. It is often seen that bad husbands, have very good wives; whether it be, that it raiseth the price of their husband's kindness, when it comes; or that the wives take a pride in their patience. But this never fails, if the bad husbands were of their own choosing, against their friends' consent; for then they will be sure to make good their own folly.

Exercise

I. Word Matching

Directions: Please choose the most appropriate ones from the given words to explain the original boldfaced words in the following sentences.

A. **greedy**   B. **silliness**   C. **hinderance**   D. **runaway**

1. He that hath wife and children hath given hostages to fortune; for they are **impediment**s to great **enterprise**s, either of virtue or mischief.

2. There are some foolish rich **covetous** men, that take a pride, in having no children, because they may be thought so much the richer.

3. They are light to run away; and almost all **fugitive**s, are of that condition.

4. If the bad husbands were of their own choosing, against their friends' consent; for then they will be sure to make good their own **folly**.

II. Blank Filling

Directions: Please fill in the following blanks with words or expressions that best express the contextual meaning of the classic dicta.

1. All colours will agree in the _____ .

—*Essays*

2. A wise man will _____ more opportunities than he finds.

—*Essays*

3. Wives are young men's mistresses, companions for _____ age, and old men's nurses.

—*Essays*

4. Unmarried men are best friends, best masters, best servants; but _____ always best subjects.

—*Essays*

5. A man that studieth revenge keeps his own wounds _____ .

—*Essays*

III. Term Defining

Directions: *Please explain the following literary terms based on Of Marriage and Single Life.*

1. argumentation
2. comparison
3. deduction

IV. Content-Based Questions

Directions: *Please give a concise and adequate answer to the following questions related to Text B.*

1. Why does Bacon argue that the unmarried or childless men will do the best work?
2. Why are there some greedy men that take pride in having no children?
3. What major cause of remaining single is given in the account?
4. What are the attributes of the best wife in Bacon's essay?

V. Discussion Question

Directions: *Please discuss the following question in pairs or groups.*

Please discuss the views of the author with your partner(s) and divide your neighboring members into two teams to debate the advantages and disadvantages of being married or unmarried.

VI. Essay Question

"Wives are young men's mistresses; companions for middle age; and old men's nurses." Please write a 200-word essay on the ideal relationship between husband and wife in your mind.

Self-Improving Reading

Of Truth by Francis Bacon

Of Beauty by Francis Bacon

Unit 4   William Shakespeare (1564–1616)

Life and Works

William Shakespeare, indisputably the world's greatest playwright and poet, was born to John Shakespeare, a leather merchant, and Mary Arden, the daughter of an aristocratic landowner in Stratford-upon-Avon, in Warwickshire, England in April 1564. In 1561, Shakespeare began his eight-year study at the King's New School, a free grammar school offering Latin grammar and classics. At the age of 18, Shakespeare married Anne Hathaway, then 26, in Stratford's Holy Trinity Church and the couple had a daughter named Susanna in 1583 and two years later, twins, Judith and Hamnet. Shakespeare appeared on the London stage around 1592 and had worked for a company named the Lord Chamberlain's Men during the reign of Queen Elizabeth and renamed the King's Men after King James I, as a shareholder, actor and playwright, for almost the next twenty years. Shakespeare died at the age of 52 of unknown causes in Stratford on April 23, 1616 and was buried in the chancel of Holy Trinity Church.

Shakespeare's first collection of sonnets was published in 1609 and *Mr. William Shakespeare's Comedies, Histories & Tragedies* for the first time in 1623. Shakespeare's works include 38 plays ranging from histories such as *Richard II*, *Henry IV* and *Henry V*, comedies

Unit 4 William Shakespeare (1564–1616)

The Merchant of Venice, *A Midsummer Night's Dream*, *As You Like It*, *Twelfth Night* and *The Winter's Tale*, to tragedies *Hamlet*, *Othello*, *King Lear* and *Macbeth*. Shakespeare is estimated to have used at least 20,000 words in his works and about 1,700 of them were coined by him.

Text A

Hamlet
Act III, Scene 1, Lines 1–102

A room in the castle.

[*Enter KING CLAUDIUS, QUEEN GERTRUDE, POLONIUS OPHELIA, ROSENCRANTZ, and GUILDENSTERN*]

KING CLAUDIUS
And can you, by no **drift of circumstance**①,
Get from him why he puts on this confusion,
Grating② so harshly all his days of quiet
With turbulent and dangerous lunacy?

ROSENCRANTZ
He does confess he feels himself distracted;
But from what cause he will by no means speak.

GUILDENSTERN
Nor do we find him **forward**③ to be sounded,
But, with a crafty madness, keeps **aloof**④,
When we would bring him on to some confession
Of his true state.

QUEEN GERTRUDE

---

① **drift of circumstance**: device of conversation.
② **Grating**: interrupting.
③ **forward**: strongly inclined.
④ **aloof**: removed or distant either physically or emotionally.

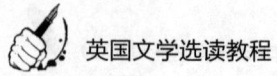

Did he receive you well?

ROSENCRANTZ
Most like a gentleman.

GUILDENSTERN
But with much forcing of his disposition.

ROSENCRANTZ
Niggard① of question; but, of our demands,
Most free in his reply.

QUEEN GERTRUDE
Did you assay him?
To any pastime?

ROSENCRANTZ
Madam, it so fell out, that certain players
We **o'er-raught**② on the way: of these we told him;
And there did seem in him a kind of joy
To hear of it: they are about the court,
And, as I think, they have already order
This night to play before him.

LORD POLONIUS
Tis most true:
And he beseech'd me to entreat your majesties
To hear and see the matter.

KING CLAUDIUS
With all my heart; and it doth much content me
To hear him so inclined.
Good gentlemen, give him a further **edge**③,
And drive his purpose on to these delights.

---

① **Niggard**: mean about spending or granting.
② **o'er-raught**: overreached.
③ **edge**: encouragement.

ROSENCRANTZ

We shall, my lord.

Exeunt ROSENCRANTZ and GUILDENSTERN

KING CLAUDIUS

Sweet Gertrude, leave us too,

For we have closely sent for Hamlet hither,

That he, as 'twere by accident, may here

Affront Ophelia:

Her father and myself, lawful **espials**[①],

Will so bestow ourselves that, seeing, unseen,

We may of their encounter frankly judge,

And gather by him, as he is behaved,

If 't be the affliction of his love or no

That thus he suffers for.

QUEEN GERTRUDE

I shall obey you.

And for your part, Ophelia, I do wish

That your good beauties be the happy cause

Of Hamlet's wildness: so shall I hope your virtues

Will bring him to his **wonted**[②] way again,

To both your honours.

OPHELIA

Madam, I wish it may.

Exit QUEEN GERTRUDE

LORD POLONIUS

Ophelia, walk you here. **Gracious**[③], so please you,

We will bestow ourselves.

---

① **espials**: spies.
② **wonted**: usual or ordinary especially by reason of established habit.
③ **Gracious**: your Grace.

To OPHELIA
Read on this book;
That show of such an exercise may colour
Your loneliness. We are oft to blame in this,—
Tis too much proved—that with devotion's visage
And pious action we do sugar o'er
The devil himself.

KING CLAUDIUS
[Aside] O, 'tis too true!
How smart a lash that speech doth give my conscience!
The harlot's cheek, beautied with **plastering**① art,
Is not more ugly to the thing that helps it
Than is my deed to my most painted word:
O heavy burthen!

LORD POLONIUS
I hear him coming: let's withdraw, my lord.

Exeunt KING CLAUDIUS and POLONIUS

Enter HAMLET

HAMLET
To be, or not to be: that is the question:
Whether 'tis nobler in the mind to suffer
The **slings**② and arrows of outrageous fortune,
Or to take arms against a sea of troubles,
And by opposing end them? To die: to sleep;
No more; and by a sleep to say we end
The heart-ache and the thousand natural shocks
That flesh is heir to, 'tis a **consummation**③
Devoutly to be wish'd. To die, to sleep;

---

① **plastering**: covering sb/sth with a wet or sticky substance.
② **slings**: instruments for throwing stones that usually consist of short straps with strings fastened to their ends and are whirled round to discharge missiles by centrifugal force.
③ **consummation**: the ultimate end.

To sleep: perchance to dream: ay, there's the **rub**①;
For in that sleep of death what dreams may come
When we have shuffled off this mortal **coil**②,
Must give us pause: there's the respect
That makes calamity of so long life;
For who would bear the whips and scorns of time,
The oppressor's wrong, the proud man's **contumely**③,
The pangs of despised love, the law's delay,
The insolence of office and the **spurns**④
That patient merit of the unworthy takes,
When he himself might his quietus make
With a bare **bodkin**⑤? who would **fardels**⑥ bear,
To grunt and sweat under a weary life,
But that the dread of something after death,
The undiscover'd country from whose bourn
No traveller returns, puzzles the will
And makes us rather bear those ills we have
Than fly to others that we know not of?
Thus conscience does make cowards of us all;
And thus the native hue of resolution
Is sicklied o'er with the pale cast of thought,
And enterprises of great pith and moment
With this regard their currents turn **awry**⑦,
And lose the name of action.—Soft you now!
The fair Ophelia! **Nymph**⑧, in thy orisons
Be all my sins remember'd.

OPHELIA
Good my lord,

---

① **rub**: obstacle; difficulty.
② **coil**: turmoil.
③ **contumely**: harsh language or treatment arising from haughtiness and contempt.
④ **spurns**: contemptuous treatment.
⑤ **bodkin**: dagger.
⑥ **fardels**: burdens.
⑦ **awry**: off the correct or expected course.
⑧ **Nymph**: (in ancient Greek and Roman stories) Spirit of nature in the form of a young woman, that lives in rivers, woods, etc.

How does your honour for this many a day?

HAMLET
I humbly thank you; well, well, well.

OPHELIA
My lord, I have remembrances of yours,
That I have longed long to re-deliver;
I pray you, now receive them.

HAMLET
No, not I;
I never gave you **aught**①.

OPHELIA
My honour'd lord, you know right well you did;
And, with them, words of so sweet breath composed
As made the things more rich: their perfume lost,
Take these again; for to the noble mind
Rich gifts **wax**② poor when givers prove unkind.
There, my lord.

Exercise

I. Word Matching

Directions: Please choose the most appropriate ones from the given words to explain the original boldfaced words in the following lines.

A. **rudeness** B. **madness** C. **pains** D. **misfortune**
E. **examine** F. **mood** G. **appearance**

1. And can you, by no drift of circumstance,
   Get from him why he puts on this confusion,
   Grating so harshly all his days of quiet
   With turbulent and dangerous **lunacy**?
2. Most like a gentleman.

---

① **aught**: anything.
② **wax**: assume a (specified) characteristic, quality, or state; become.

But with much forcing of his **disposition**.

3. Did you **assay** him?

    To any pastime?

4. 'Tis too much proved–that with devotion's **visage**

    And pious action we do sugar o'er

    The devil himself.

5. When we have shuffled off this mortal coil,

    Must give us pause: there's the respect

    That makes **calamity** of so long life;

6. The oppressor's wrong, the proud man's contumely,

    The **pangs** of despised love, the law's delay,

    The insolence of office and the spurns

II. Blank Filling

Directions: Please fill in the following blanks with words or expressions that best express the contextual meaning of the classic dicta.

1. To be, or not to be: that is the question:

    Whether 'tis nobler in the mind to suffer

    The slings and arrows of outrageous fortune,

    Or to take _____ against a sea of troubles,

    And by opposing end them?

    —*Hamlet*

2. All the world's a stage, / And all the men and women merely _____.

    —*As You Like It*

3. Be not afraid of _____. Some are born great, some achieve greatness, and some have greatness thrust upon them.

    —*Twelfth Night*

4. All things are ready if our _____ be so.

    —*Henry V*

5. Have more than you show, Speak _____ than you know.

    —*King Lear*

III. Term Defining

Directions: Please explain the following literary terms based on Hamlet.

1. act
2. round character
3. flat character
4. soliloquy

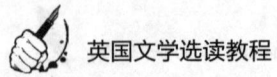

IV. Content-Based Questions

Directions: *Please give a concise and adequate answer to the following questions related to Text A.*

1. How many main characters are there in Act III, Scene 1? Who are they? What are the main reasons for their appearance in this scene?
2. Why did King Claudius ask his sweet Gertrude to leave him and Polonius for a while?
3. How did Claudius and Polonius admit of being guilty in this scene?
4. What did Polonius instruct Ophelia to do and why?

V. Discussion Question

Directions: *Please discuss the following question in pairs or groups.*

Please discuss the above excerpt of Act III, Scene 1 with your partner(s) and sum up the nature of Hamlet's "To be or not to be" soliloquy.

VI. Essay Question

Thus conscience does make cowards of us all;

And thus the native hue of resolution

Is sicklied o'er with the pale cast of thought,

And enterprises of great pith and moment

With this regard their currents turn awry,

And lose the name of action.

Please write a 200-word essay on the practical significance of these lines in Hamlet's soliloquy of Act III, Scene 1 in light of your life.

Text B

Sonnet 18

Shall I compare thee to a summer's day?
Thou art more lovely and more temperate:
Rough winds do shake the darling buds of May,
And summer's **lease**① hath all too short a date;
Sometime too hot the eye of heaven shines,
And often is his gold complexion dimm'd;
And every fair from fair sometime declines,

---

① **lease**: the period of time during which a contract conveying property to a person is in effect.

By chance or nature's changing course untrimm'd;
But thy eternal summer shall not fade,
Nor lose possession of that fair thou ow'st;
Nor shall death brag thou wander'st in his shade,
When in eternal lines to time thou grow'st:
So long as men can breathe or eyes can see,
So long lives this, and this gives life to thee.

Exercise

I. Word Matching

Directions: Please choose the most appropriate ones from the given words to explain the original boldfaced words in the following lines.

A. boast   B. beauty   C. moderate   D. face

1. Shall I compare thee to a summer's day?
   Thou art more lovely and more **temperate**.
2. Sometime too hot the eye of heaven shines,
   And often is his gold **complexion** dimm'd;
3. And every **fair** from fair sometime declines,
4. Nor shall death **brag** thou wander'st in his shade,

II. Blank Filling

Directions: Please fill in the following blanks with words or expressions that best express the contextual meaning of the classic dicta.

1. Shall I compare thee to a _____'s day?
   Thou art more lovely and more temperate.

   —*Sonnet 18*

2. Brevity is the _____ of wit.

   —*Hamlet*

3. Love does not see with the _____, but with the soul.

   —*A Midsummer Night's Dream*

4. To me, fair friend, you never can be old,
   For as you were when first your eye I ey'd,
   Such seems your _____ still.

   —*Sonnet 104*

5. The fool doth think he is _____, but the wise man knows himself to be a fool.

   —*As You Like It*

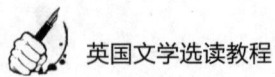

III. Term Defining

Directions: *Please explain the following literary terms based on Sonnet 18.*

1. Shakespearean sonnet
2. personification
3. hyperbole

IV. Content-Based Questions

Directions: *Please give a concise and adequate answer to the following questions related to Text B.*

1. Does the author successfully compare thee to a summer's day? Why or why not? Please present appropriate argument to support your idea.

2. In short, what are the differences between thee and summer? Please state them one by one.

3. Why does the author have the courage to say thy eternal summer shall not fade?

V. Discussion Question

Directions: *Please discuss the following question in pairs or groups.*

Please discuss Sonnet 18 by William Shakespeare and Sonnet 34 in Unit 2 by Edmund Spenser with your partner(s) and compare Shakespearean sonnet to Spenserian sonnet in detail.

VI. Essay Question

What we have learned about Shakespeare is far from enough and let us do some extra research on Shakespeare's life after class and write a 200-word essay on the difference between the themes of Shakespeare's sonnets and his plays.

Self-Improving Reading

Act IV, Scene 1 of *The Merchant of Venice* by William Shakespeare

Act II, Scene 4 of *King Lear and Macbeth* by William Shakespeare

Act III, Scene 4 of *Macbeth* by William Shakespeare

Unit 5　John Milton (1608−1674)

Life and Works

  John Milton was born in London on December 9, 1608, the son of John Milton Sr., a scrivener and composer, and Sara Jeffrey Milton. Milton enrolled at St. Paul's School in London in 1619 and was educated in Christ's College, Cambridge, graduating with a Master of Arts in 1632, who did dabble in Latin, Greek, French, Italian, and Hebrew. Over the next six years, Milton stayed with his family in Hammersmith and Horton later, where he read voraciously Greek and Latin works and tried his hand at composing poems. Milton ever met with 75-year-old blind Galileo under house arrest in Florence during his Continental tour of 1638-1639. Milton opposed the Church of England and the monarchy by writing radical pamphlets on the freedom of the press and sanctioned regicide to defend Oliver Cromwell's government in the English Civil War. In 1652, Milton was overcome by total blindness, undoubtedly due to years of eyestrain. When the monarchy was restored by Charles II in 1660, Milton was inevitably imprisoned as a defender of the Commonwealth but soon released with a fine. The remainder of his life saw the completion of Milton's immortal epic poems. Milton died in Buckinghamshire, England in November, 1674 with his monument in Poet's Corner in Westminster Abbey.

Milton ever translated *Psalm 114* in Hebrew into English at the age of 15 and later into Greek. John Milton's first published work, *On Shakespeare.1630*, was seeking to eulogize Shakespeare and his literary works as an epitaph. *Comus* also called *A Mask*, a masque by Milton was originally presented in honor of the Earl of Bridgewater becoming lord president of Wales in 1634 and published anonymously in 1637. *Lycidas*, a pastoral elegy written by Milton in 1637, was published in 1638 and republished in 1645 to memorialize Edward King, a fellow student of Milton's at Christ's College, Cambridge, who died of his capsized vessel in the Irish Sea. *Paradise Lost*, the greatest English epic poem, was initially issued in 10 books in 1667 and in 12 books in the second edition of 1674. Milton's last two opuses, *Paradise Regained* and *Samson Agonistes* were published jointly in one volume in 1671.

Text A

Paradise Lost
An Excerpt of Book 1 (1674 version)

OF Mans First Disobedience, and the Fruit
Of that Forbidden Tree, whose mortal tast
Brought Death into the World, and all our woe,
With loss of *Eden*, till one greater Man
Restore us, and regain the blissful Seat,
Sing Heav'nly Muse, that on the secret top
Of **Oreb**[①], or of *Sinai*, didst inspire
That Shepherd, who first taught the chosen Seed,
In the Beginning how the Heav'ns and Earth
Rose out of **Chaos**[②]: or if **Sion Hill**[③]
Delight thee more, and **Siloa's brook**[④] that flow'd
Fast by the **Oracle**[⑤] of God; I thence
Invoke thy aid to my adventrous Song,
That with no middle flight intends to soar

---

① **Oreb**: Mt. Horeb in the south central part of the Sinai Peninsula; Mt. Sinai.
② **Chaos**: the confused unorganized state of primordial matter before the creation of distinct forms.
③ **Sion Hill**: Mt. Zion or Mt. Sion in eastern Jerusalem.
④ **Siloa's brook**: a stream flowing from Mt. Sion.
⑤ **Oracle**: a shrine in which a deity reveals hidden knowledge or the divine purpose through such a person.

Unit 5 John Milton (1608-1674)

Above th' **Aonian**① Mount, while it pursues
Things unattempted yet in Prose or Rhime.
And chiefly Thou, O Spirit, that dost prefer
Before all Temples th' upright heart and pure,
Instruct me, for Thou know'st; Thou from the first
Wast present, and with mighty wings outspread
Dove-like satst brooding on the vast **Abyss**②
And mad'st it pregnant: What in me is dark
Illumin, what is low raise and support;
That to the highth of this great Argument
I may assert Eternal Providence,
And justifie the wayes of God to men.

Say first, for Heav'n hides nothing from thy view
Nor the deep **Tract**③ of Hell, say first what cause
Mov'd our Grand Parents in that happy State,
Favour'd of Heav'n so highly, to fall off
From thir Creator, and transgress his Will
For one restraint, Lords of the World besides?
Who first seduc'd them to that foul revolt?
Th' infernal **Serpent**④; he it was, whose guile
Stird up with Envy and Revenge, deceiv'd
The Mother of Mankind, what time his Pride
Had cast him out from Heav'n, with all his Host
Of Rebel Angels, by whose aid aspiring
To set himself in Glory above his Peers,
He trusted to have equal'd the most High,
If he oppos'd; and with ambitious aim
Against the Throne and Monarchy of God
Rais'd impious War in Heav'n and Battel proud
With vain attempt. Him the Almighty Power

---

① **Aonian**: pertaining to Aonia, or to the Muses, who were supposed to dwell there.
② **Abyss**: an immeasurably deep gulf or great space.
③ **Tract**: an area either large or small
④ **Serpent**: the personal supreme spirit of evil often represented in Christian belief as the tempter of humankind, the leader of all apostate angels, and the ruler of hell.

Hurld headlong flaming from th' **Ethereal**① Skie
With hideous ruine and combustion down
To bottomless perdition, there to dwell
In **Adamantine**② Chains and penal Fire,
Who **durst**③ defie th' Omnipotent to Arms.
Nine times the Space that measures Day and Night
To mortal men, he with his horrid crew
Lay vanquisht, rowling in the fiery Gulfe
Confounded though immortal: But his doom
Reserv'd him to more wrath; for now the thought
Both of lost happiness and lasting pain
Torments him; round he throws his baleful eyes
That witness'd huge affliction and dismay
Mixt with **obdurate**④ pride and stedfast hate:
At once as far as Angels kenn he views
The dismal Situation waste and wilde,
A Dungeon horrible, on all sides round
As one great Furnace flam'd, yet from those flames
No light, but rather darkness visible
Serv'd onely to discover sights of woe,
Regions of sorrow, doleful shades, where peace
And rest can never dwell, hope never comes
That comes to all; but torture without end
Still urges, and a fiery **Deluge**⑤, fed
With ever-burning Sulphur unconsum'd:
Such place Eternal Justice had prepar'd
For those rebellious, here thir prison ordained
In utter darkness, and thir portion set
As far remov'd from God and light of Heav'n
As from the Center thrice to th' utmost Pole.
O how unlike the place from whence they fell!
There the companions of his fall, o'rewhelm'd

---

① **Ethereal**: of or relating to the regions beyond the earth.
② **Adamantine**: made of or having the quality of a stone formerly believed to be of impenetrable hardness.
③ **durst**: *archaic and dialectal past tense of* dare.
④ **obdurate**: stubbornly persistent in wrongdoing.
⑤ **Deluge**: an overflowing of the land by water.

With Floods and Whirlwinds of tempestuous fire,
He soon discerns, and **weltring**① by his side
One next himself in power, and next in crime,
Long after known in *Palestine*, and nam'd
Beelzebub②. To whom th' Arch-Enemy,
And thence in Heav'n call'd Satan, with bold words
Breaking the horrid silence thus began.

Exercise

I. Word Matching

Directions: Please choose the most appropriate ones from the given words to explain the original boldfaced words in the following lines.

A. **hell**   B. **wheel**   C. **incubate**   D. **troubles**   E. **use**
F. **disobey**   G. **conquer**   H. **immoral**

1. OF Mans First Disobedience, and the Fruit
   Of that Forbidden Tree, whose mortal tast
   Brought Death into the World, and all our **woe**,
2. Fast by the Oracle of God; I thence
   Invoke thy aid to my adventrous Song,
   That with no middle flight intends to **soar**
   Above th'*Aonian* Mount, while it pursues
   Things unattempted yet in Prose or Rhime.
3. Instruct me, for Thou know'st; Thou from the first
   Wast present, and with mighty wings outspread
   Dove-like satst **brood**ing on the vast Abyss
4. Mov'd our Grand Parents in that happy State,
   Favour'd of Heav'n so highly, to fall off
   From thir Creator, and **transgress** his Will
5. If he oppos'd; and with ambitious aim
   Against the Throne and Monarchy of God
   Rais'd **impious** War in Heav'n and Battel proud
6. To bottomless **perdition**, there to dwell
   In Adamantine Chains and penal Fire,

---

① **weltring**: weltering; twisting (the body or a bodily part) in pain.
② **Beelzebub**: a fallen angel in *Paradise Lost* ranking next to Satan; a devil.

7. To mortal men, he with his horrid crew

　Lay **vanquisht**, rowling in the fiery Gulfe

II. Blank Filling

Directions: Please fill in the following blanks with words or expressions that best express the contextual meaning of the classic dicta.

　1. Give me the _____ to know, to utter, and to argue freely according to conscience, above all liberties.

　　　　　　　　　　　　　　　　　　　　　　　　　　　　—*Areopagitica*

　2. Solitude sometimes is best _____ .

　　　　　　　　　　　　　　　　　　　　　　　　　　　　—*Paradise Lost*

　3. Who kills a man kills a reasonable creature, … but he who destroys a good _____ kills reason itself.

　　　　　　　　　　　　　　　　　　　　　　　　　　　　—*Areopagitica*

　4. The childhood shows the _____ , as morning shows the day.

　　　　　　　　　　　　　　　　　　　　　　　　　　　　—*Paradise Regained*

　5. The stars, that nature hung in heaven, and filled their lamps with everlasting oil, give due _____ to the misled and lonely traveller.

　　　　　　　　　　　　　　　　　　　　　　　　　　　　—*Comus*

III. Term Defining

Directions: Please explain the following literary terms based on Paradise Lost.

　1. blank verse

　2. protagonist

　3. antagonist

IV. Content-Based Questions

Directions: Please give a concise and adequate answer to the following questions related to Text A.

　1. What subject does John Milton recount within the first five lines of stanza 1?

　2. What did Heav'nly Muse inspire That Shepherd in stanza 1?

　3. What does thy refer to in the expression Invoke thy aid and what's the specific meaning of aid in the discourse?

　4. What did Th' infernal Serpent do in the light of the beginning account of stanza 2?

　5. What's the aftermath of the act of Th' infernal Serpent?

　6. What status quo did Th' infernal Serpent and Rebel Angels have to face?

V. Discussion Question

Directions: Please discuss the following question in pairs or groups.

　Please study and discuss the first two stanzas of Book 1 of *Paradise Lost* with your partner(s) and point out the real purpose of the appearance of the image Heav'nly Muse in

Unit 5　John Milton (1608–1674)

Milton's *Paradise Lost*.

IV. Essay Question

John Milton presents his real pursuit in the above section of *Paradise Lost*. Please think deeply about the academic, athletic or social achievement in your mind and write a 200-word essay to elaborate it further.

Text B

When I Consider How My Light Is Spent

When I consider how my light is spent,
Ere half my days, in this dark world and wide,
And that one Talent which is death to hide
Lodged with me useless, though my Soul more bent
To serve **therewith**[①] my Maker, and present
My true account, lest he returning chide;
Doth God exact day-labour, light denied?
I fondly ask. But patience, to prevent
That murmur, soon replies, God doth not need
Either man's work or his own gifts; who best

---

① **therewith**: with that.

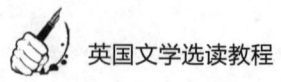

Bear his mild **yoke**①, they serve him best. His state
Is Kingly. Thousands at his bidding speed
And post o'er Land and Ocean without rest:
They also serve who only stand and wait.

Exercise

I. Word Matching

Directions: Please choose the most appropriate ones from the given words to explain the original boldfaced words in the following lines.

  A. **demand**   B. **blame**   C. **before**

1. When I consider how my light is spent,
   Ere half my days, in this dark world and wide,

2. To serve therewith my Maker, and present
   My true account, lest he returning **chide**;

3. Doth God **exact** day-labour, light denied?
   I fondly ask. But patience, to prevent

II. Blank Filling

Directions: Please fill in the following blanks with words or expressions that best express the contextual meaning of the classic dicta.

1. To live a life half dead, a living _____ .

                       —*Samson Agonistes*

2. Thou canst not touch the freedom of my _____ .

                           —*Comus*

3. Sweet is the _____ of morn, her rising sweet, With charm of earliest birds.

                          —*Paradise Lost*

4. Danger will _____ on opportunity.

                  —*The Poetical Works of John Milton*

5. Part of my soul I seek thee, and claim thee my other _____ .

                          —*Paradise Lost*

III. Term Defining

Directions: Please explain the following literary terms based on When I Consider How My Light Is Spent.

1. enjambment

---

① **yoke**: a wooden beam normally used between a pair of oxen or other animals to enable them to pull together on a load when working in pairs; servitude to a controlling person or force.

2. Petrarchan sonnet

3. allusion

IV. Content-Based Questions

Directions: *Please give a concise and adequate answer to the following questions related to Text B.*

1. What does the title *When I Consider How My Light Is Spent* really mean? Please formulate another name for it after comprehending the whole poem.

2. What is the possible reason that my light is spent, Ere half my days in your view?

3. Who is the answerer of the question Doth God exact day-labour, light denied? and why?

V. Discussion Question

Directions: *Please discuss the following question in pairs or groups.*

Please ponder on the almost 6-line answer to the question Doth God exact day-labour, light denied? Individually and discuss it with your partner(s), and share your thoughts with the whole class.

VI. Essay Question

Paradise Lost, *Paradise Regained* and *Samson Agonistes* were composed by John Milton through his dictation and transcription by others after his light was spent. Please write an essay on your reflection on the possible hardships and torments he may have undergone during this time.

Self-Improving Reading

To Mr. Cyriack Skinner Upon His Blindness by John Milton

Areopagitica by John Milton

Unit 6   Daniel Defoe (1660-1731)

Life and Works

Daniel Defoe, the Father of the English Novel, was born in the parish of St. Giles Cripplegate, London, England, in 1660 to Alice Marsh, and James Foe, a Presbyterian butcher, who, as a Nonconformist, sent his son to Newington Green Academy run by the Reverend Charles Morton to prepare for the ministry. Defoe once got stuck in the Great Plague of London in 1664 and the Great Fire of 1665, which were depicted in his *Journal of the Plague Year* of 1722 and other writings. Defoe went into business in 1683 instead of the original intention of being a minister but as a staunch supporter of freedom of religion and the press by his myriad pamphlets like *The Shortest Way with the Dissenters* in 1702. Defoe married Mary Tuffley, the daughter of a wealthy wine-cooper, gaining a huge dowry worth £3, 700 in 1684. Defoe was forced to declare bankruptcy by a debt of £17,000 due to business failure, which however, helped him to bring about the first English business manual, *The Complete English Tradesman* in 1692.

Unit 6 Daniel Defoe (1660-1731)

In 1704, Defoe founded *The Review*, a tri-weekly political journal to lash out at social injustices. Defoe published the first English novel, *Robinson Crusoe*, or *The Life and Strange Surprising Adventures of Robinson Crusoe*, inspired by a true Scottish sailor named Alexander Selkirk in 1719 and subsequently *Captain Singleton* and *Memoirs of a Cavalier* in 1720, *Colonel Jack* and *Moll Flanders* in 1722, and *Roxana* in 1724. Defoe died of lethargy on 24 April 1731, in Moorfields, London, England.

Text A

Robinson Crusoe
Chapter IX   A Boat

But first I was to prepare more land, for I had now seed enough to sow above an acre of ground. Before I did this, I had a week's work at least to make me a **spade**①, which, when it was done, was but a sorry one indeed, and very heavy, and required double labour to work with it. However, I got through that, and sowed my seed in two large flat pieces of ground, as near my house as I could find them to my mind, and fenced them in with a good hedge, the **stakes**② of which were all cut off that wood which I had set before, and knew it would grow; so that, in a year's time, I knew I should have a quick or living hedge, that would want but little repair. This work did not take me up less than three months, because a great part of that time was the wet season, when I could not go abroad. Within-doors, that is when it rained and I could not go out, I found employment in the following occupations—always observing, that all the while I was at work I **diverted**③ myself with talking to my parrot, and teaching him to speak; and I quickly taught him to know his own name, and at last to speak it out pretty loud, Poll, which was the first word I ever heard spoken in the island by any mouth but my own. This, therefore, was not my work, but an assistance to my work; for now, as I said, I had a great employment upon my hands, as follows: I had long studied to make, by some means or other, some **earthen vessels**④, which, indeed, I wanted **sorely**⑤, but knew not where to come at them. However, considering the heat of the climate, I did not doubt but if I could find out any **clay**⑥,

---

① **spade**: a tool used for digging or cutting earth.
② **stakes**: *pl.* of **stake**, slender pieces of wood used to support the hedge.
③ **diverted**: *v.* divert (**diverted, diverted**), distract from, shift.
④ **earthen vessels**: containers made from baked clay.
⑤ **sorely**: extremely, badly.
⑥ **clay**: a kind of earth that is soft but hard when fired.

I might make some pots that might, being dried in the sun, be hard enough and strong enough to bear handling, and to hold anything that was dry, and required to be kept so; and as this was necessary in the preparing corn, meal, &c., which was the thing I was doing, I resolved to make some as large as I could, and fit only to stand like jars, to hold what should be put into them.

It would make the reader pity me, or rather laugh at me, to tell how many awkward ways I took to raise this **paste**①; what odd, **misshapen**②, ugly things I made; how many of them fell in and how many fell out, the clay not being **stiff**③ enough to bear its own weight; how many **cracked**④ by the over-violent heat of the sun, being set out too **hastily**⑤; and how many fell in pieces with only removing, as well before as after they were dried; and, in a word, how, after having laboured hard to find the clay—to dig it, to **temper**⑥ it, to bring it home, and work it—I could not make above two large earthen ugly things (I cannot call them jars) in about two months' labour.

However, as the sun baked these two very dry and hard, I lifted them very gently up, and set them down again in two great wicker baskets, which I had made on purpose for them, that they might not break; and as between the pot and the basket there was a little room to spare, I stuffed it full of the rice and **barley**⑦ **straw**⑧; and these two pots being to stand always dry I thought would hold my dry corn, and perhaps the meal, when the corn was **bruised**⑨.

Though I miscarried so much in my design for large pots, yet I made several smaller things with better success; such as little round pots, flat dishes, **pitchers**⑩, and **pipkins**⑪, and any things my hand turned to; and the heat of the sun baked them quite hard.

But all this would not answer my end, which was to get an earthen pot to hold what was liquid, and bear the fire, which none of these could do. It happened after some time, making a pretty large fire for cooking my meat, when I went to put it out after I had done with it, I found a broken piece of one of my **earthenware**⑫ vessels in the fire, burnt as hard as a stone, and red as a **tile**⑬. I was agreeably surprised to see it, and said to myself, that certainly they might be made to burn whole, if they would burn broken.

---

① **paste**: a soft wet mixture of clay.
② **misshapen**: not having the normal or regular shape.
③ **stiff**: rigid, not flexible.
④ **cracked**: *v.* **crack** (**cracked, cracked**), break open or into pieces.
⑤ **hastily**: in haste, hurriedly.
⑥ **temper**: to mix the clay with water or other substances to achieve a uniform texture.
⑦ **barley**: a grain that is used to make food and beer.
⑧ **straw**: the dried, yellowish stalks from barley.
⑨ **bruised**: *v.* bruise (**bruised, bruised**), damaged by being handled roughly.
⑩ **pitchers**: *pl.* of **pitcher**, a large container with a small opening and a handle.
⑪ **pipkins**: *pl.* of **pipkin**, a small earthenware cooking pot.
⑫ **earthenware**: made of clay.
⑬ **tile**: a thin, flat piece of baked clay used for covering roofs.

Unit 6　Daniel Defoe (1660–1731)

　　This set me to study how to order my fire, so as to make it burn some pots. I had no notion of a **kiln**①, such as the **potters**② burn in, or of glazing them with **lead**③, though I had some lead to do it with; but I placed three large pipkins and two or three pots in a pile, one upon another, and placed my firewood all round it, with a great heap of **embers**④ under them. I **plied**⑤ the fire with fresh fuel round the outside and upon the top, till I saw the pots in the inside red-hot quite through, and observed that they did not crack at all. When I saw them clear red, I let them stand in that heat about five or six hours, till I found one of them, though it did not crack, did melt or **run**⑥; for the sand which was mixed with the clay melted by the violence of the heat, and would have run into glass if I had gone on; so I **slacked**⑦ my fire gradually till the pots began to **abate**⑧ of the red colour; and watching them all night, that I might not let the fire abate too fast, in the morning I had three very good (I will not say handsome) pipkins, and two other earthen pots, as hard burnt as could be desired, and one of them perfectly glazed with the running of the sand.

　　After this experiment, I need not say that I wanted no sort of earthenware for my use; but I must needs say as to the shapes of them, they were very **indifferent**⑨, as any one may suppose, when I had no way of making them but as the children make dirt pies, or as a woman would make pies that never learned to raise paste.

　　No joy at a thing of so mean a nature was ever equal to mine, when I found I had made an earthen pot that would bear the fire; and I had hardly patience to stay till they were cold before I set one on the fire again with some water in it to boil me some meat, which it did admirably well; and with a piece of a **kid**⑩ I made some very good **broth**⑪, though I wanted oatmeal, and several other ingredients requisite to make it as good as I would have had it been.

　　My next concern was to get me a stone **mortar**⑫ to stamp or beat some corn in; for as to the mill, there was no thought of arriving at that perfection of art with one pair of hands. To supply this want, I was at a great loss; for, of all the trades in the world, I was as perfectly unqualified for a stone-cutter as for any whatever; neither had I any tools to go about it with. I spent many a day to find out a great stone big enough to cut hollow, and make fit for a mortar,

---

① **kiln**: a large oven for baking clay and bricks.
② **potters**: *pl.* of potter, a person who makes clay pots by hand.
③ **lead**: a heavy soft grey metal, often used in the past for making pipes or roofing.
④ **embers**: *pl.* of ember, small pieces of burning or glowing coal or wood in a dying fire.
⑤ **plied**: *v.* ply (**plied, plied**), keep giving more of sth.
⑥ **run**: melt and flow.
⑦ **slacked**: *v.* slack (**slacked, slacked**), reduce the intensity of the fire.
⑧ **abate**: reduce, become less strong.
⑨ **indifferent**: not very good, mediocre or average.
⑩ **kid**: a young goat.
⑪ **broth**: soup made by boiling meat or vegetables.
⑫ **mortar**: a small hard bowl used for crushing and grinding grains into powder.

and could find none at all, except what was in the solid rock, and which I had no way to dig or cut out; nor indeed were the rocks in the island of hardness sufficient, but were all of a sandy, crumbling stone, which neither would bear the weight of a heavy **pestle**①, nor would break the corn without filling it with sand. So, after a great deal of time lost in searching for a stone, I gave it over, and resolved to look out for a great block of hard wood, which I found, indeed, much easier; and getting one as big as I had strength to stir, I **rounded**② it, and formed it on the outside with my axe and **hatchet**③, and then with the help of fire and infinite labour, made a hollow place in it, as the Indians in Brazil make their **canoes**④. After this, I made a great heavy pestle or beater of the wood called the iron-wood; and this I prepared and laid by against I had my next crop of corn, which I proposed to myself to grind, or rather pound into meal to make bread.

My next difficulty was to make a **sieve**⑤ or searce, to dress my meal, and to part it from the **bran**⑥ and the husk; without which I did not see it possible I could have any bread. This was a most difficult thing even to think on, for to be sure I had nothing like the necessary thing to make it—I mean fine thin **canvas**⑦ or stuff to searce the meal through. And here I was at a full stop for many months; nor did I really know what to do. **Linen**⑧ I had none left but what was mere rags; I had goat's hair, but neither knew how to weave it or **spin**⑨ it; and had I known how, here were no tools to work it with. All the remedy that I found for this was, that at last I did remember I had, among the seamen's clothes which were saved out of the ship, some neckcloths of **calico**⑩ or **muslin**⑪; and with some pieces of these I made three small sieves proper enough for the work; and thus I made shift for some years: how I did afterwards, I shall show in its place.

The baking part was the next thing to be considered, and how I should make bread when I came to have corn; for first, I had no **yeast**⑫. As to that part, there was no supplying the want, so I did not concern myself much about it. But for an oven I was indeed in great pain. At length I found out an experiment for that also, which was this: I made some earthen-vessels very broad but not deep, that is to say, about two feet diameter, and not above nine inches deep. These I

---

① **pestle**: a small heavy tool with a round end used for crushing things in a mortar.
② **rounded**: *v.* **round (rounded, rounded)**, make sth into a round shape.
③ **hatchet**: a small axe.
④ **caneos**: *pl.* of **caneo**, a light narrow boat.
⑤ **sieve**: a tool used for separating larger pieces of something from smaller ones, synonymous with *searce*.
⑥ **bran**: the outer covering of grain, synonymous with *husk*.
⑦ **canvas**: a strong, heavy and rough cloth.
⑧ **linen**: a type of cloth made from flax.
⑨ **spin**: make thread by twisting fibres such as wool or cotton.
⑩ **calico**: plain white fabric made from cotton.
⑪ **muslin**: very thin, cotton cloth.
⑫ **yeast**: a kind of fungus used to make bread rise.

burned in the fire, as I had done the other, and laid them by; and when I wanted to bake, I made a great fire upon my **hearth**①, which I had paved with some square tiles of my own baking and burning also; but I should not call them square.

When the firewood was burned pretty much into embers or live coals, I drew them forward upon this hearth, so as to cover it all over, and there I let them lie till the hearth was very hot. Then sweeping away all the embers, I set down my loaf or loaves, and **whelming**② down the earthen pot upon them, drew the embers all round the outside of the pot, to keep in and add to the heat; and thus as well as in the best oven in the world, I baked my barley-loaves, and became in little time a good **pastrycook**③ into the bargain; for I made myself several cakes and puddings of the rice; but I made no pies, neither had I anything to put into them supposing I had, except the flesh either of fowls or goats.

It need not be wondered at if all these things took me up most part of the third year of my **abode**④ here; for it is to be observed that in the intervals of these things I had my new harvest and **husbandry**⑤ to manage; for I reaped my corn in its season, and carried it home as well as I could, and laid it up in the ear, in my large baskets, till I had time to rub it out, for I had no floor to **thrash**⑥ it on, or instrument to thrash it with.

And now, indeed, my stock of corn increasing, I really wanted to build my barns bigger; I wanted a place to lay it up in, for the increase of the corn now yielded me so much, that I had of the barley about twenty **bushels**⑦, and of the rice as much or more; in so much that now I resolved to begin to use it freely; for my bread had been quite gone a great while; also I resolved to see what quantity would be sufficient for me a whole year, and to sow but once a year.

Upon the whole, I found that the forty bushels of barley and rice were much more than I could consume in a year; so I resolved to sow just the same quantity every year that I sowed the last, in hopes that such a quantity would fully provide me with bread, &c.

All the while these things were doing, you may be sure my thoughts ran many times upon the prospect of land which I had seen from the other side of the island; and I was not without secret wishes that I were on shore there, fancying that, seeing the mainland, and an inhabited country, I might find some way or other to convey myself further, and perhaps at last find some means of escape.

But all this while I made no allowance for the dangers of such an undertaking, and how I

---

① **hearth**: the floor at the bottom of a fireplace.
② **whelming**: *v.* **whelm**, turn a container upside down or place it over something else to cover it completely.
③ **pastrycook**: someone who bakes various sweet baked goods.
④ **abode**: the duration of Crusoe's stay on the island.
⑤ **husbandry**: farming, cultivation or production of plants or animals.
⑥ **thrash**: to beat or strike in order to separate grains from the husks or straw.
⑦ **bushels**: *pl.* of **bushel**, a unit for measuring grain.

might fall into the hands of savages, and perhaps such as I might have reason to think far worse than the lions and tigers of Africa: that if I once came in their power, I should run a **hazard**① of more than a thousand to one of being killed, and perhaps of being eaten; for I had heard that the people of the Caribbean coast were **cannibals**② or man-eaters, and I knew by the latitude that I could not be far from that shore. Then, supposing they were not cannibals, yet they might kill me, as many Europeans who had fallen into their hands had been served, even when they had been ten or twenty together—much more I, that was but one, and could make little or no defence; all these things, I say, which I ought to have considered well; and did come into my thoughts afterwards, yet gave me no **apprehensions**③ at first, and my head ran mightily upon the thought of getting over to the shore.

Now I wished for my boy **Xury**④, and the long-boat with shoulder-of-mutton **sail**⑤, with which I sailed above a thousand miles on the coast of Africa; but this was in vain: then I thought I would go and look at our ship's boat, which, as I have said, was blown up upon the shore a great way, in the storm, when we were first cast away. She lay almost where she did at first, but not quite; and was turned, by the force of the waves and the winds, almost bottom upward, against a high **ridge**⑥ of beachy, rough sand, but no water about her. If I had hands to have **refitted**⑦ her, and to have launched her into the water, the boat would have done well enough, and I might have gone back into the Brazils with her easily enough; but I might have foreseen that I could no more turn her and set her upright upon her bottom than I could remove the island; however, I went to the woods, and cut levers and rollers, and brought them to the boat resolving to try what I could do; suggesting to myself that if I could but turn her down, I might repair the damage she had received, and she would be a very good boat, and I might go to sea in her very easily.

I spared no pains, indeed, in this piece of fruitless toil, and spent, I think, three or four weeks about it; at last finding it impossible to heave it up with my little strength, I fell to digging away the sand, to **undermine**⑧ it, and so to make it fall down, setting pieces of wood to thrust and guide it right in the fall.

But when I had done this, I was unable to stir it up again, or to get under it, much less to move it forward towards the water; so I was forced to give it over; and yet, though I gave over

---

① **hazard**: risk, venture.
② **cannibals**: *pl.* of **cannibal**, people who eat the flesh of other human beings.
③ **apprehensions**: *pl.* of **apprehension**, anxiety or fear that something unpleasant will happen.
④ **Xury**: A boy who is a fellow captive on an enslaving vessel and escapes with Crusoe and aids in survival efforts before Crusoe sells him to a Portuguese captain under the condition of eventual freedom.
⑤ **shoulder-of-mutton sail**: a type of sail that has a triangular shape.
⑥ **ridge**: a long, narrow elevation of sand.
⑦ **refitted**: *v.* refit (**refitted, refitted**), repair or make adjustments to a ship.
⑧ **undermine**: destroy the base of the ship by digging away the sand under it.

the hopes of the boat, my desire to venture over for the main increased, rather than decreased, as the means for it seemed impossible.

This at length put me upon thinking whether it was not possible to make myself a canoe, or periagua, such as the natives of those climates make, even without tools, or, as I might say, without hands, of the trunk of a great tree. This I not only thought possible, but easy, and pleased myself extremely with the thoughts of making it, and with my having much more convenience for it than any of the negroes or Indians; but not at all considering the particular inconveniences which I lay under more than the Indians did—viz. want of hands to move it, when it was made, into the water—a difficulty much harder for me to surmount than all the consequences of want of tools could be to them; for what was it to me, if when I had chosen a vast tree in the woods, and with much trouble cut it down, if I had been able with my tools to hew and **dub**① the outside into the proper shape of a boat, and burn or cut out the inside to make it hollow, so as to make a boat of it—if, after all this, I must leave it just there where I found it, and not be able to launch it into the water?

One would have thought I could not have had the least reflection upon my mind of my circumstances while I was making this boat, but I should have immediately thought how I should get it into the sea; but my thoughts were so intent upon my voyage over the sea in it, that I never once considered how I should get it off the land: and it was really, in its own nature, more easy for me to guide it over forty-five miles of sea than about forty-five **fathoms**② of land, where it lay, to set it afloat in the water.

I went to work upon this boat the most like a fool that ever man did who had any of his senses awake. I pleased myself with the design, without determining whether I was ever able to undertake it; not but that the difficulty of launching my boat came often into my head; but I put a stop to my inquiries into it by this foolish answer which I gave myself—Let me first make it; I **warrant**③ I will find some way or other to get it along when it is done.

This was a most **preposterous**④ method; but the eagerness of my fancy prevailed, and to work I went. I **felled**⑤ a cedar-tree, and I question much whether **Solomon**⑥ ever had such a one for the building of the Temple of Jerusalem; it was five feet ten inches diameter at the lower part next the stump, and four feet eleven inches diameter at the end of twenty-two feet; after which it lessened for a while, and then parted into branches. It was not without infinite labour that I felled this tree; I was twenty days hacking and hewing at it at the bottom; I was fourteen

---

① **dub**: shape by cutting or chiseling.
② **fathoms**: *pl.* of **fathom**, a measurement of 6 feet, used to measure the depth of water.
③ **warrant**: declare with confidence; assure or promise.
④ **preposterous**: ridiculous, absurd.
⑤ **felled**: *v.* **fell** (**felled**, **felled**), cut down.
⑥ **Solomon**: the biblical King **Solomon**, renowned for his wisdom and, according to the *Old Testament*, for building the First Temple in Jerusalem.

more getting the branches and limbs and the vast spreading head cut off, which I hacked and hewed through with axe and hatchet, and inexpressible labour; after this, it cost me a month to shape it and dub it to a proportion, and to something like the bottom of a boat, that it might swim upright as it ought to do. It cost me near three months more to clear the inside, and work it out so as to make an exact boat of it; this I did, indeed, without fire, by mere **mallet**① and **chisel**②, and **by the dint of**③ hard labour, till I had brought it to be a very handsome periagua, and big enough to have carried six-and-twenty men, and consequently big enough to have carried me and all my cargo.

When I had gone through this work I was extremely delighted with it. The boat was really much bigger than ever I saw a canoe or periagua, that was made of one tree, in my life. Many a weary stroke it had cost, you may be sure; and had I gotten it into the water, I make no question, but I should have begun the maddest voyage, and the most unlikely to be performed, that ever was undertaken.

But all my devices to get it into the water failed me; though they cost me infinite labour too. It lay about one hundred yards from the water, and not more; but the first inconvenience was, it was up hill towards the creek. Well, to take away this discouragement, I resolved to dig into the surface of the earth, and so make a **declivity**④: this I began, and it cost me a **prodigious**⑤ deal of pains (but who **grudge**⑥ pains who have their deliverance in view?); but when this was worked through, and this difficulty managed, it was still much the same, for I could no more stir the canoe than I could the other boat. Then I measured the distance of ground, and resolved to cut a dock or canal, to bring the water up to the canoe, seeing I could not bring the canoe down to the water. Well, I began this work; and when I began to enter upon it, and calculate how deep it was to be dug, how broad, how the stuff was to be thrown out, I found that, by the number of hands I had, being none but my own, it must have been ten or twelve years before I could have gone through with it; for the shore lay so high, that at the upper end it must have been at least twenty feet deep; so at length, though with great reluctancy, I gave this attempt over also.

This grieved me heartily; and now I saw, though too late, the folly of beginning a work before we count the cost, and before we judge rightly of our own strength to go through with it.

In the middle of this work I finished my fourth year in this place, and kept my anniversary with the same devotion, and with as much comfort as ever before; for, by a constant study and serious application to **the Word of God**⑦, and by the assistance of His grace, I gained a

---

① **mallet**: a wooden hammer with a square head.
② **chisel**: a hand tool with a sharp edge on its end for cutting wood.
③ **by the dint of**: by means of.
④ **declivity**: a downward slope.
⑤ **prodigious**: remarkably large in size.
⑥ **grudge**: to resent, to be reluctant or unwilling to give or allow something.
⑦ **the Word of God**: the *Bible*.

Unit 6 Daniel Defoe (1660-1731)

different knowledge from what I had before. I entertained different notions of things. I looked now upon the world as a thing remote, which I had nothing to do with, no expectations from, and, indeed, no desires about: in a word, I had nothing indeed to do with it, nor was ever likely to have, so I thought it looked, as we may perhaps look upon it hereafter—viz. as a place I had lived in, but was come out of it; and well might I say, as Father Abraham to Dives, Between me and thee is a great gulf fixed.

In the first place, I was removed from all the wickedness of the world here; I had neither the lusts of the flesh, the lusts of the eye, nor the pride of life. I had nothing to **covet**①, for I had all that I was now capable of enjoying; I was lord of the whole **manor**②; or, if I pleased, I might call myself king or emperor over the whole country which I had possession of: there were no rivals; I had no competitor, none to dispute sovereignty or command with me: I might have raised ship-loadings of corn, but I had no use for it; so I let as little grow as I thought enough for my occasion. I had tortoise or turtle enough, but now and then one was as much as I could put to any use: I had **timber**③ enough to have built a fleet of ships; and I had grapes enough to have made wine, or to have cured into **raisins**④, to have loaded that fleet when it had been built.

But all I could make use of was all that was valuable: I had enough to eat and supply my wants, and what was all the rest to me? If I killed more flesh than I could eat, the dog must eat it, or vermin; if I sowed more corn than I could eat, it must be spoiled; the trees that I cut down were lying to rot on the ground; I could make no more use of them but for fuel, and that I had no occasion for but to dress my food.

In a word, the nature and experience of things dictated to me, upon just reflection, that all the good things of this world are no farther good to us than they are for our use; and that, whatever we may heap up to give others, we enjoy just as much as we can use, and no more. The most **covetous**⑤, griping **miser**⑥ in the world would have been cured of the vice of covetousness if he had been in my case; for I possessed infinitely more than I knew what to do with. I had no room for desire, except it was of things which I had not, and they were but trifles, though, indeed, of great use to me. I had, as I hinted before, a parcel of money, as well gold as silver, about thirty-six pounds sterling. Alas! there the sorry, useless stuff lay; I had no more manner of business for it; and often thought with myself that I would have given a handful of it for a gross of tobacco-pipes; or for a hand-mill to grind my corn; nay, I would have given it all for a sixpenny-worth of **turnip**⑦ and carrot seed out of England, or for a handful of peas and

---

① **covet**: strongly want sth, especially sth that belongs to another.
② **manor**: a landed estate.
③ **timber**: wood prepared for use in building and carpentry.
④ **raisins**: *pl.* of raisin, a dried grape.
⑤ **covetous**: greedy, acquisitive or grasping.
⑥ **miser**: a person who loves money but hates spending it.
⑦ **turnip**: a round root vegetable with a white or yellowish flesh.

beans, and a bottle of ink. As it was, I had not the least advantage by it or benefit from it; but there it lay in a drawer, and grew **mouldy**① with the damp of the cave in the wet seasons; and if I had had the drawer full of diamonds, it had been the same case—they had been of no manner of value to me, because of no use.

I had now brought my state of life to be much easier in itself than it was at first, and much easier to my mind, as well as to my body. I frequently sat down to meat with thankfulness, and admired the hand of God's **providence**②, which had thus spread my table in the wilderness. I learned to look more upon the bright side of my condition, and less upon the dark side, and to consider what I enjoyed rather than what I wanted; and this gave me sometimes such secret comforts, that I cannot express them; and which I take notice of here, to put those discontented people in mind of it, who cannot enjoy comfortably what God has given them, because they see and covet something that He has not given them. All our discontents about what we want appeared to me to spring from the want of thankfulness for what we have.

Another reflection was of great use to me, and doubtless would be so to any one that should fall into such distress as mine was; and this was, to compare my present condition with what I at first expected it would be; nay, with what it would certainly have been, if the good providence of God had not wonderfully ordered the ship to be cast up nearer to the shore, where I not only could come at her, but could bring what I got out of her to the shore, for my relief and comfort; without which, I had wanted for tools to work, weapons for defence, and gunpowder and shot for getting my food.

I spent whole hours, I may say whole days, in representing to myself, in the most lively colours, how I must have acted if I had got nothing out of the ship. How I could not have so much as got any food, except fish and turtles; and that, as it was long before I found any of them, I must have **perished**③ first; that I should have lived, if I had not perished, like a mere savage; that if I had killed a goat or a fowl, by any **contrivance**④, I had no way to **flay**⑤ or open it, or part the flesh from the skin and the **bowels**⑥, or to cut it up; but must **gnaw**⑦ it with my teeth, and pull it with my claws, like a beast.

These reflections made me very sensible of the goodness of Providence to me, and very thankful for my present condition, with all its hardships and misfortunes; and this part also I cannot but recommend to the reflection of those who are apt, in their misery, to say, Is any

---

① **mouldy**: covered with mold, which is a fungus that typically grows in damp or decaying conditions.
② **providence**: protective care and guidance believed to be provided by God.
③ **perished**: *v.* **perish** (**perished, perished**), to die, usually in a harsh or abrupt manner.
④ **contrivance**: a clever device or plan.
⑤ **flay**: to remove the skin from an animal.
⑥ **bowels**: *pl.* of **bowel**, the intestines of an animal or human being.
⑦ **gnaw**: to bite at or nibble something persistently.

Unit 6   Daniel Defoe (1660-1731)

affliction① like mine? Let them consider how much worse the cases of some people are, and their case might have been, if Providence had thought fit.

I had another reflection, which assisted me also to comfort my mind with hopes; and this was comparing my present situation with what I had deserved, and had therefore reason to expect from the hand of Providence. I had lived a dreadful life, perfectly destitute of the knowledge and fear of God. I had been well instructed by father and mother; neither had they been wanting to me in their early endeavours to infuse a religious awe of God into my mind, a sense of my duty, and what the nature and end of my being required of me. But, alas! falling early into the seafaring life, which of all lives is the most destitute of the fear of God, though His terrors are always before them; I say, falling early into the seafaring life, and into seafaring company, all that little sense of religion which I had entertained was laughed out of me by my **messmates**②; by a hardened **despising**③ of dangers, and the views of death, which grew habitual to me by my long absence from all manner of opportunities to converse with anything but what was like myself, or to hear anything that was good or tended towards it.

So void was I of everything that was good, or the least sense of what I was, or was to be, that, in the greatest deliverances I enjoyed—such as my escape from Sallee; my being taken up by the Portuguese master of the ship; my being planted so well in the Brazils; my receiving the cargo from England, and the like—I never had once the words Thank God! so much as on my mind, or in my mouth; nor in the greatest distress had I so much as a thought to pray to Him, or so much as to say, Lord, have mercy upon me! no, nor to mention the name of God, unless it was to swear by, and **blaspheme**④ it.

I had terrible reflections upon my mind for many months, as I have already observed, on account of my wicked and hardened life past; and when I looked about me, and considered what particular providences had attended me since my coming into this place, and how God had dealt **bountifully**⑤ with me—had not only punished me less than my **iniquity**⑥ had deserved, but had so plentifully provided for me—this gave me great hopes that my **repentance**⑦ was accepted, and that God had yet mercy in store for me.

With these reflections I worked my mind up, not only to a **resignation**⑧ to the will of God in the present disposition of my circumstances, but even to a sincere thankfulness for my condition; and that I, who was yet a living man, ought not to complain, seeing I had not the due

---

① **affliction**: hardship, tribulation.
② **messmates**: *pl.* of **messmate**, a companion with whom one shares meals.
③ **despising**: disdain, defiance.
④ **blaspheme**: to speak about God in an irreverent, impious manner.
⑤ **bountifully**: with great generosity; abundantly.
⑥ **iniquity**: wickedness or sin.
⑦ **repentance**: the action of expressing sincere regret for one's wrongdoing or sin.
⑧ **resignation**: acceptance of something undesirable but inevitable.

punishment of my sins; that I enjoyed so many mercies which I had no reason to have expected in that place; that I ought never more to **repine**① at my condition, but to **rejoice**②, and to give daily thanks for that daily bread, which nothing but a crowd of wonders could have brought; that I ought to consider I had been fed even by a miracle, even as great as that of feeding Elijah by ravens, nay, by a long series of miracles; and that I could hardly have named a place in the uninhabitable part of the world where I could have been cast more to my advantage; a place where, as I had no society, which was my affliction on one hand, so I found no **ravenous**③ beasts, no furious wolves or tigers, to threaten my life; no **venomous**④ creatures, or poisons, which I might feed on to my hurt; no savages to murder and **devour**⑤ me. In a word, as my life was a life of sorrow one way, so it was a life of mercy another; and I wanted nothing to make it a life of comfort but to be able to make my sense of God's goodness to me, and care over me in this condition, be my daily consolation; and after I did make a just improvement on these things, I went away, and was no more sad. I had now been here so long that many things which I had brought on shore for my help were either quite gone, or very much wasted and near spent.

My ink, as I observed, had been gone some time, all but a very little, which I **eked**⑥ out with water, a little and a little, till it was so pale, it scarce left any appearance of black upon the paper. As long as it lasted I made use of it to **minute down**⑦ the days of the month on which any remarkable thing happened to me; and first, by casting up times past, I remembered that there was a strange **concurrence**⑧ of days in the various providences which **befell**⑨ me, and which, if I had been **superstitiously**⑩ inclined to observe days as fatal or fortunate, I might have had reason to have looked upon with a great deal of curiosity.

First, I had observed that the same day that I broke away from my father and friends and ran away to Hull, in order to go to sea, the same day afterwards I was taken by the Sallee man-of-war, and made a slave; the same day of the year that I escaped out of the wreck of that ship in Yarmouth Roads, that same day-year afterwards I made my escape from Sallee in a boat; the same day of the year I was born on—viz. the 30th of September, that same day I had my life so miraculously saved twenty-six years after, when I was cast on shore in this island; so that my wicked life and my solitary life began both on a day.

---

① **repine**: to feel or express discontent; to fret.
② **rejoice**: to feel great joy or delight.
③ **ravenous**: extremely hungry.
④ **venomous**: capable of injecting venom.
⑤ **devour**: to eat up hungrily or quickly.
⑥ **eked**: *v.* **eke (eked, eked)**, make a small supply of sth last longer.
⑦ **minute down**: write down.
⑧ **concurrence**: the simultaneous **occurrence** of events or circumstances.
⑨ **befall**: *v.* **befall (befell, befallen)**, happen to.
⑩ **superstitiously**: having a belief in superstitions.

Unit 6 Daniel Defoe (1660-1731)

The next thing to my ink being wasted was that of my bread—I mean the biscuit which I brought out of the ship; this I had **husbanded**① to the last degree, allowing myself but one cake of bread a-day for above a year; and yet I was quite without bread for near a year before I got any corn of my own, and great reason I had to be thankful that I had any at all, the getting it being, as has been already observed, next to miraculous.

My clothes, too, began to decay; as to linen, I had had none a good while, except some **chequered**② shirts which I found in the chests of the other seamen, and which I carefully preserved; because many times I could bear no other clothes on but a shirt; and it was a very great help to me that I had, among all the men's clothes of the ship, almost three dozen of shirts. There were also, indeed, several thick watch-coats of the seamen's which were left, but they were too hot to wear; and though it is true that the weather was so violently hot that there was no need of clothes, yet I could not go quite naked—no, though I had been inclined to it, which I was not—nor could I **abide**③ the thought of it, though I was alone. The reason why I could not go naked was, I could not bear the heat of the sun so well when quite naked as with some clothes on; nay, the very heat frequently **blistered**④ my skin: whereas, with a shirt on, the air itself made some motion, and whistling under the shirt, was twofold cooler than without it. No more could I ever bring myself to go out in the heat of the sun without a cap or a hat; the heat of the sun, beating with such violence as it does in that place, would give me the headache presently, by **darting**⑤ so directly on my head, without a cap or hat on, so that I could not bear it; whereas, if I put on my hat it would presently go away.

Upon these views I began to consider about putting the few rags I had, which I called clothes, into some order; I had worn out all the waistcoats I had, and my business was now to try if I could not make jackets out of the great watch-coats which I had by me, and with such other materials as I had; so I set to work, tailoring, or rather, indeed, **botching**⑥, for I made most **piteous**⑦ work of it. However, I made shift to make two or three new waistcoats, which I hoped would serve me a great while: as for **breeches**⑧ or **drawers**⑨, I made but a very sorry shift indeed till afterwards.

I have mentioned that I saved the skins of all the creatures that I killed, I mean four-footed ones, and I had them hung up, stretched out with sticks in the sun, by which means some of

---

① **husbanded**: *v.* **husband (husbanded, husbanded)** to use sth prudently and economically.
② **chequered**: having a pattern of squares.
③ **abide**: put up with; stand.
④ **blistered**: *v.* **blister (blistered, blistered)**, to form **blisters**.
⑤ **darting**: *v.* **dart**, to thrust or move with sudden speed.
⑥ **botching**: *v.* **botch**, spoil, foul up.
⑦ **piteous**: deserving or arousing pity.
⑧ **breeches**: pants extending to the knee or just below.
⑨ **drawers**: underpants.

them were so dry and hard that they were fit for little, but others were very useful. The first thing I made of these was a great cap for my head, with the hair on the outside, to shoot off the rain; and this I performed so well, that after I made me a suit of clothes wholly of these skins—that is to say, a waistcoat, and breeches open at the knees, and both loose, for they were rather wanting to keep me cool than to keep me warm. I must not omit to acknowledge that they were **wretchedly**① made; for if I was a bad carpenter, I was a worse tailor. However, they were such as I made very good shift with, and when I was out, if it happened to rain, the hair of my waistcoat and cap being outermost, I was kept very dry.

After this, I spent a great deal of time and pains to make an umbrella; I was, indeed, in great want of one, and had a great mind to make one; I had seen them made in the Brazils, where they are very useful in the great heats there, and I felt the heats every **jot**② as great here, and greater too, being nearer the **equinox**③; besides, as I was obliged to be much abroad, it was a most useful thing to me, as well for the rains as the heats. I took a world of pains with it, and was a great while before I could make anything likely to hold: nay, after I had thought I had hit the way, I spoiled two or three before I made one to my mind: but at last I made one that answered indifferently well: the main difficulty I found was to make it let down. I could make it spread, but if it did not let down too, and draw in, it was not portable for me any way but just over my head, which would not do. However, at last, as I said, I made one to answer, and covered it with skins, the hair upwards, so that it cast off the rain like a pent-house, and kept off the sun so effectually, that I could walk out in the hottest of the weather with greater advantage than I could before in the coolest, and when I had no need of it could close it, and carry it under my arm.

Thus I lived mighty comfortably, my mind being entirely composed by resigning myself to the will of God, and throwing myself wholly upon the disposal of His providence. This made my life better than sociable, for when I began to regret the want of conversation I would ask myself, whether thus conversing mutually with my own thoughts, and (as I hope I may say) with even God Himself, by **ejaculations**④, was not better than the utmost enjoyment of human society in the world?

> Exercise

I. Word Matching

Directions: Please choose the most appropriate ones from the given words to explain the

---

① **wretchedly**: poorly or very badly.
② **jot**: a very small amount.
③ **equinox**: one of the two times in the year when the sun crosses the equator and day and night are of equal length.
④ **ejaculations**: *pl.* of **ejaculation**, sudden, short exclamations.

original boldfaced words in the following lines.

A. **clean**	B. **extend**	C. **estimate**	D. **pack**
E. **significant**	F. **work**	G. **incompetent**	

1. Within-doors, that is when it rained and I could not go out, I found **employment** in the following occupations.

2. As between the pot and the basket there was a little room to spare, I **stuff**ed it full of the rice and barley straw.

3. To supply this want, I was at a great loss; for, of all the trades in the world, I was as perfectly **unqualified** for a stone-cutter as for any whatever.

4. Then **sweep**ing away all the embers, I set down my loaf or loaves.

5. When I began to enter upon it, and **calculate** how deep it was to be dug, how broad, how the stuff was to be thrown out, I found that, by the number of hands I had, being none but my own, it must have been ten or twelve years before I could have gone through with it.

6. As long as it lasted I made use of it to minute down the days of the month on which any **remarkable** thing happened to me.

7. I could make it **spread**, but if it did not let down too, and draw in, it was not portable for me any way but just over my head, which would not do.

II. English-Chinese Translation

Directions: Please translate the following classic dicta from English into Chinese.

1. All of our discontents for what we want appear to me to spring from want of thankfulness for what we have.

—*Robinson Crusoe*

2. Thus we never see the true state of our condition till it is illustrated to us by its contraries, nor know how to value what we enjoy, but by the want of it.

—*Robinson Crusoe*

3. The soul is placed in the body like a rough diamond; and must be polished, or the lustre of it will never appear.

—*On the Education of Women*

4. Misery and distress are not, I say, capable to terrify a man of courage or resolution, but will rather animate and encourage him to action and enterprise.

—*Moll Flanders*

5. Thus fear of danger is ten thousand times more terrifying than danger itself when apparent to the eyes.

—*Robinson Crusoe*

III. Term Defining

Directions: Please explain the following literary terms based on Robinson Crusoe.

1. adventure fiction

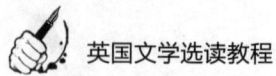

2. first-person narration

3. metaphor

IV. Content-Based Questions

Directions: *Please give a concise and adequate answer to the following questions related to the excerpt.*

1. Crusoe described creating a sieve as a most difficult thing. What reasons did he give for this, and what strategy did he employ to resolve this issue?

2. Crusoe hesitated initially despite his eagerness to explore the land visible from the island's opposite side. Can you find the reasons for his reluctance to act immediately?

3. Crusoe explored several strategies to launch his constructed boat into the water. Investigate the specific methods he attempted, and analyze the reasons behind the failure of these endeavors.

V. Discussion Question

Crusoe places significant emphasis on his various attempts to create practical items for his survival. Reflect on Crusoe's narrative about his endeavors and discuss with your partner the implications of his resourcefulness. Consider the emotions and thought processes he might have experienced during these trials. How do you think you would have approached these challenges if you were in his shoes? Share your perspectives with each other.

VI. Essay Question

Robinson Crusoe reflects on solitude enhancing his inner life, suggesting it may be preferable to the company of others. Do you align with Crusoe's perspective on solitude? Consider the potential benefits and drawbacks of such isolation on personal growth and societal interaction. Can solitude truly rival the enrichment that comes from engaging with a community? Write a 200-word essay on your reflections on Crusoe's view of solitude and provide your stance using personal insights or societal examples.

Text B

Robinson Crusoe
An Excerpt from Chapter XIV

It was one of the nights in the rainy season in March, the four-and-twentieth year of my first setting foot in this island of solitude, I was lying in my bed or hammock, awake, very well in health, had no pain, no distemper, no uneasiness of body, nor any uneasiness of mind more than ordinary, but could by no means close my eyes, that is, so as to sleep; no, not a wink all night long, otherwise than as follows:

It is impossible to set down the innumerable crowd of thoughts that **whirled**① through that great **thoroughfare**② of the brain, the memory, in this night's time. I ran over the whole history of my life in miniature, or by abridgment, as I may call it, to my coming to this island, and also of that part of my life since I came to this island. In my reflections upon the state of my case since I came on shore on this island, I was comparing the happy posture of my affairs in the first years of my habitation here, with the life of anxiety, fear, and care which I had lived in ever since I had seen the print of a foot in the sand. Not that I did not believe the savages had frequented the island even all the while, and might have been several hundreds of them at times on shore there; but I had never known it, and was incapable of any apprehensions about it; my satisfaction was perfect, though my danger was the same, and I was as happy in not knowing my danger as if I had never really been exposed to it. This furnished my thoughts with

---

① **whirled**: *v.* **whirl** (**whirled**, **whirled**), move in a circle or similar curve especially with force or speed.
② **thoroughfare**: a way or place for passage.

many very profitable reflections, and particularly this one: How infinitely good that Providence is, which has provided, in its government of mankind, such narrow bounds to his sight and knowledge of things; and though he walks in the midst of so many thousand dangers, the sight of which, if discovered to him, would distract his mind and sink his spirits, he is kept serene and calm, by having the events of things hid from his eyes, and knowing nothing of the dangers which surround him.

After these thoughts had for some time entertained me, I came to reflect seriously upon the real danger I had been in for so many years in this very island, and how I had walked about in the greatest security, and with all possible tranquillity, even when perhaps nothing but the brow of a hill, a great tree, or the casual approach of night, had been between me and the worst kind of destruction—viz. that of falling into the hands of **cannibals**① and savages, who would have seized on me with the same view as I would on a goat or turtle; and have thought it no more crime to kill and devour me than I did of a pigeon or a curlew. I would unjustly slander myself if I should say I was not sincerely thankful to my great Preserver, to whose singular protection I acknowledged, with great humanity, all these unknown deliverances were due, and without which I must inevitably have fallen into their merciless hands.

When these thoughts were over, my head was for some time taken up in considering the nature of these wretched creatures, I mean the savages, and how it came to pass in the world that the wise Governor of all things should give up any of His creatures to such inhumanity—**nay**②, to something so much below even brutality itself—as to devour its own kind: but as this ended in some (at that time) fruitless speculations, it occurred to me to inquire what part of the world these wretches lived in? how far off the coast was from whence they came? what they ventured over so far from home for? what kind of boats they had? and why I might not order myself and my business so that I might be able to go over thither, as they were to come to me?

I never so much as troubled myself to consider what I should do with myself when I went thither; what would become of me if I fell into the hands of these savages; or how I should escape them if they attacked me; no, nor so much as how it was possible for me to reach the coast, and not to be attacked by some or other of them, without any possibility of delivering myself; and if I should not fall into their hands, what I should do for provision, or whither I should bend my course; none of these thoughts, I say, so much as came in my way; but my mind was wholly bent upon the notion of my passing over in my boat to the mainland. I looked upon my present condition as the most miserable that could possibly be; that I was not able to throw myself into anything but death, that could be called worse; and if I reached the shore of the main I might perhaps meet with relief, or I might coast along, as I did on the African

---

① **cannibals**: ones that eat the flesh of its own kind.

② **nay**: (old-fashioned; literary) used to correct what has just been said by replacing a word with one that is more accurate or appropriate

shore, till I came to some inhabited country, and where I might find some relief; and after all, perhaps I might fall in with some Christian ship that might take me in: and if the worst came to the worst, I could but die, which would put an end to all these miseries at once. Pray note, all this was the fruit of a disturbed mind, an impatient temper, made desperate, as it were, by the long continuance of my troubles, and the disappointments I had met in the wreck I had been on board of, and where I had been so near obtaining what I so earnestly longed for—somebody to speak to, and to learn some knowledge from them of the place where I was, and of the probable means of my deliverance. I was agitated wholly by these thoughts; all my calm of mind, in my resignation to Providence, and waiting the issue of the dispositions of Heaven, seemed to be suspended; and I had as it were no power to turn my thoughts to anything but to the project of a voyage to the main, which came upon me with such force, and such an impetuosity of desire, that it was not to be resisted.

When this had agitated my thoughts for two hours or more, with such violence that it set my very blood into a ferment, and my pulse beat as if I had been in a fever, merely with the extraordinary fervour of my mind about it, Nature—as if I had been fatigued and exhausted with the very thoughts of it—threw me into a sound sleep. One would have thought I should have dreamed of it, but I did not, nor of anything relating to it, but I dreamed that as I was going out in the morning as usual from my castle, I saw upon the shore two canoes and eleven savages coming to land, and that they brought with them another savage whom they were going to kill in order to eat him; when, on a sudden, the savage that they were going to kill jumped away, and ran for his life; and I thought in my sleep that he came running into my little thick grove before my fortification, to hide himself; and that I seeing him alone, and not perceiving that the others sought him that way, showed myself to him, and smiling upon him, encouraged him: that he kneeled down to me, seeming to pray me to assist him; upon which I showed him my ladder, made him go up, and carried him into my cave, and he became my servant; and that as soon as I had got this man, I said to myself, now I may certainly venture to the mainland, for this fellow will serve me as a pilot, and will tell me what to do, and whither to go for provisions, and whither not to go for fear of being devoured; what places to venture into, and what to shun. I waked with this thought; and was under such inexpressible impressions of joy at the prospect of my escape in my dream, that the disappointments which I felt upon coming to myself, and finding that it was no more than a dream, were equally extravagant the other way, and threw me into a very great **dejection**① of spirits.

Upon this, however, I made this conclusion: that my only way to go about to attempt an escape was, to endeavour to get a savage into my possession: and, if possible, it should be one of their prisoners, whom they had condemned to be eaten, and should bring hither to kill.

---

① **dejection**: lowness of spirits.

But these thoughts still were attended with this difficulty: that it was impossible to effect this without attacking a whole **caravan**① of them, and killing them all; and this was not only a very desperate attempt, and might miscarry, but, on the other hand, I had greatly **scrupled**② the lawfulness of it to myself; and my heart trembled at the thoughts of shedding so much blood, though it was for my deliverance. I need not repeat the arguments which occurred to me against this, they being the same mentioned before; but though I had other reasons to offer now—viz. That those men were enemies to my life, and would devour me if they could; that it was self-preservation, in the highest degree, to deliver myself from this death of a life, and was acting in my own defence as much as if they were actually assaulting me, and the like; I say though these things argued for it, yet the thoughts of shedding human blood for my deliverance were very terrible to me, and such as I could by no means reconcile myself to for a great while. However, at last, after many secret disputes with myself, and after great perplexities about it (for all these arguments, one way and another, struggled in my head a long time), the eager prevailing desire of deliverance at length mastered all the rest; and I resolved, if possible, to get one of these savages into my hands, cost what it would. My next thing was to contrive how to do it, and this, indeed, was very difficult to resolve on; but as I could pitch upon no probable means for it, so I resolved to put myself upon the watch, to see them when they came on shore, and leave the rest to the event; taking such measures as the opportunity should present, let what would be.

With these resolutions in my thoughts, I set myself upon the **scout**③ as often as possible, and indeed so often that I was heartily tired of it; for it was above a year and a half that I waited; and for great part of that time went out to the west end, and to the south-west corner of the island almost every day, to look for canoes, but none appeared. This was very discouraging, and began to trouble me much, though I cannot say that it did in this case (as it had done some time before) **wear off**④ the edge of my desire to the thing; but the longer it seemed to be delayed, the more eager I was for it: in a word, I was not at first so careful to shun the sight of these savages, and avoid being seen by them, as I was now eager to be upon them. Besides, I fancied myself able to manage one, nay, two or three savages, if I had them, so as to make them entirely slaves to me, to do whatever I should direct them, and to prevent their being able at any time to do me any hurt. It was a great while that I pleased myself with this affair; but nothing still presented itself; all my fancies and schemes came to nothing, for no savages came near me for a great while.

About a year and a half after I entertained these notions (and by long musing had, as it were, resolved them all into nothing, for want of an occasion to put them into execution), I

---

① **caravan**: a company of travelers on a journey through desert or hostile regions.
② **scrupled**: held back in doubt or indecision.
③ **scout**: the act of observing in order to obtain information or evaluate.
④ **wear off**: gradually decrease, disappear, or stop.

was surprised one morning by seeing no less than five canoes all on shore together on my side the island, and the people who belonged to them all landed and out of my sight. The number of them broke all my measures; for seeing so many, and knowing that they always came four or six, or sometimes more in a boat, I could not tell what to think of it, or how to take my measures to attack twenty or thirty men single-handed; so lay still in my castle, perplexed and discomforted. However, I put myself into the same position for an attack that I had formerly provided, and was just ready for action, if anything had presented. Having waited a good while, listening to hear if they made any noise, at length, being very impatient, I set my guns at the foot of my ladder, and clambered up to the top of the hill, by my two stages, as usual; standing so, however, that my head did not appear above the hill, so that they could not perceive me by any means. Here I observed, by the help of my perspective glass, that they were no less than thirty in number; that they had a fire kindled, and that they had meat dressed. How they had cooked it I knew not, or what it was; but they were all dancing, in I know not how many barbarous gestures and figures, their own way, round the fire.

While I was thus looking on them, I perceived, by my perspective, two miserable wretches dragged from the boats, where, it seems, they were laid by, and were now brought out for the slaughter. I perceived one of them immediately fall; being knocked down, I suppose, with a **club**① or wooden sword, for that was their way; and two or three others were at work immediately, cutting him open for their cookery, while the other victim was left standing by himself, till they should be ready for him. In that very moment this poor wretch, seeing himself a little at liberty and unbound, nature inspired him with hopes of life, and he started away from them, and ran with incredible swiftness along the sands, directly towards me; I mean towards that part of the coast where my habitation was. I was dreadfully frightened, I must acknowledge, when I perceived him run my way; and especially when, as I thought, I saw him pursued by the whole body: and now I expected that part of my dream was coming to pass, and that he would certainly take shelter in my grove; but I could not depend, by any means, upon my dream, that the other savages would not pursue him thither and find him there. However, I kept my station, and my spirits began to recover when I found that there was not above three men that followed him; and still more was I encouraged, when I found that he outstripped them exceedingly in running, and gained ground on them; so that, if he could but hold out for half-an-hour, I saw easily he would fairly get away from them all.

There was between them and my castle the creek, which I mentioned often in the first part of my story, where I landed my cargoes out of the ship; and this I saw plainly he must necessarily swim over, or the poor wretch would be taken there; but when the savage escaping came thither, he made nothing of it, though the tide was then up; but plunging in, swam through

---

① **club**: a heavy stick with one end thicker than the other, which is used as a weapon.

in about thirty strokes, or thereabouts, landed, and ran with exceeding strength and swiftness. When the three persons came to the creek, I found that two of them could swim, but the third could not, and that, standing on the other side, he looked at the others, but went no farther, and soon after went softly back again; which, as it happened, was very well for him in the end. I observed that the two who swam were yet more than twice as strong swimming over the creek as the fellow was that fled from them. It came very warmly upon my thoughts, and indeed irresistibly, that now was the time to get me a servant, and, perhaps, a companion or assistant; and that I was plainly called by Providence to save this poor creature's life. I immediately ran down the ladders with all possible expedition, fetched my two guns, for they were both at the foot of the ladders, as I observed before, and getting up again with the same haste to the top of the hill, I crossed towards the sea; and having a very short cut, and all down hill, placed myself in the way between the pursuers and the pursued, hallowing aloud to him that fled, who, looking back, was at first perhaps as much frightened at me as at them; but I **beckoned**① with my hand to him to come back; and, in the meantime, I slowly advanced towards the two that followed; then rushing at once upon the foremost, I knocked him down with the stock of my piece. I was loath to fire, because I would not have the rest hear; though, at that distance, it would not have been easily heard, and being out of sight of the smoke, too, they would not have known what to make of it. Having knocked this fellow down, the other who pursued him stopped, as if he had been frightened, and I advanced towards him: but as I came nearer, I perceived presently he had a bow and arrow, and was fitting it to shoot at me: so I was then obliged to shoot at him first, which I did, and killed him at the first shot. The poor savage who fled, but had stopped, though he saw both his enemies fallen and killed, as he thought, yet was so frightened with the fire and noise of my piece that he stood stock still, and neither came forward nor went backward, though he seemed rather inclined still to fly than to come on. I hallooed again to him, and made signs to come forward, which he easily understood, and came a little way; then stopped again, and then a little farther, and stopped again; and I could then perceive that he stood trembling, as if he had been taken prisoner, and had just been to be killed, as his two enemies were. I beckoned to him again to come to me, and gave him all the signs of encouragement that I could think of; and he came nearer and nearer, kneeling down every ten or twelve steps, in token of acknowledgment for saving his life. I smiled at him, and looked pleasantly, and beckoned to him to come still nearer; at length he came close to me; and then he kneeled down again, kissed the ground, and laid his head upon the ground, and taking me by the foot, set my foot upon his head; this, it seems, was in token of swearing to be my slave for ever. I took him up and made much of him, and encouraged him all I could. But there was more work to do yet; for I perceived the savage whom I had knocked down was not killed,

---

① **beckoned**: *v.* **beckon**, summon or signal typically with a wave or nod.

but stunned with the blow, and began to come to himself: so I pointed to him, and showed him the savage, that he was not dead; upon this he spoke some words to me, and though I could not understand them, yet I thought they were pleasant to hear; for they were the first sound of a man's voice that I had heard, my own excepted, for above twenty-five years. But there was no time for such reflections now; the savage who was knocked down recovered himself so far as to sit up upon the ground, and I perceived that my savage began to be afraid; but when I saw that, I presented my other piece at the man, as if I would shoot him: upon this my savage, for so I call him now, made a motion to me to lend him my sword, which hung naked in a belt by my side, which I did. He no sooner had it, but he runs to his enemy, and at one blow cut off his head so cleverly, no executioner in Germany could have done it sooner or better; which I thought very strange for one who, I had reason to believe, never saw a sword in his life before, except their own wooden swords: however, it seems, as I learned afterwards, they make their wooden swords so sharp, so heavy, and the wood is so hard, that they will even cut off heads with them, ay, and arms, and that at one blow, too. When he had done this, he comes laughing to me in sign of triumph, and brought me the sword again, and with abundance of gestures which I did not understand, laid it down, with the head of the savage that he had killed, just before me. But that which astonished him most was to know how I killed the other Indian so far off; so, pointing to him, he made signs to me to let him go to him; and I bade him go, as well as I could. When he came to him, he stood like one amazed, looking at him, turning him first on one side, then on the other; looked at the wound the bullet had made, which it seems was just in his breast, where it had made a hole, and no great quantity of blood had followed; but he had bled inwardly, for he was quite dead. He took up his bow and arrows, and came back; so I turned to go away, and beckoned him to follow me, making signs to him that more might come after them. Upon this he made signs to me that he should bury them with sand, that they might not be seen by the rest, if they followed; and so I made signs to him again to do so. He fell to work; and in an instant he had **scraped**① a hole in the sand with his hands big enough to bury the first in, and then dragged him into it, and covered him; and did so by the other also; I believe he had him buried them both in a quarter of an hour. Then, calling away, I carried him, not to my castle, but quite away to my cave, on the farther part of the island: so I did not let my dream come to pass in that part, that he came into my grove for shelter. Here I gave him bread and a bunch of raisins to eat, and a draught of water, which I found he was indeed in great distress for, from his running: and having refreshed him, I made signs for him to go and lie down to sleep, showing him a place where I had laid some rice-straw, and a blanket upon it, which I used to sleep upon myself sometimes; so the poor creature lay down, and went to sleep.

---

① **scraped**: *v.* **scrape**, make a hole or hollow place in the ground.

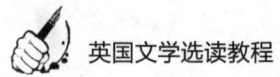

He was a **comely**①, handsome fellow, perfectly well made, with straight, strong limbs, not too large; tall, and well-shaped; and, as I reckon, about twenty-six years of age. He had a very good countenance, not a fierce and surly aspect, but seemed to have something very manly in his face; and yet he had all the sweetness and softness of a European in his countenance, too, especially when he smiled. His hair was long and black, not curled like wool; his forehead very high and large; and a great vivacity and sparkling sharpness in his eyes. The colour of his skin was not quite black, but very **tawny**②; and yet not an ugly, yellow, **nauseous**③ tawny, as the Brazilians and Virginians, and other natives of America are, but of a bright kind of a **dun**④ olive-colour, that had in it something very agreeable, though not very easy to describe. His face was round and plump; his nose small, not flat, like the negroes; a very good mouth, thin lips, and his fine teeth well set, and as white as ivory.

After he had slumbered, rather than slept, about half-an-hour, he awoke again, and came out of the cave to me, for I had been milking my goats which I had in the enclosure just by: when he **espied**⑤ me he came running to me, laying himself down again upon the ground, with all the possible signs of an humble, thankful disposition, making a great many **antic**⑥ gestures to show it. At last he lays his head flat upon the ground, close to my foot, and sets my other foot upon his head, as he had done before; and after this made all the signs to me of subjection, servitude, and submission imaginable, to let me know how he would serve me so long as he lived. I understood him in many things, and let him know I was very well pleased with him. In a little time I began to speak to him; and teach him to speak to me; and first, I let him know his name should be Friday, which was the day I saved his life; I called him so for the memory of the time. I likewise taught him to say Master; and then let him know that was to be my name; I likewise taught him to say Yes and No and to know the meaning of them. I gave him some milk in an earthen pot, and let him see me drink it before him, and **sop**⑦ my bread in it; and gave him a cake of bread to do the like, which he quickly complied with, and made signs that it was very good for him. I kept there with him all that night; but as soon as it was day I beckoned to him to come with me, and let him know I would give him some clothes; at which he seemed very glad, for he was **stark**⑧ naked. As we went by the place where he had buried the two men, he pointed exactly to the place, and showed me the marks that he had made to find them again, making signs to me that we should dig them up again and eat them. At this I appeared very angry,

---

① **comely**: having a pleasing appearance.
② **tawny**: of a warm sandy color.
③ **nauseous**: causing disgust.
④ **dun**: having a slightly brownish dark gray color.
⑤ **espied**: *v.* **espy (espied, espied)**, catch sight of.
⑥ **antic**: ludicrously odd.
⑦ **sop**: cover with liquid.
⑧ **stark**: utter.

Unit 6 Daniel Defoe (1660-1731)

expressed my abhorrence of it, made as if I would vomit at the thoughts of it, and beckoned with my hand to him to come away, which he did immediately, with great submission. I then led him up to the top of the hill, to see if his enemies were gone; and pulling out my glass I looked, and saw plainly the place where they had been, but no appearance of them or their canoes; so that it was plain they were gone, and had left their two comrades behind them, without any search after them.

But I was not content with this discovery; but having now more courage, and consequently more curiosity, I took my man Friday with me, giving him the sword in his hand, with the bow and arrows at his back, which I found he could use very dexterously, making him carry one gun for me, and I two for myself; and away we marched to the place where these creatures had been; for I had a mind now to get some further intelligence of them. When I came to the place my very blood ran chill in my veins, and my heart sunk within me, at the horror of the spectacle; indeed, it was a dreadful sight, at least it was so to me, though Friday made nothing of it. The place was covered with human bones, the ground dyed with their blood, and great pieces of flesh left here and there, half-eaten, **mangled**①, and scorched; and, in short, all the tokens of the triumphant feast they had been making there, after a victory over their enemies. I saw three skulls, five hands, and the bones of three or four legs and feet, and abundance of other parts of the bodies; and Friday, by his signs, made me understand that they brought over four prisoners to feast upon; that three of them were eaten up, and that he, pointing to himself, was the fourth; that there had been a great battle between them and their next king, of whose subjects, it seems, he had been one, and that they had taken a great number of prisoners; all which were carried to several places by those who had taken them in the fight, in order to feast upon them, as was done here by these wretches upon those they brought hither.

I caused Friday to gather all the skulls, bones, flesh, and whatever remained, and lay them together in a heap, and make a great fire upon it, and burn them all to ashes. I found Friday had still a **hankering**② stomach after some of the flesh, and was still a cannibal in his nature; but I showed so much abhorrence at the very thoughts of it, and at the least appearance of it, that he **durst**③ not discover it: for I had, by some means, let him know that I would kill him if he offered it.

≫ Exercise

I. Word Matching

Directions: Please choose the most appropriate ones from the given words to explain the

---

① **mangled**: injured with deep disfiguring wounds by cutting, tearing, or crushing.
② **hankering**: having a strong or persistent desire.
③ **durst**: archaic and dialectal past tense of dare.

original boldfaced words in the following lines.

A. **fire**   B. **expertly**   C. **attack**   D. **condensation**

E. **abhorrence**   F. **destroy**   G. **confusion**   H. **reluctant**

1. I ran over the whole history of my life in miniature, or by **abridgment**, as I may call it, to my coming to this island, and also of that part of my life since I came to this island.

2. Cannibals and savages would have seized on me with the same view as I would on a goat or turtle; and have thought it no more crime to kill and **devour** me than I did of a pigeon or a curlew.

3. It was self-preservation, in the highest degree, to deliver myself from this death of a life, and was acting in my own defence as much as if they were actually **assaulting** me, and the like.

4. After great **perplexities** about it (for all these arguments, one way and another, struggled in my head a long time), the eager prevailing desire of deliverance at length mastered all the rest.

5. I was **loath** to fire, because I would not have the rest hear; though, at that distance, it would not have been easily heard, and being out of sight of the smoke, too.

6. At this I appeared very angry, expressed my **abhorrence** of it, made as if I would vomit at the thoughts of it.

7. I took my man Friday with me, giving him the sword in his hand, with the bow and arrows at his back, which I found he could use very **dexterously**.

II. Blank Filling

Directions: Please fill in the following blanks with words or expressions that best express the contextual meaning of the classic dicta.

1. Thus fear of danger is ten thousand times more terrifying than _____ itself.

—Robinson Crusoe

2. I saw the Cloud, though I did not _____ the Storm.

—Moll Flanders

3. I am giving an account of what was, not of what ought or ought _____ to be.

—Moll Flanders

4. Today we love what tomorrow we _____, today we seek what tomorrow we shun, today we desire what tomorrow we fear, nay, even tremble at the apprehensions of.

—Robinson Crusoe

5. Pleasure is a thief to _____.

—The Complete English Tradesman

III. Term Defining

Directions: Please explain the following literary terms based on Robinson Crusoe.

1. fiction

2. adventure fiction

3. narrator

IV. Content-Based Questions

Directions: Please give a concise and adequate answer to the following questions related to the above excerpt from Chapter XIV Robinson Crusoe.

1. What happened to me on one March night of my four-and-twentieth year on the island and what reflections were my thoughts filled with?

2. What's the real danger I had encountered for so many years on this island?

3. What came upon me forcefully and could not to be resisted after my thoughts of the whole night?

4. Why did I resolve to get one savage into my hands at any cost?

5. In what way did I get rid of the other two savages pursuing the runaway one?

6. What encouragement did I make to the saved savage and how did he express his gratitude to me?

V. Discussion Question

Please analyze and discuss the plot of the excerpt of Chapter XIV with your partner(s) and give an account of the exact process of Friday being saved in a relay.

VI. Essay Question

Apparently Friday devoted himself to Robinson's heart and soul at the end of Chapter XIV. Please transform yourself into Daniel Defoe to create a sequel of the tale of Friday and Robinson keeping each other company.

Self-Improving Reading

Robinson Crusoe: Chapter 21 by Daniel Defoe

Robinson Crusoe: Chapter 1 by Daniel Defoe

Unit 7   Jonathan Swift (1667–1745)

Life and Works

    Jonathan Swift, one of the foremost prose satirists of the English language, was brought up by his uncle Godwin Swift, an esteemed attorney, due to the fact that his father, Jonathan Swift the elder, had died seven months before Jonathan's birth in Ireland in 1667. Jonathan received the best primary schooling in Ireland's Kilkenny Grammar School and entered Dublin's Trinity College at the age of 14 and earned his Bachelor of Arts degree in 1686, but the advent of the Glorious Revolution suspended his pursuit for a Master's degree. Jonathan then moved to England and with the help of his mother, had the chance of working as secretary to Sir William Temple, a famous political essayist and statesman, intermittently for a decade in Moor Park, Surrey, where he got to know his dearest Stella, Esther Johnson, the daughter of Temple's housekeeper and maintained their intimate relationship all their lives. Jonathan received his M.A. from Oxford in 1692 and a Doctor of Divinity from Dublin University in 1702. Two years later Swift published his two powerful satires on corruption in religion and learning, *A Tale of a Tub* and *The Battle of the Books*, the first of which was relentlessly condemned officially owing to its description of the religious extremes between Roman Catholicism and Calvinism, but simultaneously helped him to obtain a job with the tories as the editor of their organ, *The Examiner*.

Jonathan returned to Ireland in 1713 and was ordained as Dean of St. Patrick's Cathedral in Dublin. Jonathan's work *Gulliver's Travels*, one of the most delightful children's books, was initiated in 1720, whose manuscript was finally finished and published in 1726. The year 1729 saw the publication of Jonathan's satirical work, *A Modest Proposal*, which exposed the narrow-mindedness of Ireland's ruling class and the colonial government in England. Jonathan seemingly suffered a stroke in 1742 and never recovered from the affliction before his demise on Oct. 19, 1745.

Text A

Gulliver's Travels
Part I   A Voyage to Lilliput
Chapter I

My father had a small estate in **Nottinghamshire**[①]: I was the third of five sons. He sent me to Emanuel College in Cambridge at fourteen years old, where I resided three years, and applied myself close to my studies; but the charge of maintaining me, although I had a very **scanty**[②] **allowance**[③], being too great for a narrow fortune, I was bound **apprentice**[④] to Mr. James Bates, an eminent surgeon in London, with whom I continued four years. My father now and then sending me small sums of money, I laid them out in learning navigation, and other parts of the mathematics, useful to those who intend to travel, as I always believed it would be, some time or other, my fortune to do. When I left Mr. Bates, I went down to my father: where, by the assistance of him and my uncle John, and some other relations, I got forty pounds, and a promise of thirty pounds a year to maintain me at **Leyden**[⑤]: there I studied physic two years and seven months, knowing it would be useful in long voyages.

Soon after my return from Leyden, I was recommended by my good master, Mr. Bates, to be surgeon to the Swallow, Captain Abraham Pannel, commander; with whom I continued three

---

① **Nottinghamshire**: a county in the East Midlands of England.
② **scanty**: insufficient in amount or quantity; barely enough.
③ **allowance**: an amount of money that is given to sb regularly.
④ **apprentice**: someone who is training under a skilled employer to learn a trade or occupation.
⑤ **Leyden**: a city in the province of South Holland, Netherlands.

years and a half, making a voyage or two into the Levant, and some other parts. When I came back I resolved to settle in London; to which Mr. Bates, my master, encouraged me, and by him I was recommended to several patients. I took part of a small house in the Old Jewry; and being advised to alter my condition, I married Mrs. Mary Burton, second daughter to Mr. Edmund Burton, **hosier**①, in Newgate-street, with whom I received four hundred pounds for a **portion**②.

But my good master Bates dying in two years after, and I having few friends, my business began to fail; for my conscience would not suffer me to imitate the bad practice of too many among my **brethren**③. Having therefore consulted with my wife, and some of my acquaintance, I determined to go again to sea. I was surgeon successively in two ships, and made several voyages, for six years, to the East and West Indies, by which I got some addition to my fortune. My hours of leisure I spent in reading the best authors, ancient and modern, being always provided with a good number of books; and when I was ashore, in observing the manners and **dispositions**④ of the people, as well as learning their language; wherein I had a great facility, by the strength of my memory.

The last of these voyages not proving very fortunate, I grew weary of the sea, and intended to stay at home with my wife and family. I removed from the Old Jewry to Fetter Lane, and from thence to Wapping, hoping to get business among the sailors; but it would not turn to account. After three years expectation that things would mend, I accepted an advantageous offer from Captain William Prichard, master of the Antelope, who was making a voyage to the South Sea. We set sail from Bristol, May 4, 1699, and our voyage was at first very prosperous.

It would not be proper, for some reasons, to trouble the reader with the particulars of our adventures in those seas; let it suffice to inform him, that in our passage from thence to the East Indies, we were driven by a violent storm to the north-west of Van Diemen's Land. By an observation, we found ourselves in the latitude of 30 degrees 2 minutes south. Twelve of our crew were dead by **immoderate**⑤ labour and ill food; the rest were in a very weak condition. On the 5th of November, which was the beginning of summer in those parts, the weather being very **hazy**⑥, the seamen **spied**⑦ a rock within half a cable's length of the ship; but the wind was so strong, that we were driven directly upon it, and immediately split. Six of the crew, of whom I was one, having let down the boat into the sea, made a shift to get clear of the ship and the rock. We rowed, by my computation, about three **leagues**⑧, till we were able to work no longer,

---

① **hosier**: a person who sells garments like stockings, socks, and tights.
② **portion**: a dowry in marriage.
③ **brethren**: fellow professionals or those within his trade.
④ **dispositions**: *pl.* of **disposition**, inherent qualities of mind and character.
⑤ **immoderate**: excessive or extreme.
⑥ **hazy**: weather conditions where there is reduced visibility due to mist or light fog.
⑦ **spied**: *v.* spy (**spied**, **spied**), suddenly see or notice sth.
⑧ **leagues**: *pl.* of **league**, a unit for measuring distance, equal to about 3 miles.

Unit 7 Jonathan Swift (1667-1745)

being already spent with labour while we were in the ship. We therefore trusted ourselves to the mercy of the waves, and in about half an hour the boat was overset by a sudden **flurry**① from the north. What became of my companions in the boat, as well as of those who escaped on the rock, or were left in the vessel, I cannot tell; but conclude they were all lost. For my own part, I swam as fortune directed me, and was pushed forward by wind and tide. I often let my legs drop, and could feel no bottom; but when I was almost gone, and able to struggle no longer, I found myself within my depth; and by this time the storm was much **abated**②. The **declivity**③ was so small, that I walked near a mile before I got to the shore, which I **conjectured**④ was about eight o'clock in the evening. I then advanced forward near half a mile, but could not discover any sign of houses or inhabitants; at least I was in so weak a condition, that I did not observe them. I was extremely tired, and with that, and the heat of the weather, and about half a pint of brandy that I drank as I left the ship, I found myself much inclined to sleep. I lay down on the grass, which was very short and soft, where I slept sounder than ever I remembered to have done in my life, and, as I reckoned, about nine hours; for when I awaked, it was just daylight. I attempted to rise, but was not able to stir: for, as I happened to lie on my back, I found my arms and legs were strongly fastened on each side to the ground; and my hair, which was long and thick, tied down in the same manner. I likewise felt several slender **ligatures**⑤ across my body, from my **arm-pits**⑥ to my thighs. I could only look upwards; the sun began to grow hot, and the light offended my eyes. I heard a confused noise about me; but in the posture I lay, could see nothing except the sky. In a little time I felt something alive moving on my left leg, which advancing gently forward over my breast, came almost up to my chin; when, bending my eyes downwards as much as I could, I perceived it to be a human creature not six inches high, with a bow and arrow in his hands, and a **quiver**⑦ at his back. In the mean time, I felt at least forty more of the same kind (as I conjectured) following the first. I was in the utmost astonishment, and roared so loud, that they all ran back in a fright; and some of them, as I was afterwards told, were hurt with the falls they got by leaping from my sides upon the ground. However, they soon returned, and one of them, who ventured so far as to get a full sight of my face, lifting up his hands and eyes by way of admiration, cried out in a **shrill**⑧ but distinct voice, hekinah degul: the others repeated the same words several times, but then I knew not what they meant. I lay all this while, as the reader may believe, in great uneasiness. At length,

---

① **flurry**: a brief burst of wind.
② **abated**: *v.* **abate**, to make sth less strong.
③ **declivity**: a downward slope.
④ **conjectured**: *v.* **conjecture**, guess or speculate.
⑤ **ligatures**: *pl.* of **ligature**, binding or tie-up.
⑥ **arm-pits**: *pl.* of **arm-pit**, the hollow area under the junction where the arm joins the shoulder.
⑦ **quiver**: a container for holding arrows.
⑧ **shrill**: a sound that is high-pitched and piercing.

struggling to get loose, I had the fortune to break the strings, and **wrench**① out the **pegs**② that fastened my left arm to the ground; for, by lifting it up to my face, I discovered the methods they had taken to bind me, and at the same time with a violent pull, which gave me excessive pain, I a little loosened the strings that tied down my hair on the left side, so that I was just able to turn my head about two inches. But the creatures ran off a second time, before I could seize them; whereupon there was a great shout in a very shrill accent, and after it ceased I heard one of them cry aloud tolgo phonac; when in an instant I felt above a hundred arrows discharged on my left hand, which, **pricked**③ me like so many needles; and besides, they shot another flight into the air, as we do bombs in Europe, whereof many, I suppose, fell on my body (though I felt them not), and some on my face, which I immediately covered with my left hand. When this shower of arrows was over, I fell a groaning with grief and pain; and then striving again to get loose, they discharged another **volley**④ larger than the first, and some of them attempted with spears to stick me in the sides; but by good luck I had on a **buff**⑤ **jerkin**⑥, which they could not pierce. I thought it the most **prudent**⑦ method to lie still, and my design was to continue so till night, when, my left hand being already loose, I could easily free myself: and as for the inhabitants, I had reason to believe I might be a match for the greatest army they could bring against me, if they were all of the same size with him that I saw. But fortune disposed otherwise of me. When the people observed I was quiet, they discharged no more arrows; but, by the noise I heard, I knew their numbers increased; and about four yards from me, over against my right ear, I heard a knocking for above an hour, like that of people at work; when turning my head that way, as well as the pegs and strings would permit me, I saw a stage erected about a foot and a half from the ground, capable of holding four of the inhabitants, with two or three ladders to mount it: from whence one of them, who seemed to be a person of quality, made me a long speech, whereof I understood not one syllable. But I should have mentioned, that before the principal person began his **oration**⑧, he cried out three times, Langro dehul san (these words and the former were afterwards repeated and explained to me); whereupon, immediately, about fifty of the inhabitants came and cut the strings that fastened the left side of my head, which gave me the liberty of turning it to the right, and of observing the person and gesture of him that was to speak. He appeared to be of a middle age, and taller than any of the other three who attended him, whereof one was a page that held up his train, and seemed to be somewhat

---

① **wrench**: to pull or twist sth violently.
② **pegs**: pins or bolts used to fasten or as a bearing for sth that turns.
③ **pricked**: *v.* prick (pricked, pricked), poke or stab slightly with a sharp point.
④ **volley**: a lot of arrows that are fired at the same time.
⑤ **buff**: pale yellow-brown in colour.
⑥ **jerkin**: a short jacket without sleeves.
⑦ **prudent**: sensible and careful.
⑧ **oration**: a formal speech made in public.

Unit 7　Jonathan Swift (1667-1745)

longer than my middle finger; the other two stood one on each side to support him. He acted every part of an orator, and I could observe many periods of threatenings, and others of promises, pity, and kindness. I answered in a few words, but in the most **submissive**① manner, lifting up my left hand, and both my eyes to the sun, as calling him for a witness; and being almost **famished**② with hunger, having not eaten a **morsel**③ for some hours before I left the ship, I found the demands of nature so strong upon me, that I could not forbear showing my impatience (perhaps against the strict rules of decency) by putting my finger frequently to my mouth, to signify that I wanted food. The hurgo (for so they call a great lord, as I afterwards learnt) understood me very well. He descended from the stage, and commanded that several ladders should be applied to my sides, on which above a hundred of the inhabitants mounted and walked towards my mouth, **laden**④ with baskets full of meat, which had been provided and sent **thither**⑤ by the king's orders, upon the first intelligence he received of me. I observed there was the flesh of several animals, but could not distinguish them by the taste. There were shoulders, legs, and **loins**⑥, shaped like those of mutton, and very well dressed, but smaller than the wings of a lark. I ate them by two or three at a mouthful, and took three loaves at a time, about the bigness of **musket**⑦ bullets. They supplied me as fast as they could, showing a thousand marks of wonder and astonishment at my **bulk**⑧ and appetite. I then made another sign, that I wanted drink. They found by my eating that a small quantity would not suffice me; and being a most **ingenious**⑨ people, they **slung**⑩ up, with great **dexterity**⑪, one of their largest **hogsheads**⑫, then rolled it towards my hand, and beat out the top; I drank it off **at a draught**⑬, which I might well do, for it did not hold half a pint, and tasted like a small wine of **Burgundy**⑭, but much more delicious. They brought me a second hogshead, which I drank in the same manner, and made signs for more; but they had none to give me. When I had performed these wonders, they shouted for joy, and danced upon my breast, repeating several times as they did at first, Hekinah degul. They made me a sign that I should throw down the two hogsheads, but first warning the people below to stand out of the way, crying aloud, borach

---

① **submissive**: meekly obedient or passive.
② **famished**: extremely hungry or starved.
③ **morsel**: a small piece of food.
④ **laden**: heavily loaded.
⑤ **thither**: to that place; there.
⑥ **loins**: *pl.* of **loin**, a part of the body on both sides of the spine between the ribs and the pelvis.
⑦ **musket**: a type of long gun.
⑧ **bulk**: Gulliver's huge size compared with the residents'.
⑨ **ingenious**: cleverly inventive or resourceful.
⑩ **slung**: *v.* **sling (slung, slung)**, hang sth loosely.
⑪ **dexterity**: skill in performing tasks, especially with the hands.
⑫ **hogsheads**: *pl.* of **hogshead**, a large barrel used for storing and transporting liquids.
⑬ **at a draught**: at one go.
⑭ **Burgundy**: a type of red wine from the **Burgundy** region in France.

mevolah; and when they saw the **vessels**① in the air, there was a universal shout of Hekinah degul. I confess I was often tempted, while they were passing backwards and forwards on my body, to seize forty or fifty of the first that came in my reach, and **dash**② them against the ground. But the remembrance of what I had felt, which probably might not be the worst they could do, and the promise of honour I made them—for so I interpreted my submissive behaviour—soon drove out these imaginations. Besides, I now considered myself as bound by the laws of hospitality, to a people who had treated me with so much expense and magnificence. However, in my thoughts I could not sufficiently wonder at the **intrepidity**③ of these **diminutive**④ **mortals**⑤, who **durst**⑥ venture to mount and walk upon my body, while one of my hands was at liberty, without trembling at the very sight of so prodigious a creature as I must appear to them. After some time, when they observed that I made no more demands for meat, there appeared before me a person of high rank from his imperial majesty. His excellency, having mounted on the small of my right leg, advanced forwards up to my face, with about a dozen of his **retinue**⑦; and producing his **credentials**⑧ under the **signet**⑨ royal, which he applied close to my eyes, spoke about ten minutes without any signs of anger, but with a kind of determinate resolution, often pointing forwards, which, as I afterwards found, was towards the capital city, about half a mile distant; whither it was agreed by his majesty in council that I must be conveyed. I answered in few words, but to no purpose, and made a sign with my hand that was loose, putting it to the other (but over his excellency's head for fear of hurting him or his train) and then to my own head and body, to signify that I desired my liberty. It appeared that he understood me well enough, for he shook his head by way of **disapprobation**⑩, and held his hand in a posture to show that I must be carried as a prisoner. However, he made other signs to let me understand that I should have meat and drink enough, and very good treatment. Whereupon I once more thought of attempting to break my bonds; but again, when I felt the smart of their arrows upon my face and hands, which were all in **blisters**⑪, and many of the darts still sticking in them, and observing likewise that the number of my enemies increased, I gave tokens to let them know that they might do with me what they pleased. Upon this, the

---

① **vessels**: the hogsheads.

② **dash**: to strike or smash violently.

③ **intrepidity**: exceptional bravery and fearlessness.

④ **diminutive**: extremely small.

⑤ **mortals**: *pl.* of mortal, humans.

⑥ **durst**: a past tense of the verb dare.

⑦ **retinue**: a group of advisers or assistants accompanying the imperial commissioner.

⑧ **credentials**: *pl.* of **credential**, a document or evidence proving one's identity.

⑨ **signet**: a small seal.

⑩ **disapprobation**: strong disapproval of sth.

⑪ **blisters**: *pl.* of **blister**, a painful swelling on the surface of skins.

hurgo and his train withdrew, with much **civility**① and cheerful **countenances**②. Soon after I heard a general shout, with frequent repetitions of the words peplom selan; and I felt great numbers of people on my left side relaxing the cords to such a degree, that I was able to turn upon my right, and to ease myself with **making water**③; which I very plentifully did, to the great astonishment of the people; who, conjecturing by my motion what I was going to do, immediately opened to the right and left on that side, to avoid the **torrent**④, which fell with such noise and violence from me. But before this, they had **daubed**⑤ my face and both my hands with a sort of **ointment**⑥, very pleasant to the smell, which, in a few minutes, removed all the smart of their arrows. These circumstances, added to the refreshment I had received by their **victuals**⑦ and drink, which were very nourishing disposed me to sleep. I slept about eight hours, as I was afterwards assured; and it was no wonder, for the physicians, by the emperor's order, had mingled a sleepy **potion**⑧ in the hogsheads of wine.

It seems, that upon the first moment I was discovered sleeping on the ground, after my landing, the emperor had early notice of it by an express; and determined in council, that I should be tied in the manner I have related, which was done in the night while I slept; that plenty of meat and drink should be sent to me, and a machine prepared to carry me to the capital city.

This resolution perhaps may appear very bold and dangerous, and I am confident would not be imitated by any prince in Europe on the like occasion. However, in my opinion, it was extremely prudent, as well as generous: for, supposing these people had endeavoured to kill me with their spears and arrows, while I was asleep, I should certainly have awaked with the first sense of smart, which might so far have roused my rage and strength, as to have enabled me to break the strings wherewith I was tied; after which, as they were not able to make resistance, so they could expect no mercy.

These people are most excellent mathematicians, and arrived to a great perfection in mechanics, by the countenance and encouragement of the emperor, who is a renowned **patron**⑨ of learning. This prince has several machines fixed on wheels, for the carriage of trees and other great weights. He often builds his largest men of war, whereof some are nine feet long, in the woods where the timber grows, and has them carried on these engines three or four hundred

---

① **civility**: polite behavior.
② **countenances**: *pl.* of **countenance**, a person's facial expression.
③ **making water**: euphemism for urinating.
④ **torrent**: a strong and fast-moving stream of water, here refers to Gulliver's urine.
⑤ **daubed**: *v.* **daub** (**daubed, daubed**), to spread the ointment on the skin in a rough or careless way.
⑥ **ointment**: a thick, smooth substance rubbed to the skin for medicinal purposes.
⑦ **victuals**: supplies of food; provisions.
⑧ **potion**: a drink of medicine.
⑨ **patron**: a person who gives financial or other support to a cause; sponsor.

yards to the sea. Five hundred carpenters and engineers were immediately set at work to prepare the greatest engine they had. It was a frame of wood raised three inches from the ground, about seven feet long, and four wide, moving upon twenty-two wheels. The shout I heard was upon the arrival of this engine, which, it seems, set out in four hours after my landing. It was brought parallel to me, as I lay. But the principal difficulty was to raise and place me in this vehicle. Eighty poles, each of one foot high, were erected for this purpose, and very strong cords, of the bigness of **packthread**①, were fastened by hooks to many bandages, which the workmen had **girt**② round my neck, my hands, my body, and my legs. Nine hundred of the strongest men were employed to draw up these cords, by many **pulleys**③ fastened on the poles; and thus, in less than three hours, I was raised and slung into the engine, and there tied fast. All this I was told; for, while the operation was performing, I lay in a profound sleep, by the force of that **soporiferous**④ medicine infused into my liquor.

Fifteen hundred of the emperor's largest horses, each about four inches and a half high, were employed to draw me towards the **metropolis**⑤, which, as I said, was half a mile distant.

About four hours after we began our journey, I awaked by a very ridiculous accident; for the carriage being stopped a while, to adjust something that was out of order, two or three of the young natives had the curiosity to see how I looked when I was asleep; they climbed up into the engine, and advancing very softly to my face, one of them, an officer in the guards, put the sharp end of his **half-pike**⑥ a good way up into my left **nostril**⑦, which **tickled**⑧ my nose like a straw, and made me sneeze violently; whereupon they stole off unperceived, and it was three weeks before I knew the cause of my waking so suddenly. We made a long march the remaining part of the day, and, rested at night with five hundred guards on each side of me, half with torches, and half with bows and arrows, ready to shoot me if I should offer to stir. The next morning at sun-rise we continued our march, and arrived within two hundred yards of the city gates about noon. The emperor, and all his court, came out to meet us; but his great officers would by no means suffer his majesty to endanger his person by mounting on my body.

At the place where the carriage stopped there stood an ancient temple, **esteemed**⑨ to be the largest in the whole kingdom; which, having been polluted some years before by an unnatural

---

① **packthread**: a strong thread or twine used for bundling or tying.
② **girt**: to surround or encircle something tightly.
③ **pulleys**: *pl.* of **pulley**, a wheel or set of wheels over which a rope or chain is pulled in order to lift heavy objects.
④ **soporiferous**: causing or inducing sleep.
⑤ **metropolis**: the largest, busiest and the most important city in a country.
⑥ **half-pike**: a type of weapon; a pike with a short shaft.
⑦ **nostril**: each of the two openings at the end of a nose.
⑧ **tickled**: *v.* **tickle** (**tickled**, **tickled**), to touch lightly, causing a feeling of itching.
⑨ **esteemed**: *v.* **esteem**, to regard with great respect.

murder, was, according to the zeal of those people, looked upon as **profane**①, and therefore had been applied to common use, and all the ornaments and furniture carried away. In this **edifice**② it was determined I should lodge. The great gate fronting to the north was about four feet high, and almost two feet wide, through which I could easily creep. On each side of the gate was a small window, not above six inches from the ground: into that on the left side, the king's smith conveyed **fourscore**③ and eleven chains, like those that hang to a lady's watch in Europe, and almost as large, which were locked to my left leg with six-and-thirty **padlocks**④. Over against this temple, on the other side of the great highway, at twenty feet distance, there was a **turret**⑤ at least five feet high. Here the emperor ascended, with many principal lords of his court, to have an opportunity of viewing me, as I was told, for I could not see them. It was reckoned that above a hundred thousand inhabitants came out of the town upon the same errand; and, in spite of my guards, I believe there could not be fewer than ten thousand at several times, who mounted my body by the help of ladders. But a **proclamation**⑥ was soon issued, to forbid it upon pain of death. When the workmen found it was impossible for me to break loose, they cut all the strings that bound me; whereupon I rose up, with as **melancholy**⑦ a disposition as ever I had in my life. But the noise and astonishment of the people, at seeing me rise and walk, are not to be expressed. The chains that held my left leg were about two yards long, and gave me not only the liberty of walking backwards and forwards in a semicircle, but, being fixed within four inches of the gate, allowed me to creep in, and lie at my full length in the temple.

Exercise

I. Word Matching

Directions: Please choose the most appropriate ones from the given words to explain the original boldfaced words in the following lines.

A. **jeopardize**　　B. **prohibit**　　C. **satisfy**　　D. **successful**
E. **profitable**　　F. **differentiate**　　G. **modify**

1. Being advised to **alter** my condition, I married Mrs. Mary Burton, second daughter to Mr. Edmund Burton.

2. After three years expectation that things would mend, I accepted an **advantageous** offer from Captain William Prichard, master of the Antelope, who was making a voyage to the South

---

① **profane**: not holy because unconsecrated, impure, or defiled.
② **edifice**: a large or massive building.
③ **fourscore**: a term that means eighty (score = twenty).
④ **padlocks**: *pl.* of padlock, a portable lock with a shackle.
⑤ **turret**: a small tower on top of a building or wall, typically of a castle.
⑥ **proclamation**: an official announcement or public declaration.
⑦ **melancholy**: a feeling of deep sadness or gloom.

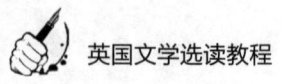

Sea.

3. We set sail from Bristol, May 4, 1699, and our voyage was at first very **prosperous**.

4. I observed there was the flesh of several animals, but could not **distinguish** them by the taste.

5. They found by my eating that a small quantity would not **suffice** me.

6. The emperor, and all his court, came out to meet us; but his great officers would by no means suffer his majesty to **endanger** his person by mounting on my body.

7. But a proclamation was soon issued, to **forbid** it upon pain of death.

II. English-Chinese Translation

Directions: Please translate the following classic dicta from English into Chinese.

1. Books, the children of the brain.

—A Tale of Tub

2. Every man desires to live long, but no man wishes to be old.

—Gulliver's Travel

3. When a great genius appears in the world you may know him by this sign; that the dunces are all in confederacy against him.

—An Argument Against Abolishing Christianity

4. Satire is a sort of glass wherein beholders do generally discover everybody's face but their own; which is the chief reason for that kind reception it meets with in the world, and that so very few are offended with it.

—The Battle of the Books

5. Difference in opinions has cost many millions of lives: for instance, whether flesh be bread, or bread be flesh; whether the juice of a certain berry be blood or wine.

—Gulliver's Travel

III. Term Defining

Directions: Please explain the following literary terms based on Robinson Crusoe.

1. travelogue
2. satire
3. hyperbole

IV. Content-Based Questions

Directions: Please give a concise and adequate answer to the following questions related to the excerpt.

1. After shifting his career to seafaring, Gulliver undertook a voyage to the South Sea, which led him to an unexpected destination. Describe the sequence of events that resulted in Gulliver's arrival in Lilliput.

2. Given Gulliver's immense size compared to the Lilliputians, providing adequate food and water for him posed a significant challenge. How did the Lilliputians address this issue?

3. Gulliver praised the Lilliputians as the most excellent mathematicians. How was their expertise in mathematics manifested through Gulliver's observations and interactions with them?

V. Discussion Question

Gulliver's tale begins in a conventional travelogue style, detailing his early life and setting him in English society. As the narrative moves to Lilliput, a fantastical element emerges. Discuss with your partner if and how this transition affects your perception of the story's authenticity. Reflect on the function of the initial realistic setup in contrast to the later magical experiences. How does this shift impact your understanding and engagement with the narrative?

VI. Essay Question

Upon discovering Gulliver, the Lilliputians bound and subdued him, which was followed by the emperor's command to transport him as a captive to their capital. In a 200-word essay, examine whether their response was justified with regard to the situation. What do their actions and attitudes reveal about their perceptions towards this alien giant? Reflect on Gulliver's treatment by the Lilliputians, and provide your own perspectives on the incident.

Text B

Gulliver's Travels
Part Four: A Voyage to the Country of the Houyhnhnms
Chapter VII

The reader may be disposed to wonder how I could **prevail on**① myself to give so free a representation of my own species, among a race of mortals who are already too apt to conceive the **vilest**② opinion of humankind, from that entire **congruity**③ between me and their Yahoos. But I must freely confess, that the many virtues of those excellent quadrupeds, placed in opposite view to human corruptions, had so far opened my eyes and enlarged my understanding, that I began to view the actions and passions of man in a very different light, and to think the honour of my own kind not worth managing; which, besides, it was impossible for me to do, before a person of so acute a judgment as my master, who daily convinced me of

---

① **prevail on**: succeed in causing (a person) to act in a certain way.
② **vilest**: **vile (viler, vilest)**, morally depraved; ignoble or wicked.
③ **congruity**: the quality or fact of being corresponding or agreeing in character or kind.

a thousand faults in myself, **whereof**① I had not the least perception before, and which, with us, would never be numbered even among human **infirmities**②. I had likewise learned, from his example, an utter detestation of all falsehood or disguise; and truth appeared so amiable to me, that I determined upon sacrificing every thing to it.

Let me deal so candidly with the reader as to confess that there was yet a much stronger motive for the freedom I took in my representation of things. I had not yet been a year in this country before I contracted such a love and **veneration**③ for the inhabitants, that I entered on a firm resolution never to return to humankind, but to pass the rest of my life among these admirable Houyhnhnms, in the contemplation and practice of every virtue, where I could have no example or **incitement**④ to vice. But it was decreed by fortune, my perpetual enemy, that so great a felicity should not fall to my share. However, it is now some comfort to reflect, that in what I said of my countrymen, I **extenuated**⑤ their faults as much as I **durst**⑥ before so strict an examiner; and upon every article gave as favourable a turn as the matter would bear. For, indeed, who is there alive that will not be swayed by his bias and partiality to the place of his birth?

I have related the substance of several conversations I had with my master during the greatest part of the time I had the honour to be in his service; but have, indeed, for brevity sake,

---

① **whereof**: of which (person or thing).
② **infirmities**: *pl.* of infirmity, physical weakness or moral flaw.
③ **veneration**: respect or awe inspired by the dignity, wisdom, dedication, or talent of a person.
④ **incitement**: an act of urging on or spurring on or rousing to action.
⑤ **extenuated**: extenuate (**extenuated, extenuated**), to make or try to make seem less serious esp. by offering excuses.
⑥ **durst**: *v.* Archaic, a past tense and a past participle of dare.

Unit 7 Jonathan Swift (1667-1745)

omitted much more than is here set down.

When I had answered all his questions, and his curiosity seemed to be fully satisfied, he sent for me one morning early, and commanded me to sit down at some distance (an honour which he had never before **conferred upon**① me). He said, he had been very seriously considering my whole story, as far as it related both to myself and my country; that he looked upon us as a sort of animals, to whose share, by what accident he could not **conjecture**②, some small **pittance**③ of reason had fallen, whereof we made no other use, than by its assistance, to **aggravate**④ our natural corruptions, and to acquire new ones, which nature had not given us; that we disarmed ourselves of the few abilities she had bestowed; had been very successful in multiplying our original wants, and seemed to spend our whole lives in vain endeavours to supply them by our own inventions; that, as to myself, it was manifest I had neither the strength nor **agility**⑤ of a common Yahoo; that I walked infirmly on my **hinder**⑥ feet; had found out a **contrivance**⑦ to make my claws of no use or defence, and to remove the hair from my chin, which was intended as a shelter from the sun and the weather: lastly, that I could neither run with speed, nor climb trees like my brethren, as he called them, the Yahoos in his country.

That our institutions of government and law were plainly owing to our gross defects in reason, and by consequence in virtue; because reason alone is sufficient to govern a rational creature; which was, therefore, a character we had no pretence to challenge, even from the account I had given of my own people; although he manifestly perceived, that, in order to favour them, I had concealed many particulars, and often said the thing which was not.

He was the more confirmed in this opinion, because, he observed, that as I agreed in every feature of my body with other Yahoos, except where it was to my real disadvantage in point of strength, speed, and activity, the shortness of my claws, and some other particulars where nature had no part; so from the representation I had given him of our lives, our manners, and our actions, he found as near a resemblance in the disposition of our minds. He said, the Yahoos were known to hate one another, more than they did any different species of animals; and the reason usually assigned was, the odiousness of their own shapes, which all could see in the rest, but not in themselves. He had therefore begun to think it not unwise in us to cover our bodies, and by that invention conceal many of our **deformities**⑧ from each other, which would else be

---

① **conferred upon**: **confer** (**conferred, conferred**), to grant something often a title or honor, on someone.
② **conjecture**: to speculate or wonder about something.
③ **pittance**: a very small amount.
④ **aggravate**: to make worse.
⑤ **agility**: the power of moving quickly and easily.
⑥ **hinder**: situated at the rear or back.
⑦ **contrivance**: something invented, as a mechanical device or a clever plan.
⑧ **deformities**: *pl.* of **deformity**, the quality or state of being distorted in form.

hardly supportable. But he now found he had been mistaken, and that the **dissensions**① of those brutes in his country were owing to the same cause with ours, as I had described them. For if, said he, you throw among five Yahoos as much food as would be sufficient for fifty, they will, instead of eating peaceably, fall together by the ears, each single one impatient to have all to itself; and therefore a servant was usually employed to stand by while they were feeding abroad, and those kept at home were tied at a distance from each other: that if a cow died of age or accident, before a Houyhnhnm could secure it for his own Yahoos, those in the neighbourhood would come in herds to seize it, and then would **ensue**② such a battle as I had described, with terrible wounds made by their claws on both sides, although they seldom were able to kill one another, for want of such convenient instruments of death as we had invented. At other times, the like battles have been fought between the Yahoos of several neighbourhoods, without any visible cause; those of one district watching all opportunities to surprise the next, before they are prepared. But if they find their project has miscarried, they return home, and, for want of enemies, engage in what I call a civil war among themselves.

That in some fields of his country there are certain shining stones of several colours, whereof the Yahoos are violently fond: and when part of these stones is fixed in the earth, as it sometimes happens, they will dig with their claws for whole days to get them out; then carry them away, and hide them by heaps in their **kennels**③; but still looking round with great caution, for fear their comrades should find out their treasure. My master said, he could never discover the reason of this unnatural appetite, or how these stones could be of any use to a Yahoo; but now he believed it might proceed from the same principle of avarice which I had **ascribed**④ to mankind. That he had once, by way of experiment, privately removed a heap of these stones from the place where one of his Yahoos had buried it; **whereupon**⑤ the **sordid**⑥ animal, missing his treasure, by his loud lamenting brought the whole herd to the place, there miserably howled, then fell to biting and tearing the rest, began to **pine**⑦ away, would neither eat, nor sleep, nor work, till he ordered a servant privately to convey the stones into the same hole, and hide them as before; which, when his Yahoo had found, he presently recovered his spirits and good humour, but took good care to remove them to a better hiding place, and has ever since been a very serviceable brute.

My master further assured me, which I also observed myself, that in the fields where the shining stones abound, the fiercest and most frequent battles are fought, occasioned by

---

① **dissensions**: *pl.* of **dissension**, disagreement, esp when leading to a quarrel.
② **ensue**: to follow in order; come afterward.
③ **kennels**: *pl.* of **kennel**, a house or shelter for a dog or a cat.
④ **ascribed**：**ascribe (ascribed, ascribed)** to attribute as a quality; consider as belonging to.
⑤ **whereupon**: upon what or upon which.
⑥ **sordid**: dirty, foul；meanly selfish.
⑦ **pine**: to become ill, feeble, or thin through worry, longing, etc.

perpetual **inroads**① of the neighbouring Yahoos.

He said, it was common, when two Yahoos discovered such a stone in a field, and were contending which of them should be the **proprietor**②, a third would take the advantage, and carry it away from them both; which my master would needs contend to have some kind of resemblance with our suits at law; wherein I thought it for our credit not to undeceive him; since the decision he mentioned was much more **equitable**③ than many decrees among us; because the **plaintiff**④ and defendant there lost nothing beside the stone they contended for: whereas our courts of equity would never have dismissed the cause, while either of them had any thing left.

My master, continuing his discourse, said, there was nothing that rendered the Yahoos more odious, than their undistinguishing appetite to devour every thing that came in their way, whether herbs, roots, berries, the corrupted flesh of animals, or all mingled together: and it was peculiar in their temper, that they were fonder of what they could get by **rapine**⑤ or stealth, at a greater distance, than much better food provided for them at home. If their prey held out, they would eat till they were ready to burst; after which, nature had pointed out to them a certain root that gave them a general **evacuation**⑥.

There was also another kind of root, very juicy, but somewhat rare and difficult to be found, which the Yahoos sought for with much eagerness, and would suck it with great delight; it produced in them the same effects that wine has upon us. It would make them sometimes hug, and sometimes tear one another; they would howl, and grin, and chatter, and **reel**⑦, and **tumble**⑧, and then fall asleep in the mud.

I did indeed observe that the Yahoos were the only animals in this country subject to any diseases; which, however, were much fewer than horses have among us, and contracted, not by any ill-treatment they meet with, but by the nastiness and greediness of that sordid brute. Neither has their language any more than a general **appellation**⑨ for those **maladies**⑩, which is borrowed from the name of the beast, and called hnea-yahoo, or Yahoo's evil; and the cure prescribed is a mixture of their own dung and urine, forcibly put down the Yahoo's throat. This I have since often known to have been taken with success, and do here freely recommend it to

---

① **inroads**: an invasion or hostile attack.
② **proprietor**: a person who has the exclusive right or title to something; an owner, as of real property.
③ **equitable**: fair to all parties.
④ **plaintiff**: a person who brings a civil action in a court of law.
⑤ **rapine**: the violent seizure and carrying off of another's property.
⑥ **evacuation**: the bodily process of discharging waste matter.
⑦ **reel**: to sway, esp under the shock of a blow or through dizziness or drunkenness.
⑧ **tumble**: to roll or twist, esp in playing; to fall helplessly down, esp. headfirst.
⑨ **appellation**: an identifying name, title, or designation.
⑩ **maladies**: *pl.* of **malady**, a disorder or disease of the body.

my countrymen for the public good, as an admirable specific against all diseases produced by **repletion**①.

As to learning, government, arts, manufactures, and the like, my master confessed, he could find little or no resemblance between the Yahoos of that country and those in ours; for he only meant to observe what **parity**② there was in our natures. He had heard, indeed, some curious Houyhnhnms observe, that in most herds there was a sort of ruling Yahoo (as among us there is generally some leading or principal **stag**③ in a park), who was always more deformed in body, and mischievous in disposition, than any of the rest; that this leader had usually a favourite as like himself as he could get, whose employment was to lick his master's feet and **posterior**④, and drive the female Yahoos to his kennel; for which he was now and then rewarded with a piece of ass's flesh. This favourite is hated by the whole herd, and therefore, to protect himself, keeps always near the person of his leader. He usually continues in office till a worse can be found; but the very moment he is discarded, his successor, at the head of all the Yahoos in that district, young and old, male and female, come in a body, and discharge their **excrements**⑤ upon him from head to foot. But how far this might be applicable to our courts, and favourites, and ministers of state, my master said I could best determine.

I durst make no return to this malicious **insinuation**⑥, which debased human understanding below the **sagacity**⑦ of a common hound, who has judgment enough to distinguish and follow the cry of the ablest dog in the pack, without being ever mistaken.

My master told me, there were some qualities remarkable in the Yahoos, which he had not observed me to mention, or at least very slightly, in the accounts I had given of humankind. He said, those animals, like other brutes, had their females in common; but in this they differed, that the she Yahoo would admit the males while she was pregnant; and that the hes would quarrel and fight with the females, as fiercely as with each other; both which practices were such degrees of infamous brutality, as no other sensitive creature ever arrived at.

Another thing he wondered at in the Yahoos, was their strange disposition to nastiness and dirt; whereas there appears to be a natural love of cleanliness in all other animals. As to the two former accusations, I was glad to let them pass without any reply, because I had not a word to offer upon them in defence of my species, which otherwise I certainly had done from

---

① **repletion**: fullness, esp excessive fullness due to overeating.
② **parity**: equivalence or correspondence; similarity.
③ **stag**: an adult male deer.
④ **posterior**: (Anatomy) the buttocks.
⑤ **excrements**: *pl.* of **excrement**, waste matter discharged from the body.
⑥ **insinuation**: an artful, indirect, often derogatory hint.
⑦ **sagacity**: showing intelligence, wisdom and good judgement.

my own inclinations. But I could have easily **vindicated**① humankind from the **imputation**② of singularity upon the last article, if there had been any swine in that country (as unluckily for me there were not), which, although it may be a sweeter quadruped than a Yahoo, cannot, I humbly conceive, in justice, pretend to more cleanliness; and so his honour himself must have owned, if he had seen their filthy way of feeding, and their custom of **wallowing**③ and sleeping in the mud.

My master likewise mentioned another quality which his servants had discovered in several Yahoos, and to him was wholly unaccountable. He said, a fancy would sometimes take a Yahoo to retire into a corner, to lie down, and howl, and groan, and **spurn**④ away all that came near him, although he were young and fat, wanted neither food nor water, nor did the servant imagine what could possibly ail him. And the only remedy they found was, to set him to hard work, after which he would **infallibly**⑤ come to himself. To this I was silent out of partiality to my own kind; yet here I could plainly discover the true seeds of **spleen**⑥, which only seizes on the lazy, the luxurious, and the rich; who, if they were forced to undergo the same **regimen**⑦, I would undertake for the cure.

His honour had further observed, that a female Yahoo would often stand behind a bank or a bush, to gaze on the young males passing by, and then appear, and hide, using many **antic**⑧ gestures and **grimaces**⑨, at which time it was observed that she had a most offensive smell; and when any of the males advanced, would slowly retire, looking often back, and with a **counterfeit**⑩ show of fear, run off into some convenient place, where she knew the male would follow her.

At other times, if a female stranger came among them, three or four of her own sex would get about her, and stare, and chatter, and grin, and smell her all over; and then turn off with gestures, that seemed to express contempt and disdain.

Perhaps my master might refine a little in these speculations, which he had drawn from what he observed himself, or had been told him by others; however, I could not reflect without some amazement, and much sorrow, that the rudiments of **lewdness**⑪, **coquetry**⑫, **censure**⑬,

---

① **vindicated**: vindicate (**vindicated, vindicated**), to maintain or defend against opposition.
② **imputation**: a statement attributing something dishonest (especially a criminal offense).
③ **wallowing**: rolling the body about or lying relaxed in water or mud.
④ **spurn**: to kick or trample with the foot.
⑤ **infallibly**: certainly.
⑥ **spleen**: the organ in the human body considered to be the seat of the emotions; melancholy.
⑦ **regimen**: a systematic way of life or course of therapy, often including exercise and a recommended diet.
⑧ **antic**: *archaic* fantastic; grotesque.
⑨ **grimaces**: an ugly or distorted facial expression, as of wry humour, disgust, etc.
⑩ **counterfeit**: pretended; unreal.
⑪ **lewdness**: being preoccupied with sexual desire.
⑫ **coquetry**: flirtation.
⑬ **censure**: an expression of strong disapproval.

and scandal, should have place by instinct in womankind.

I expected every moment that my master would accuse the Yahoos of those unnatural appetites in both sexes, so common among us. But nature, it seems, has not been so expert a school–mistress; and these politer pleasures are entirely the productions of art and reason on our side of the globe.

Exercise

I. Word Matching

Directions: Please choose the most appropriate ones from the given words to explain the original boldfaced words in the following lines.

    A. **honestly**   B. **trouble**   C. **hatred**   D. **likely**

    E. **greed**   F. **mourn**   G. **dirty**

1. The reader may be **disposed** to wonder how I could prevail on myself to give so free a representation of my own species.

2. I had likewise learned, from his example, an utter **detestation** of all falsehood or disguise.

3. Let me deal so **candidly** with the reader as to confess that there was yet a much stronger motive for the freedom I took in my representation of things.

4. Now he believed it might proceed from the same principle of **avarice** which I had ascribed to mankind.

5. The sordid animal, missing his treasure, by his loud **lament**ing brought the whole herd to the place.

6. He had seen their **filthy** way of feeding, and their custom of wallowing and sleeping in the mud.

7. Although he were young and fat, wanted neither food nor water, nor did the servant imagine what could possibly **ail** him.

II. Blank Filling

Directions: Please fill in the following blanks with words or expressions that best express the contextual meaning of the classic dicta.

1. Every man desires to live _____ , but no man wishes to be old.

—Gulliver's Travels

2. A wife should be always a reasonable and agreeable companion, because she cannot always be _____ .

—Comus

3. The use of speech was to make us _____ one another, and to receive information of facts.

—*Gulliver's Travels*

4. The different _____ of the world had different customs.

—*Gulliver's Travels*

5. I grant this food will be somewhat dear, and therefore very proper for the landlords, who, as they have already devoured most of the _____ , seem to have the best title for the children.

—*A Modest Proposal*

III. Term Defining

Directions: *Please explain the following literary terms based on Gulliver's Travels.*

1. irony
2. foreshadowing
3. tone

IV. Content-Based Questions

Directions: *Please give a concise and adequate answer to the following questions related to Part Four of Gulliver's Travels.*

1. What abilities did we disarm ourselves of that nature had bestowed as far as "my" master was concerned?

2. Who were known to hate one another more than any different species of animals in "my" master's view and why?

3. What cure do I recommend to my countrymen for the public good, which is prescribed to the Yahoos in this country subject to any disease?

V. Discussion Question

Discuss with your group partners whether we are disadvantageous in point of strength, speed, and activity, the shortness of "our claws" and some other particulars compared with Yahoos here.

VI. Essay Question

The voyage to the Country of the Houyhnhnms, one of the four voyages in Jonathan Swift's *Gulliver's Travels* presents us an in-depth depiction of the Yahoos and Swift is inclined to tell us who we could be and what we should do. Please write a 200-word essay to contribute your thought on it.

Self-Improving Reading

A Tale of a Tub by Jonathan Swift

A Modest Proposal by Jonathan Swift

Unit 8 William Blake (1757—1827)

Life and Works

William Blake, one of the most important writers and artists of the Romantic period, was born to James Blake, a hosier, and Catherine Wright Armitage Blake at 28 Broad Street, Golden Square, in London on November 28, 1757. William Blake received a brief school education, mainly taught by his mother at home and simultaneously inspired profoundly by *The Bible*. Blake's artistic potential was quite obvious during his early years and accordingly, he began his seven-year engraving apprenticeship at the age of 14. Blake was admitted to the Royal Academy of Art's Schools of Design in 1780 and published his *Poetical Sketches* three years later. In 1781, Blake married Catherine Sophia Boucher, a beautiful but illiterate Huguenot girl, who learned to read, write and draw under her husband's patient guidance and even worked as his capable assistant at length.

Blake worked as an engraver during his own lifetime, but he had been writing poetry from boyhood. Blake published all his poems in an unprecedented way by illustrating his poems with their accompanying designs and then, engraving them. In 1789, the publication of *Songs of Innocence*, a collection of poems by Blake marked the beginning of his legacy as an

Unit 8 William Blake (1757–1827)

acclaimed poet, in which *The Lamb*, *The Chimney Sweeper* and *Infant Joy* were included. In the same year, Blake's first published myth, *The Book of Thel* was also published and a year later, *The Marriage of Heaven and Hell*, his best-known prose work followed immediately. Blake's more mature poems like *London* and *The Tyger* were among the collection *Songs of Experience* published in 1793. Blake's illustrations of *The Book of Job* in 1826, and Dante in 1838, are widely recognized as his greatest achievements as an engraver. On August 12, 1827, Blake passed away in his modest London lodgings, leaving behind his incomplete watercolor illustrations of Bunyan's *Pilgrim's Progress*.

Text A

London

I wander thro' each **charter'd**[①] street,
Near where the charter'd **Thames**[②] does flow,
A mark in every face I meet
Marks of weakness, marks of woe.

In every cry of every man,
In every Infant's cry of fear,
In every voice, in every ban,
The mind-forg'd **manacles**[③] I hear.

How the **Chimney-sweeper**[④]'s cry
Every blackning Church appalls;
And the **hapless**[⑤] Soldier's sigh
Runs in blood down Palace walls.

But most thro' midnight streets I hear
How the youthful **harlot**[⑥]'s curse

---

① **charter'd**: charter (charted, charted), to hire for exclusive use.
② **Thames**: a river in southern England, flowing eastward through London to the North Sea.
③ **manacles**: handcuff.
④ **Chimney-sweeper**: a poem in the collection of poems titled Songs of Innocence by William Blake published in 1789.
⑤ **hapless**: miserable, unfortunate.
⑥ **harlot**: whore, prostitute.

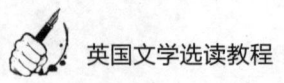

　　　　　Blasts the new-born Infant's tear,

　　　　　And **blights**① with plagues the Marriage **hearse**②.

Exercise

I. Word Matching

Directions: Please choose the most appropriate ones from the given words to explain the original boldfaced words in the following lines.

A. **formed**　　　B. **swearword**　　　C. **shocks**　　　D. **grief**

E. **pandemics**　　F. **impression**

1. A **mark** in every face I meet

2. Marks of weakness, marks of **woe**.

3. In every voice, in every ban,

　　The mind-**forg'd** manacles I hear.

4. How the Chimney-sweeper's cry

　　Every blackning Church **appalls**;

5. But most thro' midnight streets I hear

　　How the youthful harlot's **curse**.

6. And blights with **plagues** the Marriage hearse.

II. Blank Filling

Directions: Please fill in the following blanks with words or expressions that best express the contextual meaning of the classic dicta.

1. Think in the _____. Act in the noon. Eat in the evening. Sleep in the night.

　　　　　　　　　　　　　　　　　　　　—*The Marriage of Heaven and Hell*

2. To see a world in a grain of sand

　　And a heaven in a wild _____,

　　Hold infinity in the palm of your hand,

　　And eternity in an hour.

　　　　　　　　　　　　　　　　　　　　—*Auguries of Innocence*

3. He who desires, but acts _____, breeds pestilence.

　　　　　　　　　　　　　　　　　　　　—*The Marriage of Heaven and Hell*

4. I wander thro' each charter'd _____.

　　　　　　　　　　　　　　　　　　　　—*London*

5. Opposition is _____ friendship.

---

① **blights**: v. **blight**, destroy, ruin.

② **hearse**: a vehicle used to carry a coffin to a cemetery or a church.

Unit 8 William Blake (1757-1827)

—*The Marriage of Heaven and Hell*

III. Term Defining

Directions: *Please explain the following literary terms based on London.*

1. acrostic
2. repetition
3. anaphora

IV. Content-Based Questions

Directions: *Please give a concise and adequate answer to the following questions related to Text A.*

1. What does the author see when he wanders "thro' each charter'd street"?
2. What is the reaction of the author after he hear every voice in the London street?
3. Why does the author pinpoint "the Chimney-sweeper's cry" and "the hapless Soldier's sigh" in the third stanza?

V. Discussion Question

Directions: *Please discuss the following question in pairs or groups.*

Discuss with your pair partner why the author writes these unpleasant voices from all walks of life in the poem? Please imagine their life stories and share them with other classmates.

VI. Essay Question

After an in-depth reading of the poem *London* and a thorough research-based study on the societal circumstances of London during the Industrial Revolution, write a 200-word essay on the message William Blake seek to convey through the portrayal of the living conditions in the poem.

Text B

The Tyger[①]

Tyger! Tyger! burning bright
In the forests of the night,
What immortal hand or eye
Could frame thy fearful symmetry?
In what distant deeps or skies

---

① **Tyger**: tiger.

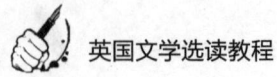

Burnt the fire of thine eyes?
On what wings dare he **aspire**①?
What the hand, dare seize the **fire**②?
And what shoulder, & what art,
Could twist the **sinews**③ of thy heart?
And when thy heart began to beat,
What dread hand? & what dread feet?
What the hammer? what the chain?
In what furnace was thy brain?
What the **anvil**④? what dread grasp
Dare its deadly terrors clasp?
When the stars threw down their spears,
And water'd heaven with their tears,
Did he smile his work to see?
Did he who made the Lamb make thee?
Tyger! Tyger! burning bright
In the forests of the night,
What immortal hand or eye
Dare frame thy fearful symmetry?

Exercise

I. Word Matching

Directions: Please choose the most appropriate ones from the given words to explain the original boldfaced words in the following lines.

A. **firebox**　　　　B. **eternal**　　　　C. **grasp**　　　　D. **balance**

1. What **immortal** hand or eye?
2. Could frame thy fearful **symmetry**?
3. In what **furnace** was thy brain?
4. Dare its deadly terrors **clasp**?

II. Blank Filling

Directions: Please fill in the following blanks with words or expressions that best express the contextual meaning of the classic dicta.

---

① **aspire**: *Archaic.* soar or rise high.
② **seize the fire**: Greek myth of Prometheus's stealing fire from the Gods.
③ **sinews**: *pl.* of **sinew**, muscular power.
④ **anvil**: a heavy iron on which metals are hammered.

1. Tyger! _____ ! burning bright.

—*The Tyger*

2. A fool sees not the same tree that a _____ man sees.

—*The Marriage of Heaven and Hell*

3. To create a little flower is the labor of _____ .

—*The Marriage of Heaven and Hell*

4. The man who _____ alters his opinion is like standing water, and breeds reptiles of the mind.

—*The Marriage of Heaven and Hell*

5. What is now proved was once only _____ .

—*The Marriage of Heaven and Hell*

III. Term Defining

Directions: *Please explain the following literary terms based on The Tyger.*

1. allusion
2. epizeuxis
3. rhetorical question

IV. Content-Based Questions

Directions: *Please give a concise and adequate answer to the following questions based on the reading of The Tyger.*

1. In what circumstances is the subject referred to by the author as a "tyger"?
2. What questions have been raised by the author about the creation of the "tyger"?
3. Who is possibly the creator of the "tyger" in the author's mind and why?

V. Discussion Question

Discuss with your group members after reading *The Lamb* and *The Tyger* by William Blake what the similarities and differences between the lamb and the tyger are and what the author's real intention is by depicting these two images?

VI. Essay Question

"What is now proved was once only imagin'd." is a sentence from *The Marriage of Heaven and Hell* by William Blake. Write a 200-word essay to express your understanding of this quotation from the perspective of social progress and scientific development in the course of human history.

Self-Improving Reading

The Lamb by Jonathan Swift

A Poison Tree by Jonathan Swift

Unit 9　William Wordsworth (1770–1850)

Life and Works

William Wordsworth, one of the founders and preeminent poets of the Romantic movement in English literature, was born in Cockermouth, Cumbria, in the Lake District of northeastern England, on April 7, 1770. His mother, Ann Cookson Wordsworth, taught him how to read, but unfortunately, she passed away when he was seven and he was enrolled first in a distinguished school for the children from esteemed households in Penrith and then in Hawkshead Grammar School. John Wordsworth, William's father, who served as a legal representative of Sir James Lowther, 1st Earl of Lonsdale, died in 1783. After four-year study at St John's College, Cambridge, William earned his B.A. degree in 1791. During and shortly after his study in Cambridge, William ever embarked on two brief sojourns to France and the French Revolution there served to advance his democratic beliefs. His poetic endeavors, including *Descriptive Sketches* published in 1793, were also initiated there during that time. Two years later Wordsworth encountered Samuel Taylor Coleridge, which led to their literary collaboration in the publication of a seminal collection, *Lyrical Ballads* first in 1798, which included renowned works such as the former's *Lines Composed a Few Miles Above Tintern Abbey* and the latter's *The Rime of the Ancient Mariner*.

Unit 9 William Wordsworth (1770-1850)

During the following years, he wrote his most notable lyrics, including *The Solitary Reaper* and *Resolution and Independence*. Wordsworth dedicated his life to writing his magnum opus, *The Prelude*, which is highly regarded as the pinnacle of English Romanticism, but it was not until after his death that the poem was eventually published by his wife, Mary Hutchinson Wordsworth. William Wordsworth perished on April 23, 1850, at Rydal Mount in England.

Text A

I Wandered Lonely as a Cloud

I wandered lonely as a cloud
That floats on high o'er **vales**① and hills,
When all at once I saw a crowd,
A host, of golden **daffodils**②;
Beside the lake, beneath the trees,
Fluttering③ and dancing in the breeze.

Continuous as the stars that shine
And twinkle on the milky way,
They stretched in never-ending line
Along the margin of a bay:
Ten thousand saw I at a glance,
Tossing their heads in **sprightly**④ dance.

The waves beside them danced; but they
Out-did the sparkling waves in **glee**⑤:
A poet could not but be gay,
In such a **jocund**⑥ company:
I gazed—and gazed—but little thought
What wealth the show to me had brought:

---

① **vales**: *pl.* of **vale**, valley.
② **daffodils**: *pl.* of **daffodil**, yellow spring flowers with a trumpetlike crown.
③ **Fluttering**: **flutter** (v.), move lightly and quickly.
④ **sprightly**: brisk, vigorous.
⑤ **glee**: joyfulness.
⑥ **jocund**: merry.

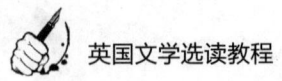

> For oft, when on my couch I lie
> In vacant or in **pensive**① mood,
> They flash upon that inward eye
> Which is the bliss of solitude;
> And then my heart with pleasure fills,
> And dances with the daffodils.

Exercise

I. Word Matching

Directions: Please choose the most appropriate ones from the given words to explain the original boldfaced words in the following lines.

A. **happiness** B. **unoccupied** C. **edge** D. **multitude**
E. **isolation** F. **shine**

1. When all at once I saw a crowd,
   A **host**, of golden daffodils ;
2. Continuous as the stars that shine
   And **twinkle** on the milky way,
3. They stretched in never-ending line
   Along the **margin** of a bay:
4. For oft, when on my couch I lie
   In **vacant** or in pensive mood,
5. They flash upon that inward eye
   Which is the **bliss** of **solitude**;

II. English-Chinese Translation

Directions: Please translate the following classic dicta from English into Chinese.

1. Poetry is the spontaneous overflow of powerful feelings: it takes its origin from emotion recollected in tranquility.

—*Lyrical Ballads*

2. Let nature be your teacher.

—*The Complete Poetical Works of William Wordsworth*

3. We live by admiration, hope and love.

—*The Complete Poetical Works of William Wordsworth*

4. The mind of man is a thousand times more beautiful than the earth on which he dwells.

—*The Prelude*

---

① **pensive**: deeply thoughtful.

5. I wandered lonely as a cloud that floats on high o'er vales and hills.

—*I Wandered Lonely as a Cloud*

III. Term Defining

Directions: *Please explain the following literary terms based on I Wandered Lonely as a Cloud.*

1. imagery

2. personification

3. assonance

IV. Content-Based Questions

Directions: *Please give a concise and adequate answer to the following questions related to Text A.*

1. What fascinating scenery comes into view "when I wandered lonely as a cloud"?

2. In what way does the narrator compare the daffodils to the stars and waves?

3. From the line like "They flash upon that inward eye", can we infer the above description on daffodils is the narrator's past experience? Why or why not?

V. Discussion Question

Can you feel the loneliness initially expressed by the narrator in the title *I Wandered Lonely as a Cloud* after reading the whole poem? Have a heart-to-heart talk with your pair partner about the emotions conveyed by the narrator in the poem and your own post-reading mood.

VI. Essay Question

It can be noticed that William Wordsworth exclaims in the poem "what wealth the show to me had brought", which reminds us of the Chinese advocacy "Lucid waters and lush mountains are valuable assets". Write a 200-word essay on the understanding of the above two sentences and also the appropriate practices in our daily lives.

Text B

The Solitary Reaper①

Behold② her, single in the field,
Yon③ solitary Highland **Lass**④!

---

① **Reaper**: a person who harvests a crop.
② **Behold**: look at or see.
③ **Yon**: yonder, over there.
④ **Lass**: a young lady who is unmarried.

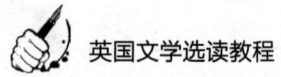

Reaping and singing by herself;
Stop here, or gently pass!
Alone she cuts and binds the grain,
And sings a melancholy strain;
O listen! for the Vale profound
Is overflowing with the sound.

No Nightingale did ever **chaunt**①
More welcome notes to weary bands
Of travellers in some shady **haunt**②,
Among Arabian sands:
A voice so thrilling ne'er was heard
In spring-time from the **Cuckoo-bird**③,
Breaking the silence of the seas
Among the farthest **Hebrides**④.

Will no one tell me what she sings? —
Perhaps the **plaintive**⑤ numbers flow
For old, unhappy, far-off things,
And battles long ago:
Or is it some more humble lay,
Familiar matter of to-day?
Some natural sorrow, loss, or pain,
That has been, and may be again?

Whate'er the theme, the Maiden sang
As if her song could have no ending;
I saw her singing at her work,
And o'er the sickle bending; —
I listened, motionless and still;
And, as I mounted up the hill,
The music in my heart I bore,

---

① **chaunt**: *Archaic*, variant of chant.
② **haunt**: a place frequently visited.
③ **Cuckoo-bird**: a bird with a characteristic two-note call, which lays its eggs in the nests of other birds.
④ **Hebrides**: a group of over 500 islands off the Northwest coast of Scotland
⑤ **plaintive**: mournful, sorrowful.

Long after it was heard no more

Exercise

I. Word Matching

Directions: Please choose the most appropriate ones from the given words to explain the original boldfaced words in the following lines.

A. **gloomy**　　B. **modest**　　C. **lonely**　　D. **balance**　　E. **miss**

1. Behold her, single in the field,
   Yon **solitary** Highland Lass!
2. Alone she cuts and binds the grain,
   And sings a **melancholy** strain;
3. Or is it some more **humble** lay,
   Familiar matter of to-day?
4. Whate'er the theme, the **Maiden** sang
   As if her song could have no ending;

II. English-Chinese Translation

Directions: Please translate the following classic dicta from English into Chinese.

1. But hearing oftentimes the still, sad music of humanity.
   　　　　　　　　　　　　—*Lines Composed a Few Miles Above Tintern Abbey*
2. This City now doth, like a garment, wear the beauty of the morning.
   　　　　　　　　　　　　—*Composed upon Westminster Bridge*
3. Strongest minds are often those whom the noisy world hears least.
   　　　　　　　　　　　　—*The Complete Poetical Works of William Wordsworth*
4. With an eye made quiet by the power of harmony, and the deep power of joy, we see into the life of things.
   　　　　　　　　　　　　—*Lines Composed a Few Miles Above Tintern Abbey*
5. A voice so thrilling ne'er was heard in spring-time from the Cuckoo-bird, breaking the silence of the seas among the farthest Hebrides.
   　　　　　　　　　　　　—*The Solitary Reaper*

III. Term Defining

Directions: Please explain the following literary terms based on The Solitary Reaper.

1. enjambment
2. rhetorical question
3. consonance

IV. Content-Based Questions

Directions: Please give a concise and adequate answer to the following questions based

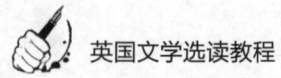

on the reading of The Solitary Reaper.

1. What figure does the narrator see at the very beginning of the poem *The Solitary Reaper*?

2. In what detailed words does the narrator depict the notes and voice of the lass's singing?

3. What possible theme does the Maiden's singing express in the narrator's mind?

V. Discussion Question

Despite his questioning "Will no one tell me what she sings?", the narrator still celebrates the lass's singing and compares it to a nightingale chanting welcome notes and even a cuckoo-bird in spring-time. Discuss with your partner the above account in the poem and the statement that music is the universal language of mankind.

VI. Essay Question

"Strongest minds are often those whom the noisy world hears least." is a quote from *The Complete Poetical Works of William Wordsworth*. Write a 200-word essay on how we can cultivate and enrich ourselves to own a powerful spiritual world and also be bold enough to speak our minds aloud in spite of the hustle and bustle of the external world.

Self-Improving Reading

Composed upon Westminster Bridge by William Wordsworth

Tintern Abbey by William Wordsworth

Unit 10　Jane Austen (1775−1817)

Life and Works

  Jane Austen, English genius author of classic novels of manners, was born to Reverend George Austen and Cassandra Austen in Steventon, Hampshire, England on December 16th, 1775. Mr. Austen brought the family with seven children together, fostering a serene and affectionate household and fundamentally establishing a setting that sparked Jane's later writing. At the age of eight, Jane began her education, together with her sister Cassandra at a local boarding school, and furthermore, they actively utilized the vast array of books available in their father's home library. Jane's early writings, now commonly recognized as *Austen's Juvenilia*, began in the year 1787, comprising a collection of short stories, poems and plays.

  Sense and Sensibility, was begun about 1795 as a novel-in-letters first called *Elinor and Marianne*, named after the Dashwood sisters in it, and published anonymously in November 1811. In December, 1795, Jane Austen fell in love with Tom Lefroy, her neighbor's nephew studying law in London, but unfortunately, their love came to an abrupt end by the interference of Tom's parents and they never had the chance to see each other for the rest of their lives. The first draft of Austen's most emblematic novel of manners, *Pride and Prejudice*, originally titled

First Impressions was completed in 1799, published anonymously in three volumes and warmly embraced by readers in 1813, which provides an insightful exploration of the social hierarchies in early 19th-century England. *Northanger Abbey*, another novel penned by Jane Austen around 1798 or 1799, and initially titled *Susan*, was not published until 1817, posthumously alongside *Persuasion*, in four volumes. In January, 1805, Jane's beloved father passed away suddenly in Bath, a city the Austen family had moved to following their three-decade residence in Steventon. Jane's three-volume *Emma* was released in 1815 and subsequently reviewed by Sir Walter Scott in *The Quarterly Review* the following year. In early 1817 Jane started her writing work of *Sanditon* with a self-mockery focus on health and illness, which was incomplete because she's inflicted with Addison disease. Jane Austen died on July 18th and was laid to rest in Winchester Cathedral.

Text A

Pride and Prejudice
Chapter I

It is a truth universally acknowledged, that a single man in possession of a good fortune, must be in want of a wife.

However little known the feelings or views of such a man may be on his first entering a neighbourhood, this truth is so well fixed in the minds of the surrounding families, that he is considered the rightful property of some one or other of their daughters.

My dear Mr. Bennet, said his lady to him one day, have you heard that Netherfield Park is let at last?

Mr. Bennet replied that he had not.

But it is, returned she; for Mrs. Long has just been here, and she told me all about it.

Mr. Bennet made no answer.

Do you not want to know who has taken it? cried his wife impatiently.

You want to tell me, and I have no objection to hearing it.

This was invitation enough.

Why, my dear, you must know, Mrs. Long says that Netherfield is taken by a young man of large fortune from the north of England; that he came down on Monday in a **chaise**[①] and four to see the place, and was so much delighted with it, that he agreed with Mr. Morris

---

① **chaise**: a light open two-wheel carriage.

immediately; that he is to take possession before **Michaelmas**①, and some of his servants are to be in the house by the end of next week.

What is his name?

Bingley.

Is he married or single?

Oh! Single, my dear, to be sure! A single man of large fortune; four or five thousand a year. What a fine thing for our girls!

How so? How can it affect them?

My dear Mr. Bennet, replied his wife, how can you be so tiresome! You must know that I am thinking of his marrying one of them.

Is that his design in settling here?

Design! Nonsense, how can you talk so! But it is very likely that he may fall in love with one of them, and therefore you must visit him as soon as he comes.

I see no occasion for that. You and the girls may go, or you may send them by themselves, which perhaps will be still better, for as you are as handsome as any of them, Mr. Bingley may like you the best of the party.

My dear, you flatter me. I certainly have had my share of beauty, but I do not pretend to be anything extraordinary now. When a woman has five grown-up daughters, she ought to give over thinking of her own beauty.

In such cases, a woman has not often much beauty to think of.

But, my dear, you must indeed go and see Mr. Bingley when he comes into the neighbourhood.

It is more than I engage for, I assure you.

But consider your daughters. Only think what an establishment it would be for one of them. Sir William and Lady Lucas are determined to go, merely on that account, for in general, you know, they visit no newcomers. Indeed you must go, for it will be impossible for us to visit him if you do not.

You are **over-scrupulous**②, surely. I dare say Mr. Bingley will be very glad to see you; and I will send a few lines by you to assure him of my hearty consent to his marrying whichever he chooses of the girls; though I must throw in a good word for my little Lizzy.

I desire you will do no such thing. Lizzy is not a bit better than the others; and I am sure she is not half so handsome as Jane, nor half so good-humoured as Lydia. But you are always giving her the preference.

They have none of them much to recommend them, replied he; they are all silly and

---

① **Michaelmas**: Sept. 29, a Christian holy day honoring the archangel Michael.
② **scrupulous**: showing care, meticulous.

ignorant like other girls; but Lizzy has something more of quickness than her sisters.

Mr. Bennet, how can you abuse your own children in such a way? You take delight in vexing me. You have no compassion for my poor nerves.

You mistake me, my dear. I have a high respect for your nerves. They are my old friends. I have heard you mention them with consideration these last twenty years at least.

Ah, you do not know what I suffer.

But I hope you will get over it, and live to see many young men of four thousand a year come into the neighbourhood.

It will be no use to us, if twenty such should come, since you will not visit them.

Depend upon it, my dear, that when there are twenty, I will visit them all.

Mr. Bennet was so odd a mixture of quick parts, sarcastic humour, reserve, and **caprice**①, that the experience of three-and-twenty years had been insufficient to make his wife understand his character. Her mind was less difficult to develop. She was a woman of mean understanding, little information, and uncertain temper. When she was discontented, she fancied herself nervous. The business of her life was to get her daughters married; its **solace**② was visiting and news.

Chapter 34

When they were gone, Elizabeth, as if intending to **exasperate**③ herself as much as possible against Mr. Darcy, chose for her employment the examination of all the letters which Jane had written to her since her being in Kent. They contained no actual complaint, nor was there any revival of past occurrences, or any communication of present suffering. But in all, and in almost every line of each, there was a want of that cheerfulness which had been used to characterise her style, and which, proceeding from the serenity of a mind at ease with itself and kindly disposed towards everyone, had been scarcely ever clouded. Elizabeth noticed every sentence conveying the idea of uneasiness, with an attention which it had hardly received on the first **perusal**④. Mr. Darcy's shameful boast of what misery he had been able to inflict, gave her a keener sense of her sister's sufferings. It was some consolation to think that his visit to Rosings was to end on the day after the next—and, a still greater, that in less than a fortnight she should herself be with Jane again, and enabled to contribute to the recovery of her spirits, by all that affection could do.

She could not think of Darcy's leaving Kent without remembering that his cousin was to go with him; but Colonel Fitzwilliam had made it clear that he had no intentions at all, and

---

① **caprice**: a tendency to change one's mind, inconstancy.
② **solace**: comfort in misery.
③ **exasperate**: annoy greatly.
④ **perusal**: reading with care.

Unit 10 Jane Austen (1775–1817)

agreeable as he was, she did not mean to be unhappy about him.

While settling this point, she was suddenly roused by the sound of the door-bell, and her spirits were a little **fluttered**① by the idea of its being Colonel Fitzwilliam himself, who had once before called late in the evening, and might now come to inquire particularly after her. But this idea was soon **banished**②, and her spirits were very differently affected, when, to her utter amazement, she saw Mr. Darcy walk into the room. In an hurried manner he immediately began an inquiry after her health, **imputing**③ his visit to a wish of hearing that she were better. She answered him with cold **civility**④. He sat down for a few moments, and then getting up, walked about the room. Elizabeth was surprised, but said not a word. After a silence of several minutes, he came towards her in an agitated manner, and thus began:

In vain I have struggled. It will not do. My feelings will not be repressed. You must allow me to tell you how ardently I admire and love you.

Elizabeth's astonishment was beyond expression. She stared, coloured, doubted, and was silent. This he considered sufficient encouragement; and the **avowal**⑤ of all that he felt, and had long felt for her, immediately followed. He spoke well; but there were feelings besides those of the heart to be detailed; and he was not more eloquent on the subject of tenderness than of pride. His sense of her inferiority-of its being a degradation-of the family obstacles which had always opposed to inclination, were dwelt on with a warmth which seemed due to the consequence he was wounding, but was very unlikely to recommend his suit.

In spite of her deeply-rooted dislike, she could not be insensible to the compliment of such a man's affection, and though her intentions did not vary for an instant, she was at first sorry for the pain he was to receive; till, roused to resentment by his subsequent language, she lost all compassion in anger. She tried, however, to **compose**⑥ herself to answer him with patience, when he should have done. He concluded with representing to her the strength of that attachment which, in spite of all his endeavours, he had found impossible to conquer; and with expressing his hope that it would now be rewarded by her acceptance of his hand. As he said this, she could easily see that he had no doubt of a favourable answer. He spoke of apprehension and anxiety, but his countenance expressed real security. Such a circumstance could only exasperate farther, and, when he ceased, the colour rose into her cheeks, and she said:

In such cases as this, it is, I believe, the established mode to express a sense of obligation

---

① **Fluttered**: **flutter** (*v.*), vibrate rapidly.
② **banished**: **banish** (*v.*), throw out.
③ **imputing**: **impute** (*v.*), attribute to a cause.
④ **civility**: politeness.
⑤ **avowal**: an open admission.
⑥ **compose**: make (oneself) calm.

for the sentiments avowed, however unequally they may be returned. It is natural that obligation should be felt, and if I could feel gratitude, I would now thank you. But I cannot—I have never desired your good opinion, and you have certainly bestowed it most unwillingly. I am sorry to have **occasion**①ed pain to anyone. It has been most unconsciously done, however, and I hope will be of short duration. The feelings which, you tell me, have long prevented the acknowledgment of your regard, can have little difficulty in overcoming it after this explanation.

Mr. Darcy, who was leaning against the **mantelpiece**② with his eyes fixed on her face, seemed to catch her words with no less resentment than surprise. His complexion became pale with anger, and the disturbance of his mind was visible in every feature. He was struggling for the appearance of composure, and would not open his lips till he believed himself to have attained it. The pause was to Elizabeth's feelings dreadful. At length, with a voice of forced calmness, he said:

And this is all the reply which I am to have the honour of expecting! I might, perhaps, wish to be informed why, with so little endeavour at civility, I am thus rejected. But it is of small importance.

I might as well inquire, replied she, why with so evident a desire of offending and insulting me, you chose to tell me that you liked me against your will, against your reason, and even against your character? Was not this some excuse for incivility, if I was uncivil? But I have other **provocations**③. You know I have. Had not my feelings decided against you—had they been indifferent, or had they even been favourable, do you think that any consideration would tempt me to accept the man who has been the means of ruining, perhaps for ever, the happiness of a most beloved sister?

As she pronounced these words, Mr. Darcy changed colour; but the emotion was short, and he listened without attempting to interrupt her while she continued:

I have every reason in the world to think ill of you. No motive can excuse the unjust and ungenerous part you acted there. You dare not, you cannot deny, that you have been the principal, if not the only means of dividing them from each other—of exposing one to the **censure**④ of the world for caprice and instability, and the other to its **derision**⑤ for disappointed hopes, and involving them both in misery of the acutest kind.

She paused, and saw with no slight **indignation**⑥ that he was listening with an air which

---

① **occasion**: bring about.
② **mantelpiece**: shelf above a fireplace.
③ **provocations**: *pl.* of *provocation*, something that causes anger.
④ **censure**: severe disapproval.
⑤ **derision**: scorn.
⑥ **indignation**: intense displeasure.

proved him wholly unmoved by any feeling of **remorse**①. He even looked at her with a smile of affected incredulity.

Can you deny that you have done it? she repeated.

With assumed tranquillity he then replied: I have no wish of denying that I did everything in my power to separate my friend from your sister, or that I rejoice in my success. Towards him I have been kinder than towards myself.

Elizabeth disdained the appearance of noticing this civil reflection, but its meaning did not escape, nor was it likely to **conciliate**② her.

But it is not merely this affair, she continued, on which my dislike is founded. Long before it had taken place my opinion of you was decided. Your character was unfolded in the **recital**③ which I received many months ago from Mr. Wickham. On this subject, what can you have to say? In what imaginary act of friendship can you here defend yourself? or under what misrepresentation can you here impose upon others?

You take an eager interest in that gentleman's concerns, said Darcy, in a less tranquil tone, and with a heightened colour.

Who that knows what his misfortunes have been, can help feeling an interest in him?

His misfortunes! repeated Darcy **contemptuously**④; yes, his misfortunes have been great indeed.

And of your infliction, cried Elizabeth with energy. You have reduced him to his present state of poverty-comparative poverty. You have withheld the advantages which you must know to have been designed for him. You have deprived the best years of his life of that independence which was no less his due than his desert. You have done all this! and yet you can treat the mention of his misfortune with contempt and ridicule.

And this, cried Darcy, as he walked with quick steps across the room, is your opinion of me! This is the estimation in which you hold me! I thank you for explaining it so fully. My faults, according to this calculation, are heavy indeed! But perhaps, added he, stopping in his walk, and turning towards her, these offenses might have been overlooked, had not your pride been hurt by my honest confession of the scruples that had long prevented my forming any serious design. These bitter accusations might have been suppressed, had I, with greater policy, concealed my struggles, and flattered you into the belief of my being impelled by unqualified, **unalloyed**⑤ inclination; by reason, by reflection, by everything. But disguise of every sort

---

① **remorse**: painful regret.
② **conciliate**: win over.
③ **recital**: account, description.
④ **contemptuously**: without respect.
⑤ **unalloyed**: pure.

is my **abhorrence**①. Nor am I ashamed of the feelings I related. They were natural and just. Could you expect me to rejoice in the inferiority of your connections?—to congratulate myself on the hope of relations, whose condition in life is so decidedly beneath my own?

Elizabeth felt herself growing more angry every moment; yet she tried to the utmost to speak with composure when she said:

You are mistaken, Mr. Darcy, if you suppose that the mode of your declaration affected me in any other way, than as it spared the concern which I might have felt in refusing you, had you behaved in a more gentlemanlike manner.

She saw him start at this, but he said nothing, and she continued:

You could not have made the offer of your hand in any possible way that would have tempted me to accept it.

Again his astonishment was obvious; and he looked at her with an expression of mingled incredulity and **mortification**②. She went on:

From the very beginning—from the first moment, I may almost say—of my acquaintance with you, your manners, impressing me with the fullest belief of your arrogance, your conceit, and your selfish disdain of the feelings of others, were such as to form the groundwork of **disapprobation**③ on which succeeding events have built so immovable a dislike; and I had not known you a month before I felt that you were the last man in the world whom I could ever be prevailed on to marry.

You have said quite enough, madam. I perfectly comprehend your feelings, and have now only to be ashamed of what my own have been. Forgive me for having taken up so much of your time, and accept my best wishes for your health and happiness.

And with these words he hastily left the room, and Elizabeth heard him the next moment open the front door and quit the house.

The **tumult**④ of her mind, was now painfully great. She knew not how to support herself, and from actual weakness sat down and cried for half-an-hour. Her astonishment, as she reflected on what had passed, was increased by every review of it. That she should receive an offer of marriage from Mr. Darcy! That he should have been in love with her for so many months! So much in love as to wish to marry her in spite of all the objections which had made him prevent his friend's marrying her sister, and which must appear at least with equal force in his own case—was almost incredible! It was gratifying to have inspired unconsciously so strong an affection. But his pride, his **abominable**⑤ pride–his shameless avowal of what he

---

① **abhorrence**: strong feelings of dislike.
② **mortification**: shame, embarrassment.
③ **disapprobation**: disapproval.
④ **tumult**: violent disturbance.
⑤ **abominable**: dreadful, detestable.

had done with respect to Jane-his unpardonable assurance in acknowledging, though he could not justify it, and the unfeeling manner in which he had mentioned Mr. Wickham, his cruelty towards whom he had not attempted to deny, soon overcame the pity which the consideration of his attachment had for a moment excited. She continued in very agitated reflections till the sound of Lady Catherine's carriage made her feel how unequal she was to encounter Charlotte's observation, and hurried her away to her room.

Exercise

I. Word Matching

Directions: Please choose the most appropriate ones from the given words to explain the original boldfaced words in the following lines.

A. **disbelief** B. **annoy** C. **admit** D. **excited**
E. **serenity** F. **dread**

1. It is a truth universally **acknowledged**, that a single man in possession of a good fortune, must be in want of a wife.
2. You take delight in **vex**ing me.
3. After a silence of several minutes, he came towards her in an **agitated** manner.
4. He spoke of **apprehension** and anxiety, but his countenance expressed real security.
5. He even looked at her with a smile of affected **incredulity**.
6. With assumed **tranquillity** he then replied.

II. English-Chinese Translation

Directions: Please translate the following classic dicta from English into Chinese.

1. It is a truth universally acknowledged that a single man in possession of a good fortune, must be in want of a wife.

—*Pride and Prejudice*

2. One half of the world cannot understand the pleasures of the other.

—*Emma*

3. Life seems but a quick succession of busy nothings.

—*Mansfield Park*

4. Laugh as much as you choose, but you will not laugh me out of my opinion.

—*Pride and Prejudice*

5. Friendship is certainly the finest balm for the pangs of disappointed love.

—*Northanger Abbey*

III. Term Defining

Directions: Please explain the following literary terms based on Pride and Prejudice.

1. novel of matters

2. verbal irony

3. omniscient narrator

IV. Content-Based Questions

Directions: *Please give a concise and adequate answer to the following questions related to Text A.*

1. What news made Mrs. Bennet so excited and then what was Mr. Bennet's reaction to it?

2. What was Elizabeth's response when Mr. Darcy called late in the evening, boldly confesses his feelings for her, and expresses his desire to marry her?

3. What objections made Mr. Darcy prevent Bingley's marrying Elizabeth's sister, Jane?

V. Role-Playing Activity

As we read in Chapter 34 of *Pride and Prejudice*, Elizabeth responded with a refusal to Mr. Darcy's sudden love confession and marriage proposal. Please have a careful re-reading of the sharp twist to the plot of this chapter and engage in a role-playing practice with your group members.

VI. Essay Question

It is evident in the above two excerpted chapters of *Pride and Prejudice* that Mrs. Bennet's extremely concerned about marrying off her daughters due to the fact that marriage was the only choice for a woman to change her economic status and social role at that age. Write a 200-word essay on the difference between the heroine, Elizabeth and the 21st-century women regarding marriage option.

Text B

Sense and Sensibility
Chapter I

The family of Dashwood had long been settled in **Sussex**①. Their estate was large, and their residence was at Norland Park, in the centre of their property, where, for many generations, they had lived in so respectable a manner as to engage the general good opinion of their surrounding acquaintance. The late owner of this estate was a single man, who lived to a very advanced age, and who for many years of his life, had a constant companion and housekeeper in his sister. But her death, which happened ten years before his own, produced a great alteration in his home; for to supply her loss, he invited and received into his house

---

① **Sussex**: an Anglo-Saxon kingdom of southern England bordering on the English Channel.

the family of his nephew Mr. Henry Dashwood, the legal inheritor of the Norland estate, and the person to whom he intended to bequeath it. In the society of his nephew and niece, and their children, the old Gentleman's days were comfortably spent. His attachment to them all increased. The constant attention of Mr. and Mrs. Henry Dashwood to his wishes, which proceeded not merely from interest, but from goodness of heart, gave him every degree of solid comfort which his age could receive; and the cheerfulness of the children added a **relish**① to his existence.

By a former marriage, Mr. Henry Dashwood had one son: by his present lady, three daughters. The son, a steady respectable young man, was amply provided for by the fortune of his mother, which had been large, and half of which **devolved**② on him on his coming of age. By his own marriage, likewise, which happened soon afterwards, he added to his wealth. To him therefore the succession to the Norland estate was not so really important as to his sisters; for their fortune, independent of what might arise to them from their father's inheriting that property, could be but small. Their mother had nothing, and their father only seven thousand pounds in his own disposal; for the remaining **moiety**③ of his first wife's fortune was also secured to her child, and he had only a life-interest in it.

The old gentleman died: his will was read, and like almost every other will, gave as much disappointment as pleasure. He was neither so unjust, nor so ungrateful, as to leave his estate from his nephew; —but he left it to him on such terms as destroyed half the value of the **bequest**④. Mr. Dashwood had wished for it more for the sake of his wife and daughters than for himself or his son; —but to his son, and his son's son, a child of four years old, it was secured, in such a way, as to leave to himself no power of providing for those who were most dear to him, and who most needed a provision by any charge on the estate, or by any sale of its valuable woods. The whole was tied up for the benefit of this child, who, in occasional visits with his father and mother at Norland, had so far gained on the affections of his uncle, by such attractions as are by no means unusual in children of two or three years old; an imperfect **articulation**⑤, an earnest desire of having his own way, many cunning tricks, and a great deal of noise, as to outweigh all the value of all the attention which, for years, he had received from his niece and her daughters. He meant not to be unkind, however, and, as a mark of his affection for the three girls, he left them a thousand pounds a-piece.

Mr. Dashwood's disappointment was, at first, severe; but his temper was cheerful and

---

① **relish**: a keen liking.
② **devolved**: **devolve** (*v.*), pass on.
③ **moiety**: a half.
④ **bequest**: a legacy.
⑤ **articulation**: the act of speaking in words.

sanguine①; and he might reasonably hope to live many years, and by living economically, lay by a considerable sum from the produce of an estate already large, and capable of almost immediate improvement. But the fortune, which had been so **tardy**② in coming, was his only one twelvemonth. He survived his uncle no longer; and ten thousand pounds, including the late legacies, was all that remained for his widow and daughters.

His son was sent for as soon as his danger was known, and to him Mr. Dashwood recommended, with all the strength and urgency which illness could command, the interest of his mother-in-law and sisters.

Mr. John Dashwood had not the strong feelings of the rest of the family; but he was affected by a recommendation of such a nature at such a time, and he promised to do everything in his power to make them comfortable. His father was rendered easy by such an assurance, and Mr. John Dashwood had then leisure to consider how much there might **prudently**③ be in his power to do for them.

He was not an ill-disposed young man, unless to be rather cold hearted and rather selfish is to be ill-disposed: but he was, in general, well respected; for he conducted himself with **propriety**④ in the discharge of his ordinary duties. Had he married a more amiable woman, he might have been made still more respectable than he was: —he might even have been made amiable himself; for he was very young when he married, and very fond of his wife. But Mrs. John Dashwood was a strong **caricature**⑤ of himself; —more narrow-minded and selfish.

When he gave his promise to his father, he meditated within himself to increase the fortunes of his sisters by the present of a thousand pounds a-piece. He then really thought himself equal to it. The prospect of four thousand a-year, in addition to his present income, besides the remaining half of his own mother's fortune, warmed his heart, and made him feel capable of generosity. Yes, he would give them three thousand pounds: it would be liberal and handsome! It would be enough to make them completely easy. Three thousand pounds! he could spare so considerable a sum with little inconvenience. He thought of it all day long, and for many days successively, and he did not repent.

No sooner was his father's funeral over, than Mrs. John Dashwood, without sending any notice of her intention to her mother-in-law, arrived with her child and their attendants. No one could dispute her right to come; the house was her husband's from the moment of his father's **decease**⑥; but the **indelicacy**⑦ of her conduct was so much the greater, and to a woman in Mrs.

---

① **sanguine**: optimistic.
② **tardy**: not on time.
③ **prudently**: wisely.
④ **propriety**: rightness.
⑤ **caricature**: a distorted imitation.
⑥ **decease**: death.
⑦ **indelicacy**: the quality of being offensive.

Unit 10 Jane Austen (1775-1817)

Dashwood's situation, with only common feelings, must have been highly unpleasing; —but in her mind there was a sense of honor so keen, a generosity so romantic, that any offence of the kind, by whomsoever given or received, was to her a source of immovable disgust. Mrs. John Dashwood had never been a favourite with any of her husband's family; but she had had no opportunity, till the present, of showing them with how little attention to the comfort of other people she could act when occasion required it.

So acutely did Mrs. Dashwood feel this ungracious behaviour, and so earnestly did she despise her daughter-in-law for it, that, on the arrival of the latter, she would have quitted the house for ever, had not the **entreaty**① of her eldest girl induced her first to reflect on the propriety of going, and her own tender love for all her three children determined her afterwards to stay, and for their sakes avoid a **breach**② with their brother.

Elinor, this eldest daughter, whose advice was so effectual, possessed a strength of understanding, and coolness of judgment, which qualified her, though only nineteen, to be the counsellor of her mother, and enabled her frequently to counteract, to the advantage of them all, that eagerness of mind in Mrs. Dashwood which must generally have led to imprudence. She had an excellent heart; —her disposition was affectionate, and her feelings were strong; but she knew how to govern them: it was a knowledge which her mother had yet to learn; and which one of her sisters had resolved never to be taught.

Marianne's abilities were, in many respects, quite equal to Elinor's. She was sensible and clever; but eager in everything: her sorrows, her joys, could have no moderation. She was generous, amiable, interesting: she was everything but prudent. The resemblance between her and her mother was strikingly great.

Elinor saw, with concern, the excess of her sister's sensibility; but by Mrs. Dashwood it was valued and cherished. They encouraged each other now in the violence of their affliction. The agony of grief which overpowered them at first, was voluntarily renewed, was sought for, was created again and again. They gave themselves up wholly to their sorrow, seeking increase of wretchedness in every reflection that could afford it, and resolved against ever admitting consolation in future. Elinor, too, was deeply afflicted; but still she could struggle, she could exert herself. She could consult with her brother, could receive her sister-in-law on her arrival, and treat her with proper attention; and could strive to rouse her mother to similar exertion, and encourage her to similar forbearance.

Margaret, the other sister, was a good-humored, well-disposed girl; but as she had already **imbibed**③ a good deal of Marianne's romance, without having much of her sense, she did not, at thirteen, bid fair to equal her sisters at a more advanced period of life.

---

① **entreaty**: an earnest request.
② **bleach**: separation.
③ **imbibed**: imbibe (*v.*), receive.

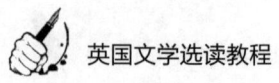

> **Exercise**

I. Word Matching

Directions: Please choose the most appropriate ones from the given words to explain the original boldfaced words in the following lines.

    A. **affection**   B. **inheritance**   C. **ponder**   D. **change**   E. **regret**

1. But her death, which happened ten years before his own, produced a great **alteration** in his home.

2. His **attachment** to them all increased.

3. To him therefore the **succession** to the Norland estate was not so really important as to his sisters.

4. He **meditated** within himself to increase the fortunes of his sisters by the present of a thousand pounds a-piece.

5. He thought of it all day long, and for many days successively, and he did not **repent**.

II. English-Chinese Translation

Directions: Please translate the following classic dicta from English into Chinese.

1. It isn't what we say or think that defines us, but what we do.

                                                      —*Sense and Sensibility*

2. If a book is well written, I always find it too short.

                                                      —*Juvenilia*

3. A woman is not to marry a man merely because she is asked, or because he is attached to her, and can write a tolerable letter.

                                                      —*Emma*

4. One man's ways may be as good as another's, but we all like our own best.

                                                      —*Persuasion*

5. The person, be it gentleman or lady, who has not pleasure in a good novel, must be intolerably stupid.

                                                     —*Northanger Abbey*

III. Term Defining

Directions: Please explain the following literary terms based on The Solitary Reaper.

1. protagonist

2. allusion

3. motif

IV. Content-Based Questions

Directions: Please give a concise and adequate answer to the following questions based on the reading of Text B.

1. Please provide the detailed information about the composition and status of Mr. Henry

Dashwood's children from his two marriages.

2. What did the eldest girl, Elinor advise her mother to do when Mrs. John Dashwood arrived at Norland Park unexpectedly after the death of Mr. Henry Dashwood? What remarkable personality was exposed with regard to the way she tackled the above matter?

3. In what respect did the second girl, Marianne resemble her mother, Mrs. Henry Dashwood noticeably?

V. Discussion Question

What does the narrator want to express with the words "The old gentleman died: his will was read, and like almost every other will, gave as much disappointment as pleasure." in chapter 1 of *Sense and Sensibility*? Discuss this chapter with your partner and figure out the intricate causes of disappointment and pleasure based on the specific plot of the context.

VI. Essay Question

Almost opposite personalities are shown in the protagonists in *Sense and Sensibility* by Jane Austen. Write a 200-word essay to express your reflection on the potential impact of such attributes as Elinor's strength of understanding and coolness of judgment, eagerness of mind in Mrs. Dashwood and Marianne's everything but prudence at a critical moment.

Self-Improving Reading

Northanger Abbey by Jane Austen

Emma by Jane Austen

Unit 11　Percy Bysshe Shelley (1792–1822)

Life and Works

Percy Bysshe Shelley, one of the most esteemed poets of English Romantic era, was born as the eldest son of Timothy Shelly and Elizabeth Shelley, in Broadbridge Heath, West Sussex, England on August 4, 1792. Shelley first received his education at Syon House Academy in 1802 and two years later began his 6-year study at Eton College, where he made commendable attempts in literature. Upon his admission to University College, Oxford in 1810, Shelley already established himself as a published writer. But unfortunately, Shelly was expelled together with his friend Thomas Jefferson Hogg by University College due to their authorship of a prose pamphlet titled *The Necessity of Atheism* early the following year. In the same year, Shelly ran away with Harriet Westbrook, a 16-year-old girl attempting to commit suicide, defying the strong opposition of his parents.

In 1812, Shelly had the privilege of meeting William Godwin, a prestigious political philosopher authoring *Political Justice*. The next year Shelley published *Queen Mab*, his first major poem in blank verse and lyric measures, describing the utopian society he envisioned. In 1814, Shelley inevitably fell in love with Mary Wollstonecraft Godwin, daughter of William

Godwin and Mary Wollstonecraft, the writer of *A Vindication of the Rights of Woman*. Shelley and Mary left London together to embark on a journey to explore France, Switzerland, Germany and Holland despite the disapproval of Godwin, and as a consequence, Harriet had no other option but to seek a divorce. In the year 1815, Shelley composed a poem titled *Alastor*, or *The Spirit of Solitude*, encompassing a total of 720 lines, and now widely acknowledged as his inaugural great work. Shelley forged a deep friendship with Byron during the stay near Lake Geneva in Switzerland and wrote *Hymn to Intellectual Beauty*. Following a further expedition alongside Byron through the French Alps, Shelley penned *Mont Blanc*, an introspective composition of humanity and the awe-inspiring nature. In the winter of 1816, Mary and Shelley were married, warmly embraced by the Godwins and moved to Buckinghamshire's Marlow, where Shelley cultivated deep friendships with John Keats and Leigh Hunt. In 1818, Shelly published *The Revolt of Islam* with its emphases on religion and socialist political ideal in a poetic way. During his residence in Italy around 1819, Shelly completed his four-act lyric drama, *Prometheus Unbound*, which explores the mythological tale of Prometheus defying Zeus by stealing fire from heaven to bestow upon humanity. In 1820, a compilation of Shelley's most remarkable shorter poems, including *Ode to Liberty*, *Ode to the West Wind*, *The Cloud*, and *To a Sky-Lark* were published together with his magnum opus *Prometheus Unbound*. Shelley drowned accidentally during his sailing return from Livorno to Lerici, after a discussion with Leigh Hunt regarding *The Liberal*, their recently launched journal on July 8, 1822. After more than a century, Shelley's legacy was commemorated with a memorial in Poet's Corner in Westminster Abbey.

Text A

Ode to the West Wind

I

O wild West Wind, thou breath of Autumn's being,
Thou, from whose unseen presence the leaves dead
Are driven, like ghosts from an **enchanter**[①] fleeing,

Yellow, and black, and pale, and **hectic**[②] red,

---

① **enchanter**: one that bewitches.
② **hectic**: flushed associated with tuberculosis.

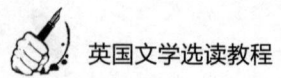

Pestilence①-stricken multitudes: O thou,
Who chariotest② to their dark wintry bed

The winged seeds, where they lie cold and low,
Each like a corpse within its grave, until
Thine azure③ sister of the Spring shall blow

Her clarion④ o'er the dreaming earth, and fill
(Driving sweet buds like flocks to feed in air)
With living hues and odours plain and hill:

Wild Spirit, which art moving everywhere;
Destroyer and preserver; hear, oh hear!

II

Thou on whose stream, mid the steep sky's commotion⑤,
Loose clouds like earth's decaying leaves are shed,
Shook from the tangled boughs of Heaven and Ocean,

Angels of rain and lightning: there are spread
On the blue surface of thine aëry surge,
Like the bright hair uplifted from the head

Of some fierce Maenad⑥, even from the dim verge
Of the horizon to the zenith⑦'s height,
The locks⑧ of the approaching storm. Thou dirge⑨

Of the dying year, to which this closing night

---

① **Pestilence**: a deadly epidemic disease.
② **chariotest**: chariot (after the second personal pronouns in ancient English), convey in a chariot.
③ **azure**: a clear blue sky.
④ **clarion**: an ancient trumpet.
⑤ **commotion**: noisy disturbance.
⑥ **Maenad**: (*Greek Mythology*) a mad woman.
⑦ **zenith**: the upper region of the sky.
⑧ **locks**: hair of the head.
⑨ **dirge**: a funeral song.

Will be the dome of a vast **sepulchre**①,
Vaulted② with all thy **congregated**③ might

Of vapours, from whose solid atmosphere
Black rain, and fire, and hail will burst: oh hear!

III

Thou who didst waken from his summer dreams
The blue Mediterranean, where he lay,
Lull'd by the coil of his **crystalline**④ streams,

Beside a **pumice**⑤ isle in **Baiae**⑥'s bay,
And saw in sleep old palaces and towers
Quivering within the wave's intenser day,

All overgrown with azure moss and flowers
So sweet, the sense faints picturing them! Thou
For whose path the Atlantic's level powers

Cleave⑦ themselves into **chasms**⑧, while far below
The sea-blooms and the **oozy**⑨ woods which wear
The **sapless**⑩ foliage of the ocean, know

Thy voice, and suddenly grow gray with fear,
And tremble and **despoil**⑪ themselves: oh hear!

IV

If I were a dead leaf thou mightest bear;

---

① **sepulchre**: grave.
② **Vaulted**: **vault** (past tense), build in the shape of an arch.
③ **congregated**: **congregate** (past tense), bring together.
④ **crystalline**: transparent, like crystal.
⑤ **pumice**: a light porous acid volcanic rock.
⑥ **Baiae**: an ancient Roman town situated on the northwest shore of the Gulf of Naples.
⑦ **Cleave**: split something in two.
⑧ **chasms**: **chasm** (*pl.*), a deep opening in the earth's surface.
⑨ **oozy**: of soft mud.
⑩ **sapless**: lacking liquid in a plant.
⑪ **despoil**: strip of things of value.

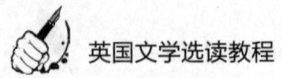

If I were a swift cloud to fly with thee;
A wave to **pant**① beneath thy power, and share

The impulse of thy strength, only less free
Than thou, O uncontrollable! If even
I were as in my boyhood, and could be

The comrade of thy wanderings over Heaven,
As then, when to outstrip thy **skiey**② speed
Scarce seem'd a vision; I would ne'er have striven

As thus with thee in prayer in my sore need.
Oh, lift me as a wave, a leaf, a cloud!
I fall upon the thorns of life! I bleed!

A heavy weight of hours has chain'd and bow'd
One too like thee: tameless, and swift, and proud.

V

Make me thy **lyre**③, even as the forest is:
What if my leaves are falling like its own!
The **tumult**④ of thy mighty harmonies

Will take from both a deep, autumnal tone,
Sweet though in sadness. Be thou, Spirit fierce,
My spirit! Be thou me, **impetuous**⑤ one!

Drive my dead thoughts over the universe
Like wither'd leaves to quicken a new birth!
And, by the **incantation**⑥ of this verse,

---

① **pant**: breathe with deep gasps.
② **skiey**: lofty.
③ **lyre**: an ancient Greek stringed instrument.
④ **tumult**: violent disturbance, uproar.
⑤ **impetuous**: impulsive, rash.
⑥ **incantation**: a verbal spell.

Unit 11 Percy Bysshe Shelley (1792–1822)

Scatter, as from an unextinguish'd **hearth**①

Ashes and sparks, my words among mankind!

Be through my lips to unawaken'd earth

The trumpet of a prophecy! O Wind,

If Winter comes, can Spring be far behind?

Exercise

I. Word Matching

Directions: Please choose the most appropriate ones from the given words to explain the original boldfaced words in the following lines.

A. **body**　　　　B. **forecast**　　　　C. **leaf**　　　　D. **mass**

E. **calm**　　　　F. **powerful**

1. Pestilence-stricken **multitudes**: O thou,

   Who chariotest to their dark wintry bed

2. Each like a **corpse** within its grave, until

   Thine azure sister of the Spring shall blow

3. **Lull**'d by the coil of his crystalline streams,

4. The sea-blooms and the oozy woods which wear

   The sapless **foliage** of the ocean, know

5. The tumult of thy **mighty** harmonies

   Will take from both a deep, autumnal tone,

6. The trumpet of a **prophecy**! O Wind,

   If Winter comes, can Spring be far behind?

II. English-Chinese Translation

Directions: Please translate the following classic dicta from English into Chinese.

1. O, wind, if winter comes, can spring be far behind?

   —*Ode to the West Wind*

2. Power, like a desolating pestilence,

   Pollutes whate'er it touches.

   —*Queen Mab*

3. Familiar acts are beautiful through love.

   —*Prometheus Unbound*

---

① **hearth**: a fireplace.

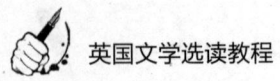

4. Reason respects the differences, and imagination the similitudes of things.

—*A Defence of Poetry*

5. Oh lift me as a wave, a leaf, a cloud! I fall upon the thorns of life! I bleed!

—*Ode to the West Wind*

III. Term Defining

Directions: Please explain the following literary terms based on *Ode to the West Wind*.

1. anastrophe
2. alliteration
3. visual imagery

IV. Content-Based Questions

Directions: Please give a concise and adequate answer to the following questions related to Text A.

1. Why does the author express such exclamation as "O wild West Wind, thou breath of Autumn's being" at the very beginning of the poem *Ode to the West Wind*?

2. How did the west wind wake the Mediterranean from his summer dreams based on the account of the third stanza?

3. For what purpose does the author earnestly request the west wind to "lift me as a wave, a leaf, a cloud"?

V. Discussion Question

From the lines "Wild Spirit, which art moving everywhere; Destroyer and preserver; hear, oh hear!" at the end of the first stanza of the poem *Ode to the West Wind,* we can infer that the author compares the west wind to "Destroyer and preserver". Discuss the whole poem with your other group members after a thorough reading and sum up the multifarious destroying and preserving impacts of the west wind on the world.

VI. Essay Question

The renowned quotes like "Wild Spirit, which art moving everywhere; Destroyer and preserver; and O Wind, If Winter comes, can Spring be far behind?" remind us of our Chinese idiom "Without destroying the old, one cannot build the new". Write a 200-word essay to exemplify some social and economic activities aiming at breaking the status quo and meeting the new challenges in our era.

Unit 11　Percy Bysshe Shelley (1792-1822)

Text B

To a Skylark

Hail to thee, blithe Spirit!
Bird thou never **wert**①,
That from Heaven, or near it,
Pourest thy full heart
In **profuse**② strains of **unpremeditated**③ art.

Higher still and higher
From the earth thou springest
Like a cloud of fire;
The blue deep thou wingest,
And singing still dost soar, and soaring ever singest.

In the golden lightning
Of the sunken sun,
O'er which clouds are bright'ning,
Thou dost float and run;
Like an unbodied joy whose race is just begun.

The pale purple even
Melts around thy flight;
Like a star of Heaven,
In the broad day-light
Thou art unseen, but yet I hear thy shrill delight,

Keen as are the arrows
Of that silver sphere,
Whose intense lamp narrows
In the white dawn clear

---

① **wert**: *Archaic* a singular form of the past tense of be.
② **profuse**: abundantly, extravagant.
③ **unpremeditated**: not thought out beforehand.

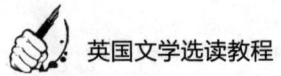

Until we hardly see, we feel that it is there.

All the earth and air
With thy voice is loud,
As, when night is bare,
From one lonely cloud
The moon rains out her beams, and Heaven is overflow'd.

What thou art we know not;
What is most like thee?
From rainbow clouds there flow not
Drops so bright to see
As from thy presence showers a rain of melody.

Like a Poet hidden
In the light of thought,
Singing hymns unbidden,
Till the world is wrought
To sympathy with hopes and fears it **heed**[①]ed not:

Like a high-born maiden
In a palace-tower,
Soothing her love-laden
Soul in secret hour
With music sweet as love, which overflows her **bower**[②]:

Like a glow-worm golden
In a **dell**[③] of dew,
Scattering unbeholden
Its aëreal hue
Among the flowers and grass, which screen it from the view:

Like a rose **embower'd**[④]

---

① **heed**: pay close attention to.
② **bower**: *literary* a lady's private chamber.
③ **dell**: wooded valley.
④ **embower'd**: **embowered** (the past tense of **embower**), enclosed in.

Unit 11　Percy Bysshe Shelley (1792–1822)

In its own green leaves,
By warm winds deflower'd,
Till the scent it gives
Makes faint with too much sweet those heavy-winged thieves:

Sound of **vernal**① showers
On the twinkling grass,
Rain-awaken'd flowers,
All that ever was
Joyous, and clear, and fresh, thy music doth surpass.

Teach us, **Sprite**② or Bird,
What sweet thoughts are thine:
I have never heard
Praise of love or wine
That panted forth a flood of **rapture**③ so divine.

Chorus **Hymeneal**④,
Or triumphal chant,
Match'd with thine would be all
But an empty **vaunt**⑤,
A thing wherein we feel there is some hidden want.

What objects are the fountains
Of thy happy **strain**⑥?
What fields, or waves, or mountains?
What shapes of sky or plain?
What love of thine own kind? what ignorance of pain?

With thy clear keen joyance
Languor⑦ cannot be:

---

① **vernal**: relating to the spring.
② **Sprite**: an elf, a spirit.
③ **rapture**: bliss, ecstatic delight.
④ **Hymeneal**: *Archaic* a wedding.
⑤ **vaunt**: a boastful remark.
⑥ **strain**: a tune.
⑦ **Languor**: physical or mental laziness or weariness.

Shadow of annoyance
Never came near thee:
Thou lovest: but ne'er knew love's sad **satiety**①.

Waking or asleep,
Thou of death must deem
Things more true and deep
Than we mortals dream,
Or how could thy notes flow in such a crystal stream?

We look before and after,
And **pine**② for what is not:
Our sincerest laughter
With some pain is **fraught**③;
Our sweetest songs are those that tell of saddest thought.

Yet if we could scorn
Hate, and pride, and fear;
If we were things born
Not to shed a tear,
I know not how thy joy we ever should come near.

Better than all measures
Of delightful sound,
Better than all treasures
That in books are found,
Thy skill to poet were, thou scorner of the ground!

Teach me half the gladness
That thy brain must know,
Such harmonious madness
From my lips would flow
The world should listen then, as I am listening now.

---

① **satiety**: the condition of being filled.
② **pine**: *archaic* grieve for.
③ **fraught**: filled with.

Unit 11 Percy Bysshe Shelley (1792–1822)

Exercise

I. Word Matching

Directions: Please choose the most appropriate ones from the given words to explain the original boldfaced words in the following lines.

A. **cheerful**   B. **despise**   C. **fly**   D. **greet**
E. **relieve**   F. **lack**

1. **Hail** to thee, **blithe** Spirit!
2. Thou art unseen, but yet I hear thy **shrill** delight,
3. **Sooth**ing her love-laden
   Soul in secret hour
4. A thing wherein we feel there is some hidden **want**.
5. Yet if we could **scorn**
   Hate, and pride, and fear;

II. English-Chinese Translation

Directions: Please translate the following classic dicta from English into Chinese.

1. Hail to thee, blithe spirit!

   —*To a Skylark*

2. Poets are the unacknowledged legislators of the world.

   —*A Defence of Poetry*

3. A single word even may be a spark of inextinguishable thought.

   —*A Defence of Poetry*

4. Poetry is the record of the best and happiest moments of the happiest and best minds.

   —*A Defence of Poetry*

5. Our sweetest songs are those that tell of saddest thought.

   —*To a Skylark*

III. Term Defining

Directions: Please explain the following literary terms based on To a Skylark.

1. rhetorical question
2. assonance
3. enjambment

IV. Content-Based Questions

Directions: Please give a concise and adequate answer to the following questions based on the reading of Text B.

1. Please enunciate the causes of "Bird thou never wert" in the first stanza of the poem *To a Skylark* with the lines the author employs.
2. As we can notice that the word "sky" is indispensable in the composition of the bird's

name "skylark", what is the detailed illustration of the skylark's interaction with the sky in the poem?

3. How does the speaker answer his own question "What objects are the fountains Of thy happy strain?" nearly at the end of the verse?

V. Discussion Question

The speaker employs a series of similes led by the expression "like a" such as "Like a Poet hidden In the light of thought" and "Like a high-born maiden In a palace-tower". Discern all the similes and discuss the similarities between these images and the skylark itself with your other group members and present your perception to your classmates in detail.

VI. Essay Question

In the poem *To a Skylark*, the author crafts such classic lines "And singing still dost soar, and soaring ever singest". After interpreting its contextual clues thoroughly, write a 200-word essay on the enlightenment the skylark and other kindred objects in the nature render us, and the positive changes we can take into account to discipline and improve ourselves.

Self-Improving Reading

Ode to Liberty by Percy Bysshe Shelley

Prometheus Unbound by Percy Bysshe Shelley

Unit 12　John Keats (1795-1821)

Life and Works

John Keats, a venerated English Romantic lyric poet, was born in London, England, on 31 October 1795, the son of Frances Jennings Keats, and Thomas Keats, a livery-stable manager. At the age of eight, John's father died unexpectedly at work. His mother entered into a new marriage without delay and chose to entrust all her four children to the care of her mother after the dissolution of her second marriage. John attended a school at Enfield, Middlesex, where his passion for reading flourished, but in 1811, one year after the death of his mother, he reluctantly initiated his three-year apprenticeship to a surgeon at Edmonton and subsequently, worked as a dresser at Guy's and St. Thomas's hospitals in London. Through the recommendation of Cowden Clarke, the son of John Clarke, the headmaster of Enfield school, John got to know Leigh Hunt, the publisher of *The Examiner*, who introduced such renowned poets as Percy Bysshe Shelley and Williams Wordsworth to the budding young poet.

In 1818, Keats published his 4,000-line poem, *Endymion* in loose rhymed couplets, based on the Greek Legend of the same title, merely slashed out by those major journals like *The Quarterly Review* and *Blackwood's Magazine*. Keats embarked on a walking expedition in the Lake District and Scotland with his friend that summer and shortly after that, returned home to attend to Tom, his brother severely inflicted with tuberculosis, while writing his poetry calmly despite the scathing criticism from the above magazines. John's poem, *Isabella* was published, recounting an appealing tale of a lady in love with a man from a lower status against the disapproval of her family. At this juncture, John fell in love with Fanny Brawne, a neighboring resident in Hampstead which culminated in their engagement in October 1819. Just between 1819 and 1820, Keats yielded an extraordinary array of poetic masterpieces, including *Lamia*, *The Eve of St. Agnes*, a collection of exquisite odes like *To Psyche*, *To a Nightingale*, *To Autumn*, *On Melancholy*, and *On Indolence*, *On a Grecian Urn*, and his two-version poetic epic of *Hyperion* and its subsequent *The Fall of Hyperion*. Keats had contracted tuberculosis as early as the year 1819 and his health declined at a rapid pace. He set off on a voyage to Italy to seek a warmer climate, accompanied by an intimate friend. Nevertheless, death still arrived on February 23, 1821.

Text A

Ode to a Nightingale

My heart aches, and a **drowsy**① numbness pains
My sense, as though of **hemlock**② I had drunk,
Or emptied some dull **opiate**③ to the drains
One minute past, and **Lethe**④-wards had sunk:
'Tis not through envy of thy happy lot,
But being too happy in thine happiness,—
That thou, light-winged **Dryad**⑤ of the trees
In some melodious plot
Of **beechen**⑥ green, and shadows numberless,
Singest of summer in full-throated ease.

---

① **drowsy**: dozy, sleepy.
② **hemlock**: a poisonous drink made from a Eurasian poisonous plant.
③ **opiate**: a drug containing opium.
④ **Lethe**: *Greek myth* a river of forgetfulness in Hades (the underworld).
⑤ **Dryad**: *Greek myth* a nymph of the woods.
⑥ **beechen**: of the beech tree.

Unit 12 John Keats (1795–1821)

O, for a draught of **vintage**①! that hath been
Cool'd a long age in the deep-delved earth,
Tasting of **Flora**② and the country green,
Dance, and **Provençal**③ song, and sunburnt **mirth**④!
O for a beaker full of the warm South,
Full of the true, the blushful **Hippocrene**⑤,
With **beaded**⑥ bubbles winking at the brim,
And purple-stained mouth;
That I might drink, and leave the world unseen,
And with thee fade away into the forest dim:

Fade far away, dissolve, and quite forget
What thou among the leaves hast never known,
The weariness, the fever, and the **fret**⑦
Here, where men sit and hear each other groan;
Where **palsy**⑧ shakes a few, sad, last gray hairs,
Where youth grows pale, and spectre-thin, and dies;
Where but to think is to be full of sorrow
And leaden-eyed despairs,
Where Beauty cannot keep her lustrous eyes,
Or new Love **pine**⑨ at them beyond to-morrow.

Away! away! for I will fly to thee,
Not charioted by **Bacchus**⑩ and his **pards**⑪,
But on the viewless wings of **Poesy**⑫,
Though the dull brain perplexes and retards:
Already with thee! tender is the night,

---

① **vintage**: grape wine of high quality.
② **Flora**: *Roman Mythology* the goddess of flowers.
③ **Provençal**: of Provence (a former province of southeast France on the Mediterranean).
④ **mirth**: laughter, merriment.
⑤ **Hippocrene**: a spring on Mount Helicon, Greece, regarded as a source of poetic inspiration.
⑥ **beaded**: furnished with beads.
⑦ **fret**: a state of anxiety or annoyance.
⑧ **palsy**: paralysis, esp. characterized by loss of sensation and tremors.
⑨ **pine**: wither, fail gradually.
⑩ **Bacchus**: an ancient Greek and Roman god of wine.
⑪ **pards**: leopards.
⑫ **Poesy**: poetry.

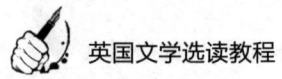

And **haply**① the Queen-Moon is on her throne,
Cluster'd around by all her starry **Fays**②;
But here there is no light,
Save what from heaven is with the breezes blown
Through **verdurous**③ glooms and winding mossy ways.

I cannot see what flowers are at my feet,
Nor what soft incense hangs upon the boughs,
But, in **embalmed**④ darkness, guess each sweet
Wherewith the seasonable month endows
The grass, the **thicket**⑤, and the fruit-tree wild;
White hawthorn, and the pastoral **eglantine**⑥;
Fast fading violets cover'd up in leaves;
And mid-May's eldest child,
The coming **musk-rose**⑦, full of dewy wine,
The murmurous haunt of flies on summer eves.

Darkling⑧ I listen; and, for many a time
I have been half in love with easeful Death,
Call'd him soft names in many a mused rhyme,
To take into the air my quiet breath;
Now more than ever seems it rich to die,
To cease upon the midnight with no pain,
While thou art pouring forth thy soul abroad
In such an ecstasy!
Still wouldst thou sing, and I have ears in vain—
To thy high **requiem**⑨ become a **sod**⑩.

---

① **haply**: by accident.
② **Fays**: *pl.* of fay (a fairy or sprite).
③ **verdurous**: vigorously green.
④ **embalmed**: *v.* embalm (embalmed, embalmed), fill with sweet odors.
⑤ **thicket**: a dense growth of bushes or small trees.
⑥ **eglantine**: Eurasian hedge roses.
⑦ **musk-rose**: a Mediterranean rose with a musky odor.
⑧ **Darkling**: in the dark.
⑨ **requiem**: a solemn chant for the repose of the dead.
⑩ **sod**: the grass-covered surface soil, turf.

Unit 12　John Keats (1795–1821)

Thou wast not born for death, immortal Bird!
No hungry generations tread thee down;
The voice I hear this passing night was heard
In ancient days by emperor and clown:
Perhaps the self-same song that found a path
Through the sad heart of **Ruth**①, when, sick for home,
She stood in tears amid the alien corn;
The same that oft-times hath
Charm'd magic **casements**②, opening on the foam
Of perilous seas, in faery lands **forlorn**③.

Forlorn! the very word is like a bell
To toll me back from thee to my sole self!
Adieu④! the fancy cannot cheat so well
As she is fam'd to do, deceiving elf.
Adieu! adieu! thy **plaintive**⑤ **anthem**⑥ fades
Past the near meadows, over the still stream,
Up the hill-side; and now'tis buried deep
In the next valley-glades:
Was it a vision, or a waking dream?
Fled is that music: —Do I wake or sleep?

Exercise

I. Word Matching

Directions: Please choose the most appropriate ones from the given words to explain the original boldfaced words in the following lines.

| A. **gleaming** | B. **grassland** | C. **invest** | D. **risky** |
| E. **vanish** | F. **puzzle** | G. **delight** | |

1. And with thee **fade** away into the forest dim:
   Fade far away, dissolve, and quite forget

---

① **Ruth**: the great-grandmother of king David, who stayed with her mother-in-law Naomi after her husband died.
② **casements**: window frames hinged on one side.
③ **forlorn**: deserted, abandoned.
④ **Adieu**: *French* farewell.
⑤ **plaintive**: mournful, woeful.
⑥ **anthem**: hymn.

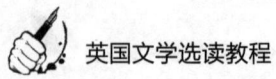

2. Where Beauty cannot keep her **lustrous** eyes,

   Or new Love pine at them beyond to-morrow.

3. Though the dull brain **perplex**es and retards:

   Already with thee! tender is the night,

4. But, in embalmed darkness, guess each sweet

   Wherewith the seasonable month **endows**

   The grass, the thicket, and the fruit-tree wild;

5. While thou art pouring forth thy soul abroad

   In such an **ecstasy**!

   Still wouldst thou sing, and I have ears in vain —

6. The same that oft-times hath

   Charm'd magic casements, opening on the foam

   Of **perilous** seas, in faery lands forlorn.

7. Adieu! adieu! thy plaintive anthem fades

   Past the near **meadow**s, over the still stream,

   Up the hill-side; and now 'tis buried deep

II. English-Chinese Translation

Directions: Please translate the following classic dicta from English into Chinese.

1. Season of mists and mellow fruitfulness,

   Close bosom-friend of the maturing sun;

   Conspiring with him how to load and bless

   With fruit the vines that round the thatch-eves run;

   —*Ode to Autumn*

2. Fade far away, dissolve, and quite forget.

   —*Ode to a Nightingale*

3. A thing of beauty is a joy for ever: Its loveliness increases; it will never Pass into nothingness.

   —*Endymion*

4. Already with thee! tender is the night,

   And haply the Queen-Moon is on her throne,

   Cluster'd around by all her starry Fays;

   —*Ode to a Nightingale*

5. Ah, happy, happy boughs! that cannot shed

   Your leaves, nor ever bid the Spring adieu;

   —*Ode on a Grecian Urn*

III. Term Defining

Directions: Please explain the following literary terms based on Ode to a Nightingale.

1. ode

2. rhetorical quesion

3. alliteration

IV. Content-Based Questions

Directions: Please give a concise and adequate answer to the following questions related to Text A.

1. In what stark contrast am "I" with "thou" at the first stanza of the poem *Ode to a Nightingale*?

2. Please paraphrase the line "What thou among the leaves hast never known", in the third stanza with the expressions in the poem.

3. How does the speaker convince the readers that "Thou wast not born for death, immortal Bird!" in the seventh stanza?

V. Discussion Question

There are such lines as "My heart aches, and a drowsy numbness pains and That thou, light-winged Dryad of the trees In some melodious plot," in the poem *Ode to a Nightingale*, which unfolds all the way from the perspectives "I" and "thou", describing their respective states. Please divide your group into Side "I" and Side "thou" and state "my" reactions to "thee", i.e. the nightingale.

VI. Essay Question

The poem *Ode to a Nightingale* impresses us with the classic line "Already with thee! tender is the night". As we know, American writer, F. Scott Fitzgerald, found the title to his novel, *Tender is the Night* from *Ode to a Nightingale* by John Keats. Write a 200-word essay to fully express the tenderness that natural objects like a nightingale bestow upon each of us.

Text B

Ode on a Grecian① Urn②

Thou still **unravish'd**③ bride of quietness,
Thou foster-child of silence and slow time,
Sylvan④ historian, who canst thus express

---

① **Grecian**: Greek.
② **Urn**: a decorated container for various purposes.
③ **unravish'd**: not ravished, not yet engaging in sexual actions.
④ **Sylvan**: of the forest, wooded.

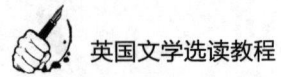

A flowery tale more sweetly than our rhyme:
What **leaf-fring'd**① legend haunts about thy shape
Of deities or mortals, or of both,
In **Tempe**② or the dales of **Arcady**③?
What men or gods are these? What maidens loth?
What mad pursuit? What struggle to escape?
What pipes and **timbrels**④? What wild ecstasy?

Heard melodies are sweet, but those unheard
Are sweeter; therefore, ye soft pipes, play on;
Not to the sensual ear, but, more endear'd,
Pipe to the spirit **ditties**⑤ of no tone:
Fair youth, beneath the trees, thou canst not leave
Thy song, nor ever can those trees be bare;
Bold Lover, never, never canst thou kiss,
Though winning near the goal yet, do not grieve;
She cannot fade, though thou hast not thy bliss,
For ever wilt thou love, and she be fair!

Ah, happy, happy boughs! that cannot shed
Your leaves, nor ever bid the Spring adieu;
And, happy melodist, unwearied,
For ever piping songs for ever new;
More happy love! more happy, happy love!
For ever warm and still to be enjoy'd,
For ever panting, and for ever young;
All breathing human passion far above,
That leaves a heart high-sorrowful and **cloy'd**⑥,
A burning forehead, and a **parching**⑦ tongue.

Who are these coming to the sacrifice?

---

① **fring'd**: **fringed**, decorated with a border.
② **Tempe**: a wooded valley in east Greece.
③ **Arcady**: Arcadia, a mountainous region of ancient Greece as a place of pastoral life.
④ **timbrels**: *pl*. **timbrel**, an ancient small hand drum.
⑤ **ditties**: *pl*. of **ditty**, a short simple song.
⑥ **cloy'd**: *v*. **cloy** (**cloyed**, **cloyed**), make weary by excess.
⑦ **parching**: become very dry.

Unit 12 John Keats (1795-1821)

  To what green altar, O mysterious priest,
  Lead'st thou that **heifer**① lowing at the skies,
  And all her silken **flanks**② with **garlands**③ drest?
  What little town by river or sea shore,
  Or mountain-built with peaceful **citadel**④,
  Is emptied of this folk, this pious morn?
  And, little town, thy streets for evermore
  Will silent be; and not a soul to tell
  Why thou art desolate, can e'er return.

  O **Attic**⑤ shape! Fair attitude! with **brede**⑥
  Of marble men and maidens overwrought,
  With forest branches and the trodden weed;
  Thou, silent form, dost tease us out of thought
  As doth eternity: Cold Pastoral!
  When old age shall this generation waste,
  Thou shalt remain, in midst of other woe
  Than ours, a friend to man, to whom thou say'st,
  Beauty is truth, truth beauty,—that is all
  Ye know on earth, and all ye need to know.

Exercise

I. Word Matching

Directions: Please choose the most appropriate ones from the given words to explain the original boldfaced words in the following lines.

  A. **lonely**   B. **obsess**   C. **farewell**   D. **grief**
  E. **gods**   F. **happiness**

1. A flowery tale more sweetly than our rhyme:
  What leaf-fring'd legend **haunt**s about thy shape
  Of **deities** or mortals, or of both,
2. Though winning near the goal yet, do not grieve;

---

① **heifer**: a young cow.
② **flanks**: *pl.* of **flank**, the side of an animal or a person between the rib and the hip.
③ **garlands**: *pl.* of **garland**, wreath of flowers or leaves.
④ **citadel**: fortress or castle.
⑤ **Attic**: of Athens or its ancient civilization.
⑥ **brede**: *archaic* embroidery.

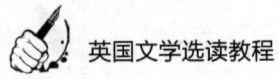

  She cannot fade, though thou hast not thy **bliss**,

  For ever wilt thou love, and she be fair!

3. Ah, happy, happy boughs! that cannot shed

  Your leaves, nor ever bid the Spring **adieu**

4. And, little town, thy streets for evermore

  Will silent be; and not a soul to tell

  Why thou art **desolate**, can e'er return.

5. When old age shall this generation waste,

  Thou shalt remain, in midst of other **woe**

  Than ours, a friend to man, to whom thou say'st,

II. English-Chinese Translation

Directions: Please translate the following classic dicta from English into Chinese.

1. Beauty is truth, truth beauty, —that is all

  Ye know on earth, and all ye need to know.

—Ode on a Grecian Urn

2. Thou, silent form, dost tease us out of thought As doth eternity.

—Ode on a Grecian Urn

3. To bend with apples the mossed cottage-trees,

  And fill all fruit with ripeness to the core;

  To swell the gourd, and plump the hazel shells

  With a sweet kernel;

—To Autumn

4. Where are the songs of spring? Ay, Where are they?

  Think not of them, thou hast thy music too,—

—To Autumn

5. Heard melodies are sweet, but those unheard Are sweeter.

—Ode on a Grecian Urn

III. Term Defining

Directions: Please explain the following literary terms based on Ode on a Grecian Urn.

1. allusion

2. caesura

3. imperative

IV. Content-Based Questions

Directions: Please give a concise and adequate answer to the following questions based on the reading of Text B.

  1. How can we understand the speaker's description of the Grecian urn as "still unravish'd bride of quietness, foster-child of silence and slow time and Sylvan historian" in the opening of

the poem *Ode to a Grecian Urn*.

2. In what way does the speaker express his comfort and admiration for the fair youth in romance especially in the second and third stanzas of the poem?

3. What details does the speaker employ to portray the sacrifice ceremony, particularly in regards to the sacrificial ox and that exact town in the fourth stanza?

V. Discussion Question

The speaker concludes the entire poem with the memorable words "Beauty is truth, truth beauty", which indicates the beauty and truth earnestly sought by him is eventually found in the Grecian urn. Discuss and analyze with your partner the five stanzas and present your individual understanding of the truth and beauty of the Grecian urn.

VI. Essay Question

We have read these two poems, *To a Skylark* by Percy Bysshe Shelley in unit 10 and *To a Nightingale* by John Keats in this unit, either of which extols the beauty of a bird. Write a 200-word essay on the poets' aspirations by means of depiction of their favorite birds, and the enlightenment we can obtain after a thorough reading.

Self-Improving Reading

Ode On Melancholy by John Keats

Ode On Indolence by John Keats

Unit 13 Charles Dickens (1812–1870)

Life and Works

Charles Dickens, the greatest English novelist of the Victorian era, was born as the eldest son of eight children of John Dickens and Elizabeth Barrow in Portsmouth, Hampshire, England on February 7, 1812. At the age of 12, Charles witnessed his father ending up in debtors' prison due to extravagant expenditures despite his well-paid job as a navy pay clerk. Dickens had no choice but to abandon his education and work at a boot-blacking factory. It was only after his father's release from debtors' prison that he was able to continue schooling, which came to an end at the age of 15. Charles had a diverse professional background, serving as a clerk in a solicitor's office, a lawcourt stenographer and a journalist.

His written sketches including *A Dinner at Poplar Walk* were published in a collection titled *Sketches by Boz* in 1836 and the following year Charles managed to wed Catherine Hogarth, the daughter of a newspaper editor. Dickens was so prolific that after releasing his debut novel in serial, *The Pickwick Papers* in 1836, he proceeded to create *Oliver Twist* and *Nicholas Nickleby* in 1839, and then *The Old Curiosity Shop* in 1841. Seizing his increasing popularity in America, he initiated his trip to America in 1842. Dickens published his renowned five-stave *A Christmas Carol* just before Christmas of 1843, which was called a national benefit by William Makepeace Thackeray. Following his travels across Europe in the mid-1840s, Charles Dickens ushered in his second decade of literary excellence. *David Copperfield*, drawing heavily from his own hard upbringing, was fully published in 1850, *Bleak House* in 1853, almost his most complex novel, exposes the prevalent social hypocrisy in Britain, *Hard Times* in 1854 denounces the execrable effects of industrialization on laborers, *A Tale of Two Cities* in 1859, his great historical novel, is set in the French Revolution, and *Great Expectations* in 1861 was eulogized by George Bernard Shaw as Dickens's most compactly perfect book. Dickens was debilitated on account of a train accident around 1865. Charles Dickens died of a stroke at Gad's Hill Place in Kent, England on June 9, 1870 and was eventually interred in Poet's Corner at Westminster Abbey.

Text A

David Copperfield
Chapter I
I am Born

Whether I shall turn out to be the hero of my own life, or whether that station will be held by anybody else, these pages must show. To begin my life with the beginning of my life, I record that I was born (as I have been informed and believe) on a Friday, at twelve o'clock at night. It was remarked that the clock began to strike, and I began to cry, simultaneously.

In consideration of the day and hour of my birth, it was declared by the nurse, and by some sage women in the neighbourhood who had taken a lively interest in me several months before there was any possibility of our becoming personally acquainted, first, that I was destined to be unlucky in life; and secondly, that I was privileged to see ghosts and spirits; both these gifts inevitably attaching, as they believed, to all unlucky infants of either gender, born towards the small hours on a Friday night.

I need say nothing here, on the first head, because nothing can show better than my history whether that prediction was verified or falsified by the result. On the second branch of the question, I will only remark, that unless I ran through that part of my inheritance while I was still a baby, I have not come into it yet. But I do not at all complain of having been kept out of this property; and if anybody else should be in the present enjoyment of it, he is heartily welcome to keep it.

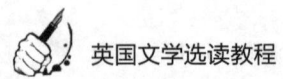

I was born with a **caul**①, which was advertised for sale, in the newspapers, at the low price of fifteen **guineas**②. Whether sea-going people were short of money about that time, or were short of faith and preferred cork **jackets**③, I don't know; all I know is, that there was but one solitary bidding, and that was from an attorney connected with the bill-broking business, who offered two pounds in cash, and the balance in sherry, but declined to be guaranteed from drowning on any higher bargain. Consequently the advertisement was withdrawn at a dead loss—for as to sherry, my poor dear mother's own sherry was in the market then—and ten years afterwards, the caul was put up in a **raffle**④ down in our part of the country, to fifty members at half-a-crown a head, the winner to spend five shillings. I was present myself, and I remember to have felt quite uncomfortable and confused, at a part of myself being disposed of in that way. The caul was won, I recollect, by an old lady with a hand-basket, who, very reluctantly, produced from it the stipulated five shillings, all in halfpence, and twopence halfpenny short—as it took an immense time and a great waste of arithmetic, to endeavour without any effect to prove to her. It is a fact which will be long remembered as remarkable down there, that she was never drowned, but died triumphantly in bed, at ninety-two. I have understood that it was, to the last, her proudest boast, that she never had been on the water in her life, except upon a bridge; and that over her tea (to which she was extremely partial) she, to the last, expressed her indignation at the impiety of mariners and others, who had the presumption to go '**meandering**⑤' about the world. It was in vain to represent to her that some conveniences, tea perhaps included, resulted from this objectionable practice. She always returned, with greater emphasis and with an instinctive knowledge of the strength of her objection, 'Let us have no meandering.'

Not to meander myself, at present, I will go back to my birth.

I was born at Blunderstone, in Suffolk, or 'there by', as they say in Scotland. I was a **posthumous**⑥ child. My father's eyes had closed upon the light of this world six months, when mine opened on it. There is something strange to me, even now, in the reflection that he never saw me; and something stranger yet in the shadowy remembrance that I have of my first childish associations with his white grave-stone in the churchyard, and of the indefinable compassion I used to feel for it lying out alone there in the dark night, when our little parlour was warm and bright with fire and candle, and the doors of our house were—almost cruelly, it seemed to me sometimes—bolted and locked against it.

An aunt of my father's, and consequently a great-aunt of mine, of whom I shall have

---

① **caul**: embryonic membrane, a part of the amnion sometimes covering the head of a child at birth.
② **guineas**: *pl.* of **guinea**, a British gold coin worth 21 shillings issued from 1663 to 1813.
③ **cork jackets**: *pl.* of **cork jacket**, life vest.
④ **raffle**: drawing, lottery.
⑤ **meandering**: *v.* **meander**, wander aimlessly.
⑥ **posthumous**: occurring after one's death.

Unit 13 Charles Dickens (1812–1870)

more to relate by and by, was the principal **magnate**① of our family. Miss Trotwood, or Miss Betsey, as my poor mother always called her, when she sufficiently overcame her dread of this formidable personage to mention her at all (which was seldom), had been married to a husband younger than herself, who was very handsome, except in the sense of the homely **adage**②, 'handsome is, that handsome does'—for he was strongly suspected of having beaten Miss Betsey, and even of having once, on a disputed question of supplies, made some hasty but determined arrangements to throw her out of a two pair of stairs' window. These evidences of an **incompatibility**③ of temper induced Miss Betsey to pay him off, and effect a separation by mutual consent. He went to India with his capital, and there, according to a wild legend in our family, he was once seen riding on an elephant, in company with a **Baboon**④; but I think it must have been a **Baboo**⑤—or a **Begum**⑥. Anyhow, from India tidings of his death reached home, within ten years. How they affected my aunt, nobody knew; for immediately upon the separation, she took her maiden name again, bought a cottage in a **hamlet**⑦ on the sea-coast a long way off, established herself there as a single woman with one servant, and was understood to live secluded, ever afterwards, in an inflexible retirement.

My father had once been a favourite of hers, I believe; but she was mortally **affronted**⑧ by his marriage, on the ground that my mother was 'a wax doll'. She had never seen my mother, but she knew her to be not yet twenty. My father and Miss Betsey never met again. He was double my mother's age when he married, and of but a delicate constitution. He died a year afterwards, and, as I have said, six months before I came into the world.

This was the state of matters, on the afternoon of, what I may be excused for calling, that eventful and important Friday. I can make no claim therefore to have known, at that time, how matters stood; or to have any remembrance, founded on the evidence of my own senses, of what follows.

My mother was sitting by the fire, but poorly in health, and very low in spirits, looking at it through her tears, and **desponding**⑨ heavily about herself and the fatherless little stranger, who was already welcomed by some grosses of prophetic pins, in a drawer upstairs, to a world not at all excited on the subject of his arrival; my mother, I say, was sitting by the fire, that bright, windy March afternoon, very timid and sad, and very doubtful of ever coming alive out of the

---

① **magnate**: a person of great influence.
② **adage**: proverb.
③ **incompatibility**: the state of not being in harmony.
④ **Baboon**: a large monkey with a dog-like face.
⑤ **Baboo**: a Hindi courtesy title for a man.
⑥ **Begum**: a Muslim woman of high rank.
⑦ **hamlet**: a small village.
⑧ **affronted**: affront (**affronted, affronted**), hurt, offend.
⑨ **desponding**: v. **despond**, be discouraged.

trial that was before her, when, lifting her eyes as she dried them, to the window opposite, she saw a strange lady coming up the garden.

My mother had a sure foreboding at the second glance, that it was Miss Betsey. The setting sun was glowing on the strange lady, over the garden-fence, and she came walking up to the door with a fell rigidity of figure and composure of countenance that could have belonged to nobody else.

When she reached the house, she gave another proof of her identity. My father had often hinted that she seldom conducted herself like any ordinary Christian; and now, instead of ringing the bell, she came and looked in at that identical window, pressing the end of her nose against the glass to that extent, that my poor dear mother used to say it became perfectly flat and white in a moment.

She gave my mother such a turn, that I have always been convinced I am indebted to Miss Betsey for having been born on a Friday.

My mother had left her chair in her agitation, and gone behind it in the corner. Miss Betsey, looking round the room, slowly and inquiringly, began on the other side, and carried her eyes on, like a **Saracen**[①]'s Head in a Dutch clock, until they reached my mother. Then she made a frown and a gesture to my mother, like one who was accustomed to be obeyed, to come and open the door. My mother went.

Mrs. David Copperfield, I think, said Miss Betsey; the emphasis referring, perhaps, to my mother's mourning **weeds**[②], and her condition.

Yes, said my mother, faintly.

Miss Trotwood, said the visitor. You have heard of her, I dare say?

My mother answered she had had that pleasure. And she had a disagreeable consciousness of not appearing to imply that it had been an overpowering pleasure.

Now you see her, said Miss Betsey. My mother bent her head, and begged her to walk in.

They went into the parlour my mother had come from, the fire in the best room on the other side of the passage not being lighted—not having been lighted, indeed, since my father's funeral; and when they were both seated, and Miss Betsey said nothing, my mother, after vainly trying to restrain herself, began to cry. Oh **tut**[③], tut, tut! said Miss Betsey, in a hurry. Don't do that! Come, come!

My mother couldn't help it notwithstanding, so she cried until she had had her cry out.

Take off your cap, child, said Miss Betsey, and let me see you.

My mother was too much afraid of her to refuse compliance with this odd request, if she had any disposition to do so. Therefore she did as she was told, and did it with such nervous

---

① **Saracen**: a Muslim from the Middle East.

② **weeds**: black mourning clothes.

③ **tut**: *interj.* used to express impatience, disapproval.

Unit 13　Charles Dickens (1812–1870)

hands that her hair (which was luxuriant and beautiful) fell all about her face.

Why, bless my heart! exclaimed Miss Betsey. You are a very Baby!

My mother was, no doubt, unusually youthful in appearance even for her years; she hung her head, as if it were her fault, poor thing, and said, sobbing, that indeed she was afraid she was but a childish widow, and would be but a childish mother if she lived. In a short pause which ensued, she had a fancy that she felt Miss Betsey touch her hair, and that with no ungentle hand; but, looking at her, in her timid hope, she found that lady sitting with the skirt of her dress tucked up, her hands folded on one knee, and her feet upon the **fender**①, frowning at the fire.

In the name of Heaven, said Miss Betsey, suddenly, why **Rookery**②?

Do you mean the house, ma'am? asked my mother.

Why Rookery? said Miss Betsey. **Cookery**③ would have been more to the purpose, if you had had any practical ideas of life, either of you.

The name was Mr. Copperfield's choice, returned my mother. When he bought the house, he liked to think that there were rooks about it.

The evening wind made such a disturbance just now, among some tall old elm-trees at the bottom of the garden, that neither my mother nor Miss Betsey could forbear glancing that way. As the elms bent to one another, like giants who were whispering secrets, and after a few seconds of such repose, fell into a violent **flurry**④, tossing their wild arms about, as if their late confidences were really too wicked for their peace of mind, some weatherbeaten ragged old rooks'-nests, burdening their higher branches, swung like wrecks upon a stormy sea.

Where are the birds? asked Miss Betsey.

The—My mother had been thinking of something else.

The rooks—what has become of them? asked Miss Betsey.

There have not been any since we have lived here, said my mother. We thought—Mr. Copperfield thought—it was quite a large rookery; but the nests were very old ones, and the birds have deserted them a long while.

David Copperfield all over! cried Miss Betsey. David Copperfield from head to foot! Calls a house a rookery when there's not a rook near it, and takes the birds on trust, because he sees the nests!

Mr. Copperfield, returned my mother, is dead, and if you dare to speak unkindly of him to me—

My poor dear mother, I suppose, had some momentary intention of committing an assault

---

① **fender**: a metal frame before an open fireplace.
② **Rookery**: a nesting place of rooks (crows).
③ **Cookery**: a place for cooking.
④ **flurry**: a sudden gust of wind.

and **battery**① upon my aunt, who could easily have settled her with one hand, even if my mother had been in far better training for such an encounter than she was that evening. But it passed with the action of rising from her chair; and she sat down again very meekly, and fainted.

When she came to herself, or when Miss Betsey had restored her, whichever it was, she found the latter standing at the window. The twilight was by this time shading down into darkness; and dimly as they saw each other, they could not have done that without the aid of the fire.

Well? said Miss Betsey, coming back to her chair, as if she had only been taking a casual look at the prospect; and when do you expect—

I am all in a tremble, **faltered**② my mother. I don't know what's the matter. I shall die, I am sure!

No, no, no, said Miss Betsey. Have some tea.

Oh dear me, dear me, do you think it will do me any good? cried my mother in a helpless manner.

Of course it will, said Miss Betsey. It's nothing but fancy. What do you call your girl?

I don't know that it will be a girl, yet, ma'am, said my mother innocently.

Bless the Baby! exclaimed Miss Betsey, unconsciously quoting the second sentiment of the **pincushion**③ in the drawer upstairs, but applying it to my mother instead of me, I don't mean that. I mean your servant-girl.

Peggotty, said my mother.

Peggotty! repeated Miss Betsey, with some indignation. Do you mean to say, child, that any human being has gone into a Christian church, and got herself named Peggotty? It's her surname, said my mother, faintly. Mr. Copperfield called her by it, because her Christian name was the same as mine.

Here! Peggotty! cried Miss Betsey, opening the parlour door. Tea. Your mistress is a little unwell. Don't **dawdle**④.

Having issued this mandate with as much potentiality as if she had been a recognized authority in the house ever since it had been a house, and having looked out to confront the amazed Peggotty coming along the passage with a candle at the sound of a strange voice, Miss Betsey shut the door again, and sat down as before: with her feet on the fender, the skirt of her dress tucked up, and her hands folded on one knee.

You were speaking about its being a girl, said Miss Betsey. I have no doubt it will be a girl. I have a presentiment that it must be a girl. Now child, from the moment of the birth of this

---

① **battery**: the act of beating.

② **faltered**: *v.* (**faltered, faltered**), speak weakly.

③ **pincushion**: a small pad for sticking pins ready for use

④ **dawdle**: move aimlessly.

Unit 13　Charles Dickens (1812–1870)

girl—

Perhaps boy, my mother took the liberty of putting in.

I tell you I have a presentiment that it must be a girl, returned Miss Betsey. Don't contradict. From the moment of this girl's birth, child, I intend to be her friend. I intend to be her godmother, and I beg you'll call her Betsey Trotwood Copperfield. There must be no mistakes in life with THIS Betsey Trotwood. There must be no trifling with HER affections, poor dear. She must be well brought up, and well guarded from reposing any foolish confidences where they are not deserved. I must make that MY care.

There was a **twitch**① of Miss Betsey's head, after each of these sentences, as if her own old wrongs were working within her, and she repressed any plainer reference to them by strong constraint. So my mother suspected, at least, as she observed her by the low glimmer of the fire: too much scared by Miss Betsey, too uneasy in herself, and too subdued and bewildered altogether, to observe anything very clearly, or to know what to say.

And was David good to you, child? asked Miss Betsey, when she had been silent for a little while, and these motions of her head had gradually ceased. Were you comfortable together?

We were very happy, said my mother. Mr. Copperfield was only too good to me.

What, he spoilt you, I suppose? returned Miss Betsey.

For being quite alone and dependent on myself in this rough world again, yes, I fear he did indeed, sobbed my mother.

Well! Don't cry! said Miss Betsey. You were not equally matched, child—if any two people can be equally matched—and so I asked the question. You were an orphan, weren't you? Yes.

And a governess?

I was nursery-governess in a family where Mr. Copperfield came to visit. Mr. Copperfield was very kind to me, and took a great deal of notice of me, and paid me a good deal of attention, and at last proposed to me. And I accepted him. And so we were married, said my mother simply.

Ha! Poor Baby! mused Miss Betsey, with her frown still bent upon the fire. Do you know anything?

I beg your pardon, ma'am, faltered my mother.

About keeping house, for instance, said Miss Betsey.

Not much, I fear, returned my mother. Not so much as I could wish. But Mr. Copperfield was teaching me—

(Much he knew about it himself!) said Miss Betsey in a parenthesis. —And I hope I should have improved, being very anxious to learn, and he very patient to teach me, if the great

---

① **twitch**: a slight jerk of a body part.

misfortune of his death—my mother broke down again here, and could get no farther.

Well, well! said Miss Betsey. —I kept my housekeeping-book regularly, and balanced it with Mr. Copperfield every night, cried my mother in another burst of distress, and breaking down again.

Well, well! said Miss Betsey. Don't cry any more. —And I am sure we never had a word of difference respecting it, except when Mr. Copperfield objected to my threes and fives being too much like each other, or to my putting curly tails to my sevens and nines, resumed my mother in another burst, and breaking down again.

You'll make yourself ill, said Miss Betsey, and you know that will not be good either for you or for my god-daughter. Come! You mustn't do it!

This argument had some share in quieting my mother, though her increasing **indisposition**① had a larger one. There was an interval of silence, only broken by Miss Betsey's occasionally ejaculating Ha! as she sat with her feet upon the fender.

David had bought an **annuity**② for himself with his money, I know, said she, by and by. What did he do for you?

Mr. Copperfield, said my mother, answering with some difficulty, was so considerate and good as to secure the reversion of a part of it to me.

How much? asked Miss Betsey.

A hundred and five pounds a year, said my mother.

He might have done worse, said my aunt.

The word was appropriate to the moment. My mother was so much worse that Peggotty, coming in with the teaboard and candles, and seeing at a glance how ill she was, —as Miss Betsey might have done sooner if there had been light enough, —conveyed her upstairs to her own room with all speed; and immediately dispatched Ham Peggotty, her nephew, who had been for some days past secreted in the house, unknown to my mother, as a special messenger in case of emergency, to fetch the nurse and doctor.

Those allied powers were considerably astonished, when they arrived within a few minutes of each other, to find an unknown lady of **portentous**③ appearance, sitting before the fire, with her bonnet tied over her left arm, stopping her ears with jewellers' cotton. Peggotty knowing nothing about her, and my mother saying nothing about her, she was quite a mystery in the parlour; and the fact of her having a magazine of jewellers' cotton in her pocket, and sticking the article in her ears in that way, did not detract from the solemnity of her presence.

The doctor having been upstairs and come down again, and having satisfied himself, I suppose, that there was a probability of this unknown lady and himself having to sit there,

---

① **indisposition**: unwellness.

② **annuity**: an investment that bears a fixed return yearly.

③ **portentous**: more impressive than it really is.

face to face, for some hours, laid himself out to be polite and social. He was the meekest of his sex, the mildest of little men. He **sidled**① in and out of a room, to take up the less space. He walked as softly as the Ghost in Hamlet, and more slowly. He carried his head on one side, partly in modest **depreciation**② of himself, partly in modest **propitiation**③ of everybody else. It is nothing to say that he hadn't a word to throw at a dog. He couldn't have thrown a word at a mad dog. He might have offered him one gently, or half a one, or a fragment of one; for he spoke as slowly as he walked; but he wouldn't have been rude to him, and he couldn't have been quick with him, for any earthly consideration.

Mr. Chillip, looking mildly at my aunt with his head on one side, and making her a little bow, said, in allusion to the jewellers' cotton, as he softly touched his left ear:

Some local irritation, ma'am?

What! replied my aunt, pulling the cotton out of one ear like a cork.

Mr. Chillip was so alarmed by her abruptness—as he told my mother afterwards—that it was a mercy he didn't lose his presence of mind. But he repeated sweetly:

Some local irritation, ma'am?'

Nonsense! replied my aunt, and corked herself again, at one blow.

Mr. Chillip could do nothing after this, but sit and look at her feebly, as she sat and looked at the fire, until he was called upstairs again. After some quarter of an hour's absence, he returned.

Well? said my aunt, taking the cotton out of the ear nearest to him.

Well, ma'am, returned Mr. Chillip, we are—we are progressing slowly, ma'am.

Ba—a—ah! said my aunt, with a perfect shake on the contemptuous **interjection**④. And corked herself as before.

Really—really—as Mr. Chillip told my mother, he was almost shocked; speaking in a professional point of view alone, he was almost shocked. But he sat and looked at her, notwithstanding, for nearly two hours, as she sat looking at the fire, until he was again called out. After another absence, he again returned.

Well? said my aunt, taking out the cotton on that side again.

Well, ma'am, returned Mr. Chillip, we are—we are progressing slowly, ma'am.

Ya—a—ah! said my aunt. With such a snarl at him, that Mr. Chillip absolutely could not bear it. It was really **calculated**⑤ to break his spirit, he said afterwards. He preferred to go and

---

① **sidled**: *v.* **sidle** (**sidled, sidled**), move sideways.
② **depreciation**: a decrease in value.
③ **propitiation**: the act of satisfying or reconciling.
④ **interjection**: an expression used in exclamation.
⑤ **calculated**: *adj.* deliberately planned.

sit upon the stairs, in the dark and a strong **draught**①, until he was again sent for.

Ham Peggotty, who went to the national school, and was a very dragon at his **catechism**②, and who may therefore be regarded as a credible witness, reported next day, that happening to peep in at the parlour-door an hour after this, he was instantly descried by Miss Betsey, then walking to and fro in a state of agitation, and **pounced upon**③ before he could make his escape. That there were now occasional sounds of feet and voices overhead which he inferred the cotton did not exclude, from the circumstance of his evidently being clutched by the lady as a victim on whom to expend her superabundant agitation when the sounds were loudest. That, marching him constantly up and down by the collar (as if he had been taking too much **laudanum**④), she, at those times, shook him, **rumpled**⑤ his hair, made light of his linen, stopped his ears as if she **confounded**⑥ them with her own, and otherwise **tousled**⑦ and maltreated him. This was in part confirmed by his aunt, who saw him at half past twelve o'clock, soon after his release, and affirmed that he was then as red as I was.

The mild Mr. Chillip could not possibly bear malice at such a time, if at any time. He sidled into the parlour as soon as he was at liberty, and said to my aunt in his meekest manner:

Well, ma'am, I am happy to congratulate you.

What upon? said my aunt, sharply.

Mr. Chillip was **fluttered**⑧ again, by the extreme severity of my aunt's manner; so he made her a little bow and gave her a little smile, to **mollify**⑨ her.

Mercy on the man, what's he doing! cried my aunt, impatiently. Can't he speak?

Be calm, my dear ma'am, said Mr. Chillip, in his softest accents.

There is no longer any occasion for uneasiness, ma'am. Be calm.

It has since been considered almost a miracle that my aunt didn't shake him, and shake what he had to say, out of him. She only shook her own head at him, but in a way that made him **quail**⑩.

Well, ma'am, resumed Mr. Chillip, as soon as he had courage, I am happy to congratulate you. All is now over, ma'am, and well over.

During the five minutes or so that Mr. Chillip devoted to the delivery of this oration, my

---

① **draught**: variant of draft, a current of air in a room.
② **catechism**: instruction on the principles of the Christian religion, usually in question-and-answer form.
③ **pounced upon**: *past tense* of pounce upon, seize somebody or something; attack somebody verbally.
④ **laudanum**: a drug made from opium.
⑤ **rumpled**: *v.* **rumple (rumpled, rumpled)**, make hair in a messy way.
⑥ **confounded**: *v.* **confound (confounded, confounded)**, frustrate, perplex.
⑦ **tousled**: *v.* **tousle (tousled, tousled)**, twist, disarrange.
⑧ **fluttered**: *v.* **flutter (fluttered, fluttered)**, make nervous.
⑨ **mollify**: soothe in temper.
⑩ **quail**: shrink back with fear.

aunt eyed him narrowly.

How is she? said my aunt, folding her arms with her bonnet still tied on one of them.

Well, ma'am, she will soon be quite comfortable, I hope, returned Mr. Chillip. Quite as comfortable as we can expect a young mother to be, under these melancholy domestic circumstances. There cannot be any objection to your seeing her presently, ma'am. It may do her good.

And SHE. How is SHE? said my aunt, sharply.

Mr. Chillip laid his head a little more on one side, and looked at my aunt like an amiable bird.

The baby, said my aunt. How is she?

Ma'am, returned Mr. Chillip, I apprehended you had known. It's a boy.

My aunt said never a word, but took her bonnet by the strings, in the manner of a sling, aimed a blow at Mr. Chillip's head with it, put it on bent, walked out, and never came back. She vanished like a discontented fairy; or like one of those supernatural beings, whom it was popularly supposed I was entitled to see; and never came back any more.

No. I lay in my basket, and my mother lay in her bed; but Betsey Trotwood Copperfield was for ever in the land of dreams and shadows, the tremendous region whence I had so lately travelled; and the light upon the window of our room shone out upon the earthly **bourne**① of all such travellers, and the **mound**② above the ashes and the dust that once was he, without whom I had never been.

Exercise

I. Word Matching

Directions: Please choose the most appropriate ones from the given words to explain the original boldfaced words in the following lines.

| A. **followed** | B. **visage** | C. **good-tempered** | D. **harshness** |
| E. **confirmed** | F. **attack** | E. **agreement** | |

1. I need say nothing here, on the first head, because nothing can show better than my history whether that prediction was **verified** or falsified by the result.

2. She came walking up to the door with a fell rigidity of figure and composure of **countenance** that could have belonged to nobody else.

3. My mother was too much afraid of her to refuse **compliance** with this odd request, if she had any disposition to do so.

---

① **bourne**: destination; border.

② **mound**: a heap of earth over a tomb.

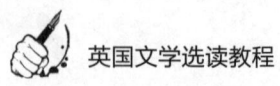

4. In a short pause which **ensued**, she had a fancy that she felt Miss Betsey touch her hair, and that with no ungentle hand.

5. My poor dear mother, I suppose, had some momentary intention of committing an **assault** and battery upon my aunt, who could easily have settled her with one hand.

6. The mild Mr. Chillip could not possibly bear **malice** at such a time, if at any time.

7. Mr. Chillip laid his head a little more on one side, and looked at my aunt like an **amiable** bird.

II. English-Chinese Translation

Directions: Please translate the following classic dicta from English into Chinese.

1. I hope that real love and truth are stronger in the end than any evil or misfortune in the world.

—*David Copperfield*

2. I will live in the past, the present, and the future. The spirits of all three shall strive within me.

—*A Christmas Carol*

3. While there is infection in disease and sorrow, there is nothing in the world so irresistibly contagious as laughter and good-humour.

—*A Christmas Carol*

4. It was the best of times, it was the worst of times, it was the age of wisdom, it was the age of foolishness, it was the epoch of belief, it was the epoch of incredulity, it was the season of light, it was the season of darkness, it was the spring of hope, it was the winter of despair.

—*A Tale of Two Cities*

5. A loving heart is the truest wisdom.

—*David Copperfield*

III. Term Defining

Directions: Please explain the following literary terms based on David Copperfield.

1. foil
2. bildungsroman
3. allusion

IV. Content-Based Questions

Directions: Please give a concise and adequate answer to the following questions related to Text A.

1. What predictions had some sage women in the neighborhood made to "my" life in consideration of the day and hour of "my" birth?

2. How did "my" aunt, Miss Betsey torture Mr. Chillip during "my" mother's delivery instead of his being "partly in modest depreciation of himself, partly in modest propitiation of everybody else"?

3. Why did Miss Betsey vanish "like a discontented fairy; or like one of those supernatural beings" when Mr. Chillip informed her that it's a boy?

V. Discussion Question

Three female main characters come on the stage in the first chapter of *David Copperfield*, who are David's mother, Clara Copperfield, his aunt, Betsey Trotwood, and the servant-girl, Clara Peggotty. Discuss with your partner your understanding of their personalities and sort out their strengths and weaknesses based on a thorough reading.

VI. Essay Question

In *David Copperfield*, aunt Betsey, as the principal magnate of our family, disapproved of my parents' marriage on the ground that my mother was 'a wax doll' and ever asked my mother whether she knew anything about keeping house. Write a 200-word essay on the development in the society's expectations of women's role in marriage from Charles Dickens's era to ours.

Text B

Oliver Twist or
The Parish Boy's Progress
Chapter I

Treats of the Place Where Oliver Twist Was Born
And of the Circumstances Attending His Birth

Among other public buildings in a certain town, which for many reasons it will be prudent to refrain from mentioning, and to which I will assign no **fictitious**① name, there is one anciently common to most towns, great or small: to wit, a workhouse; and in this workhouse was born; on a day and date which I need not trouble myself to repeat, **inasmuch as**② it can be of no possible consequence to the reader, in this stage of the business at all events; the item of mortality whose name is prefixed to the head of this chapter.

For a long time after it was ushered into this world of sorrow and trouble, by the parish surgeon, it remained a matter of considerable doubt whether the child would survive to bear any name at all; in which case it is somewhat more than probable that these memoirs would never have appeared; or, if they had, that being comprised within a couple of pages, they would have

---

① **fictitious**: assumed, counterfeit.
② **inasmuch as**: in view of the fact that, since.

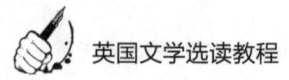

possessed the inestimable merit of being the most concise and faithful specimen of biography, **extant**① in the literature of any age or country.

Although I am not disposed to maintain that the being born in a workhouse, is in itself the most fortunate and enviable circumstance that can possibly befall a human being, I do mean to say that in this particular instance, it was the best thing for Oliver Twist that could by possibility have occurred. The fact is, that there was considerable difficulty in inducing Oliver to take upon himself the office of **respiration**②, —a troublesome practice, but one which custom has rendered necessary to our easy existence; and for some time he lay gasping on a little flock mattress, rather unequally **poised**③ between this world and the next: the balance being decidedly in favour of the latter. Now, if, during this brief period, Oliver had been surrounded by careful grandmothers, anxious aunts, experienced nurses, and doctors of profound wisdom, he would most inevitably and **indubitably**④ have been killed in no time. There being nobody by, however, but a **pauper**⑤ old woman, who was rendered rather misty by an **unwonted**⑥ allowance of beer; and a parish surgeon who did such matters by contract; Oliver and Nature fought out the point between them. The result was, that, after a few struggles, Oliver breathed, sneezed, and proceeded to advertise to the inmates of the workhouse the fact of a new burden having been imposed upon the parish, by setting up as loud a cry as could reasonably have been expected from a male infant who had not been possessed of that very useful appendage, a voice, for a much longer space of time than three minutes and a quarter.

As Oliver gave this first proof of the free and proper action of his lungs, the patchwork **coverlet**⑦ which was carelessly flung over the iron bedstead, rustled; the pale face of a young woman was raised feebly from the pillow; and a faint voice imperfectly articulated the words, Let me see the child, and die.

The surgeon had been sitting with his face turned towards the fire: giving the palms of his hands a warm and a rub alternately. As the young woman spoke, he rose, and advancing to the bed's head, said, with more kindness than might have been expected of him:

Oh, you must not talk about dying yet.

Lor bless her dear heart, no! interposed the nurse, hastily depositing in her pocket a green glass bottle, the contents of which she had been tasting in a corner with evident satisfaction.

Lor bless her dear heart, when she has lived as long as I have, sir, and had thirteen children of her own, and all on 'em dead except two, and them in the wurkus with me, she'll know better

---

① **extant**: surviving, existing.

② **respiration**: breathing.

③ **poised**: poise (**poised**, **poised**), be balanced.

④ **indubitably**: undoubtedly, assuredly.

⑤ **pauper**: a person supported by public charity.

⑥ **unwonted**: unaccustomed.

⑦ **coverlet**: bed cover.

than to take on in that way, bless her dear heart! Think what it is to be a mother, there's a dear young lamb do.

Apparently this consolatory perspective of a mother's prospects failed in producing its due effect. The patient shook her head, and stretched out her hand towards the child.

The surgeon deposited it in her arms. She imprinted her cold white lips passionately on its forehead; passed her hands over her face; gazed wildly round; shuddered; fell back—and died. They **chafed**① her breast, hands, and **temples**②; but the blood had stopped forever. They talked of hope and comfort. They had been strangers too long.

It's all over, Mrs. Thingummy! said the surgeon at last.

Ah, poor dear, so it is! said the nurse, picking up the **cork**③ of the green bottle, which had fallen out on the pillow, as she stooped to take up the child. Poor dear!

You needn't mind sending up to me, if the child cries, nurse, said the surgeon, putting on his gloves with great **deliberation**④. It's very likely it will be troublesome. Give it a little **gruel**⑤ if it is. He put on his hat, and, pausing by the bed-side on his way to the door, added, She was a good-looking girl, too; where did she come from?

She was brought here last night, replied the old woman, by the overseer's order. She was found lying in the street. She had walked some distance, for her shoes were worn to pieces; but where she came from, or where she was going to, nobody knows.

The surgeon leaned over the body, and raised the left hand. The old story, he said, shaking his head: no wedding-ring, I see. Ah! Good-night!

The medical gentleman walked away to dinner; and the nurse, having once more applied herself to the green bottle, sat down on a low chair before the fire, and proceeded to dress the infant.

What an excellent example of the power of dress, young Oliver Twist was! Wrapped in the blanket which had **hitherto**⑥ formed his only covering, he might have been the child of a nobleman or a beggar; it would have been hard for the haughtiest stranger to have assigned him his proper station in society. But now that he was enveloped in the old **calico**⑦ robes which had grown yellow in the same service, he was badged and **ticketed**⑧, and fell into his place at

---

① **chafed**: **chafe** (**chafed**, **chafed**), warm by rubbing.
② **temples**: *pl.* of **temple**, the flat part on each side of the forehead.
③ **cork**: a small round object used for closing a bottle.
④ **deliberation**: absence of hurry in movement.
⑤ **gruel**: a thin porridge.
⑥ **hitherto**: so far, until now.
⑦ **calico**: white cotton cloth.
⑧ **ticketed**: **ticket** (**ticketed**, **ticketed**), tag.

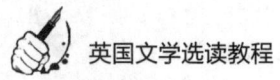

once—a parish child—the orphan of a workhouse—the humble, half-starved **drudge**①—to be **cuffed**② and **buffeted**③ through the world—despised by all, and pitied by none.

Oliver cried lustily. If he could have known that he was an orphan, left to the tender mercies of **church-wardens**④ and overseers, perhaps he would have cried the louder.

Exercise

I. Word Matching

Directions: Please choose the most appropriate ones from the given words to explain the original boldfaced words in the following lines.

A. **comforting**　　B. **utter**　　　　C. **prone**　　　　D. **cautious**
E. **hunch**　　　　F. **weakly**

1. Among other public buildings in a certain town, which for many reasons it will be **prudent** to refrain from mentioning.

2. The pale face of a young woman was raised **feebly** from the pillow; and a faint voice imperfectly **articulated** the words, Let me see the child, and die.

3. Apparently this **consolatory** perspective of a mother's prospects failed in producing its due effect.

4. Ah, poor dear, so it is! said the nurse, picking up the cork of the green bottle, which had fallen out on the pillow, as she **stoop**ed to take up the child.

5. Although I am not **disposed** to maintain that the being born in a workhouse, is in itself the most fortunate and enviable circumstance that can possibly befall a human being.

II. English-Chinese Translation

Directions: Please translate the following classic dicta from English into Chinese.

1. There is a wisdom of the head, and a wisdom of the heart.

　　　　　　　　　　　　　　　　　　　　　　　　　　　　　—*Hard Times*

2. We need never be ashamed of our tears.

　　　　　　　　　　　　　　　　　　　　　　　　　　　—*Great Expectations*

3. My advice is to never do tomorrow what you can do today. Procrastination is the thief of time.

　　　　　　　　　　　　　　　　　　　　　　　　　　　—*David Copperfield*

4. Suffering has been stronger than all other teaching, and has taught me to understand what your heart used to be.

---

① **drudge**: manual laborer.
② **cuffed**: *v.* **cuff** (**cuffed, cuffed**), slap.
③ **buffeted**: *v.* **buffet** (**buffeted, buffeted**), hit with the fist.
④ **church-wardens**: *pl.* of **church-warden**, one of two parish officers in Anglican churches with secular responsibilities.

—*Great Expectations*

5. Surprises, like misfortunes, seldom come alone.

—*Oliver Twist*

III. Term Defining

Directions: *Please explain the following literary terms based on Oliver Twist.*

1. protagonist

2. anaphora

3. irony

IV. Content-Based Questions

Directions: *Please give a concise and adequate answer to the following questions based on the reading of Text B.*

1. Where was Oliver Twist exactly born? And who was present to deliver and welcome our infant protagonist?

2. What details do we know about Oliver's family background, especially his biological parents?

3. Why would Oliver have cried louder if he could have known that he was "an orphan, left to the tender mercies of church-wardens"? What does the above expression imply?

V. Discussion Question

The births of the protagonists, David Copperfield and Oliver Twist are related in detail at the beginning of these two bildungsromans, in which the growth of the main characters is in focus. Discuss with your group members the differences between the two births based on a thorough reading and a rigorous comparison of Texts A and B.

VI. Essay Question

The hardships suffered by the protagonists in that era in Charles Dickens's classic novels have earned our readers' tears of sympathy. Write a 200-word essay to illustrate the maxim by Dickens "suffering has been stronger than all other teaching in the light of your personally experienced events".

Self-Improving Reading

Great Expectations by Charles Dickens

A Tale of Two Cities by Charles Dickens

Unit 14　Charlotte Brontë (1816–1855)

Life and Works

Charlotte Brontë, the English Victorian women novelist celebrated for *Jane Eyre*, was born in the village of Thornton, West Riding, Yorkshire on April 21, 1816, who is the third of six children born to the Rev. Patrick Brontë and Maria Branwell Brontë. Her mother died when Charlotte was five years old and the youngest Anne just around one year old. In 1824, the four older Brontë sisters, were enrolled in the Clergy Daughters' School located in Cowan Bridge, but unfortunately, Charlotte's older sisters, Maria and Elizabeth, died of the subsequent school outbreak of a typhoid fever. In 1831, Charlotte attended Roe Head School, Mirfield and her academic performance is remarkable, so she was presented with an opportunity to be a teacher there in 1835. Three years later she had to return home again owing to the school relocation. In 1839, Charlotte started working briefly as a governess and around this time, two proposals were rejected by the marriage-age lady. In 1842 Charlotte and her little sister, Emily went to Brussels to study French in a school for young ladies run by Madame Zoë Heger with the support of their mother's sister, Elizabeth Branwell, who actually had been taking care of the Brontës after the death of Charlotte's mother. Their exceptional talents won the recognition of Madam Héger and her husband, Constantin Héger and the Brontë sisters were even invited to teach some disciplines like English and music. Charlotte fell in love with Mr. Héger, their French literature instructor and wrote several love letters after she left Brussels, even if her attachment was not returned.

In 1846 Charlotte, Emily and Anne Brontë published their selected poems as *Poems by Currer, Ellis and Acton Bell* financed by the bequest from aunt Branwell. In 1847 Emily's novel, *Wuthering Heights* and Anne's *Agnes Grey* were approved for publication, still under the above pseudonym Bell while Charlotte's *The Professor* unexpectedly not. Despite the temporary setback, Charlotte produced *Jane Eyre: An Autobiography*, the first edition of classic *Jane Eyre* in the same year and it achieved instant success. A series of subsequent tragic events occurred in the Brontës with the little brother Branwell passing away in September 1848, Emily in December, and Anne in May 1849. Charlotte kept the lamentation of losing the beloved siblings in her heart and finished her *Shirley: A Tale* in August of the same year. Charlotte's three-volume *Villette* was published in January 1853, which apparently draws its materials from her own teaching experience in Brussels. Charlotte eventually married Arthur Bell Nicholls, her father's curate, in June 1854, taking care of her father went on as usual and the writing of *Emma* was proceeding in an orderly manner. Charlotte Brontë was struck by a sudden severe illness the next year and died while pregnant on March 31.

Text A

Jane Eyer
An Autobiography
Chapter I

There was no possibility of taking a walk that day. We had been wandering, indeed, in the leafless shrubbery an hour in the morning; but since dinner (Mrs. Reed, when there was no company, dined early) the cold winter wind had brought with it clouds so sombre, and a rain so penetrating, that further outdoor exercise was now out of the question.

I was glad of it: I never liked long walks, especially on chilly afternoons: dreadful to me was the coming home in the **raw**[①] twilight, with **nipped**[②] fingers and toes, and a heart

---

① **raw**: (of the weather) disagreeably cold and damp.
② **nipped**: *v.* **nip** (**nipped**, **nipped**), make numb with cold.

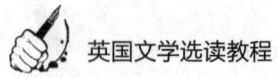

saddened by the **chidings**① of Bessie, the nurse, and humbled by the consciousness of my physical inferiority to Eliza, John, and Georgiana Reed.

The said Eliza, John, and Georgiana were now clustered round their mama in the drawing-room: she lay **reclined**② on a sofa by the fireside, and with her darlings about her (for the time neither quarrelling nor crying) looked perfectly happy. Me, she had dispensed from joining the group; saying, She regretted to be under the necessity of keeping me at a distance; but that until she heard from Bessie, and could discover by her own observation, that I was endeavouring in good earnest to acquire a more sociable and childlike disposition, a more attractive and **sprightly**③ manner—something lighter, franker, more natural, as it were—she really must exclude me from privileges intended only for contented, happy, little children.

What does Bessie say I have done? I asked.

Jane, I don't like **cavillers**④ or questioners; besides, there is something truly forbidding in a child taking up her elders in that manner. Be seated somewhere; and until you can speak pleasantly, remain silent.

A breakfast-room adjoined the drawing-room, I slipped in there. It contained a bookcase: I soon possessed myself of a volume, taking care that it should be one stored with pictures. I mounted into the window-seat: gathering up my feet, I sat cross-legged, like a Turk; and, having drawn the red **moreen**⑤ curtain nearly close, I was shrined in double retirement.

Folds of scarlet **drapery**⑥ shut in my view to the right hand; to the left were the clear panes of glass, protecting, but not separating me from the **drear**⑦ November day. At intervals, while turning over the leaves of my book, I studied the aspect of that winter afternoon. Afar, it offered a pale blank of mist and cloud; near a scene of wet lawn and storm-beat shrub, with ceaseless rain sweeping away wildly before a long and lamentable blast.

I returned to my book—Bewick's History of British Birds: the letterpress thereof I cared little for, generally speaking; and yet there were certain introductory pages that, child as I was, I could not pass quite as a blank. They were those which treat of the haunts of sea-fowl; of the solitary rocks and **promontories**⑧ by them only inhabited; of the coast of Norway, **studded**⑨ with isles from its southern extremity, the Lindeness, or Naze, to the North Cape—

Where the Northern Ocean, in vast whirls,

---

① **chidings**: *pl.* of **chiding**, scolding.
② **reclined**: *v.* **recline (reclined, reclined)**, lean back.
③ **sprightly**: lively, animated.
④ **cavillers**: *pl.* of **caviller**, someone who raises trivial objections
⑤ **moreen**: a heavy fabric of wool or cotton used especially for furnishing.
⑥ **drapery**: hanging cloth used as a curtain.
⑦ **drear**: dismal, gloomy.
⑧ **promontories**: *pl.* of **promontory**, a high land projecting into the sea.
⑨ **studded**: v. **stud (studded, studded)**, scatter like dots.

Unit 14   Charlotte Brontë (1816-1855)

Boils round the naked, melancholy isles

Of farthest **Thule**①; and the Atlantic surge

Pours in among the stormy **Hebrides**②.

Nor could I pass unnoticed the suggestion of the bleak shores of **Lapland**③, Siberia, **Spitzbergen**④, Nova **Zembla**⑤, Iceland, Greenland, with the vast sweep of the Arctic Zone, and those **forlorn**⑥ regions of dreary space, —that reservoir of frost and snow, where firm fields of ice, the accumulation of centuries of winters, glazed in **Alpine**⑦ heights above heights, surround the pole, and **concentre**⑧ the multiplied rigours of extreme cold. Of these death-white realms I formed an idea of my own: shadowy, like all the half-comprehended notions that float dim through children's brains, but strangely impressive. The words in these introductory pages connected themselves with the succeeding **vignettes**⑨, and gave significance to the rock standing up alone in a sea of billow and spray; to the broken boat stranded on a desolate coast; to the cold and ghastly moon glancing through bars of cloud at a wreck just sinking.

I cannot tell what sentiment haunted the quite solitary churchyard, with its inscribed **headstone**⑩; its gate, its two trees, its low horizon, **girdled**⑪ by a broken wall, and its newly-risen **crescent**⑫, **attesting**⑬ the hour of **eventide**⑭.

The two ships becalmed on a **torpid**⑮ sea, I believed to be marine **phantoms**⑯.

The **fiend**⑰ pinning down the thief's pack behind him, I passed over quickly: it was an object of terror.

So was the black horned thing seated **aloof**⑱ on a rock, surveying a distant crowd surrounding a **gallows**⑲.

Each picture told a story; mysterious often to my undeveloped understanding and

---

① **Thule**: the northernmost part of the inhabited ancient world.
② **Hebrides**: islands western and northwest Scotland in the Atlantic.
③ **Lapland**: a region of extreme northern Europe.
④ **Spitzbergen**: Norwegian islands to the east of northern Greenland.
⑤ **Nova Zembla**: two Russian islands.
⑥ **forlorn**: abandoned, deserted.
⑦ **Alpine**: of the Alps.
⑧ **concentre**: converge, concentrate.
⑨ **vignettes**: *pl.* of **vignette**, a small illustrative sketch.
⑩ **headstone**: a memorial stone at the head of a grave.
⑪ **girdled**: *v.* **girdle (girdled, girdled)**, surround.
⑫ **crescent**: the moon during its first and last quarters
⑬ **attesting**: *v.* **attest**, demonstrate, certify.
⑭ **eventide**: evening.
⑮ **torpid**: inactive, motionless.
⑯ **phantoms**: ghosts.
⑰ **fiend**: demon, devil.
⑱ **aloof**: distantly, indifferently.
⑲ **gallows**: a wooden structure on which criminals are executed by hanging.

imperfect feelings, yet ever profoundly interesting: as interesting as the tales Bessie sometimes narrated on winter evenings, when she chanced to be in good humour; and when, having brought her ironing-table to the nursery **hearth**①, she allowed us to sit about it, and while she got up Mrs. Reed's lace **frills**②, and **crimped**③ her nightcap borders, fed our eager attention with passages of love and adventure taken from old fairy tales and other ballads; or (as at a later period I discovered) from the pages of **Pamela**④, and **Henry, Earl of Moreland**⑤.

With Bewick on my knee, I was then happy: happy at least in my way. I feared nothing but interruption, and that came too soon. The breakfast-room door opened.

Boh! Madam **Mope**⑥! cried the voice of John Reed; then he paused: he found the room apparently empty.

Where the dickens is she! he continued. Lizzy! Georgy! (calling to his sisters) Joan is not here: tell mama she is run out into the rain—bad animal!

It is well I drew the curtain, thought I; and I wished **fervently**⑦ he might not discover my hiding-place: nor would John Reed have found it out himself; he was not quick either of vision or conception; but Eliza just put her head in at the door, and said at once—

She is in the window-seat, to be sure, Jack.

And I came out immediately, for I trembled at the idea of being dragged forth by the said Jack.

What do you want? I asked, with awkward **diffidence**⑧.

Say, 'What do you want, Master Reed?' was the answer. I want you to come here; and seating himself in an arm-chair, he **intimated**⑨ by a gesture that I was to approach and stand before him.

John Reed was a schoolboy of fourteen years old; four years older than I, for I was but ten: large and stout for his age, with a dingy and **unwholesome**⑩ skin; thick **lineaments**⑪ in a spacious visage, heavy limbs and large **extremities**⑫. He gorged himself habitually at table,

---

① **hearth**: a fireplace.

② **frills**: *pl*. of **frill**, a strip of cloth with many folds on the edge of a dress.

③ **crimp**: *v*. **crimp** (**crimped, crimped**), press cloth or paper into small folds.

④ **Pamela**: a novel written by Samuel Richardson in 1740.

⑤ **Henry, Earl of Moreland**: *The History of Henry, Earl of Moreland* is a sentimental novel by an Irishman named Henry Brook.

⑥ **Mope**: *n*. **mope**, a gloomy person.

⑦ **fervently**: earnestly, heartfeltly.

⑧ **diffidence**: timidity, fear.

⑨ **intimated**: *v*. **intimate** (**intimated, intimated**), hint, suggest.

⑩ **unwholesome**: unhealthy.

⑪ **lineaments**: features.

⑫ **extremities**: hands and feet.

which made him **bilious**①, and gave him a dim and **bleared**② eye and **flabby**③ cheeks. He ought now to have been at school; but his mama had taken him home for a month or two, on account of his delicate health. Mr. Miles, the master, affirmed that he would do very well if he had fewer cakes and sweetmeats sent him from home; but the mother's heart turned from an opinion so harsh, and inclined rather to the more refined idea that John's **sallowness**④ was owing to over-**application**⑤ and, perhaps, to **pining after**⑥ home.

John had not much affection for his mother and sisters, and an antipathy to me. He bullied and punished me; not two or three times in the week, nor once or twice in the day, but continually: every nerve I had feared him, and every **morsel**⑦ of flesh in my bones shrank when he came near. There were moments when I was bewildered by the terror he inspired, because I had no appeal whatever against either his **menaces**⑧ or his **inflictions**⑨; the servants did not like to offend their young master by taking my part against him, and Mrs. Reed was blind and deaf on the subject: she never saw him strike or heard him abuse me, though he did both now and then in her very presence, more frequently, however, behind her back.

Habitually obedient to John, I came up to his chair: he spent some three minutes in thrusting out his tongue at me as far as he could without damaging the roots: I knew he would soon strike, and while dreading the blow, I mused on the disgusting and ugly appearance of him who would presently deal it. I wonder if he read that notion in my face; for, all at once, without speaking, he struck suddenly and strongly. I **tottered**⑩, and on regaining my **equilibrium**⑪ retired back a step or two from his chair.

That is for your **impudence**⑫ in answering mama awhile since, said he, and for your sneaking way of getting behind curtains, and for the look you had in your eyes two minutes since, you rat!

Accustomed to John Reed's abuse, I never had an idea of replying to it; my care was how to endure the blow which would certainly follow the insult.

What were you doing behind the curtain? he asked.

I was reading.

---

① **bilious**: liverish.
② **bleared**: dim, blur.
③ **flabby**: loose, lacking firmness.
④ **sallowness**: a sickly yellowish skin color.
⑤ **application**: diligence.
⑥ **pining after**: longing for.
⑦ **morsel**: a small piece.
⑧ **menaces**: *pl.* of **menace**, threat, danger.
⑨ **inflictions**: *pl.* of **infliction**, an act causing pain or damage.
⑩ **tottered**: v. **totter** (**tottered**, **tottered**), stagger, move unsteadily.
⑪ **equilibrium**: a state of steadiness the body.
⑫ **impudence**: rudeness.

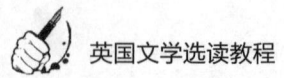

Show the book.

I returned to the window and fetched it thence.

You have no business to take our books; you are a dependent, mama says; you have no money; your father left you none; you ought to beg, and not to live here with gentlemen's children like us, and eat the same meals we do, and wear clothes at our mama's expense. Now, I'll teach you to **rummage**① my bookshelves: for they are mine; all the house belongs to me, or will do in a few years. Go and stand by the door, out of the way of the mirror and the windows.

I did so, not at first aware what was his intention; but when I saw him lift and **poise**② the book and stand in act to **hurl**③ it, I instinctively started aside with a cry of alarm: not soon enough, however; the volume was flung, it hit me, and I fell, striking my head against the door and cutting it. The cut bled, the pain was sharp: my terror had passed its climax; other feelings succeeded.

Wicked and cruel boy! I said. You are like a murderer—you are like a slave-driver—you are like the Roman emperors!

I had read **Goldsmith**④'s *History of Rome*, and had formed my opinion of **Nero**⑤, **Caligula**⑥, &c. Also I had drawn parallels in silence, which I never thought thus to have declared aloud.

What! what! he cried. Did she say that to me? Did you hear her, Eliza and Georgiana? Won't I tell mama? but first—

He ran headlong at me: I felt him grasp my hair and my shoulder: he had closed with a desperate thing. I really saw in him a tyrant, a murderer. I felt a drop or two of blood from my head trickle down my neck, and was sensible of somewhat **pungent**⑦ suffering: these sensations for the time predominated over fear, and I received him in frantic sort. I don't very well know what I did with my hands, but he called me Rat! Rat! and **bellowed**⑧ out aloud. Aid was near him: Eliza and Georgiana had run for Mrs. Reed, who was gone upstairs: she now came upon the scene, followed by Bessie and her maid Abbot. We were parted: I heard the words—

Dear! dear! What a fury to fly at Master John!

Did ever anybody see such a picture of passion!

Then Mrs. Reed subjoined—

Take her away to the red-room, and lock her in there. Four hands were immediately laid

---

① **rummage**: search thoroughly, often causing disorder.
② **poise**: cause to be balanced.
③ **hurl**: throw with force, cast.
④ **Goldsmith**: Oliver **Goldsmith** (1730-1774), Anglo-Irish essayist and poet.
⑤ **Nero**: (37-68), an ancient Roman emperor infamous for personal cruelty and tyrannical acts.
⑥ **Caligula**: (12-41), an ancient Roman emperor partly presented as an insane tyrant.
⑦ **pungent**: biting, sharp.
⑧ **bellowed**: roared, shouted.

upon me, and I was borne upstairs.

Exercise

I. Word Matching

Directions: Please choose the most appropriate ones from the given words to explain the original boldfaced words in the following lines.

A. **hangout**   B. **cast**   C. **mournful**   D. **flow**
E. **aversion**   F. **neighbor**   E. **plump**

1. A breakfast-room **adjoin**ed the drawing-room, I slipped in there.

2. Afar, it offered a pale blank of mist and cloud; near a scene of wet lawn and storm-beat shrub, with ceaseless rain sweeping away wildly before a long and **lamentable** blast.

3. They were those which treat of the **haunt**s of sea-fowl; of the solitary rocks and promontories by them only inhabited.

4. John Reed was a schoolboy of fourteen years old; four years older than I, for I was but ten: large and **stout** for his age, with a dingy and unwholesome skin.

5. John had not much affection for his mother and sisters, and an **antipathy** to me.

6. I instinctively started aside with a cry of alarm: not soon enough, however; the volume was **flung**, it hit me, and I fell, striking my head against the door and cutting it.

7. I felt a drop or two of blood from my head **trickle** down my neck, and was sensible of somewhat pungent suffering.

II. English-Chinese Translation

Directions: Please translate the following classic dicta from English into Chinese.

1. I am no bird; and no net ensnares me; I am a free human being with an independent will.

—*Jane Eyre*

2. Oh madam, when you put bread and cheese, instead of burnt porridge, into these children's mouths, you may indeed feed their vile bodies, but you little think how you starve their immortal souls!

—*Jane Eyre*

3. Peril, loneliness, an uncertain future, are not oppressive evils, so long as the frame is healthy and the faculties are employed; so long, especially, as Liberty lends us her wings, and Hope guides us by her star.

—*Villette*

4. Life appears to me too short to be spent in nursing animosity, or registering wrongs.

—*Jane Eyre*

5. Old maids like the houseless and unemployed poor, should not ask for a place and an

occupation in the world: the demand disturbs the happy and the rich.

—Shirley

III. Term Defining

Directions: *Please explain the following literary terms based on Jane Eyre.*

1. static characters
2. allusion
3. irony

IV. Content-Based Questions

Directions: *Please give a concise and adequate answer to the following questions related to Text A.*

1. Why was "I" glad of the fact that "further outdoor exercise was now out of the question that day"?

2. Where did she seat herself and what was she engrossed in after Jane was mercilessly forbidden to join the kids of Mrs. Reed in the drawing room?

3. How did Master Reed, the 14-year-old schoolboy bully and punish Jane when he discovered her hiding place with the help of his sister, Eliza?

V. Discussion Question

Jane devoted a great deal of space to introducing *Bewick's History of British Birds*, her beloved book in this chapter. Retell it to your partner in as much detail as possible after a second reading of her compelling narration.

VI. Essay Question

The account "He bullied and punished me; not two or three times in the week, nor once or twice in the day, but continually" in Chapter 1 of *Jane Eyre* leaves a horrible impression on us, uncovering 14-year-old John's frequent bullying behavior towards 10-year-old Jane. Write a 200-word essay on your reflection on the narration and related social phenomena, and provide suggestions to reduce and even eliminate this vice.

Unit 14 Charlotte Brontë (1816–1855)

Text B

Jane Eyer
An Autobiography
Chapter XXIII

A splendid Midsummer shone over England: skies so pure, suns so radiant as were then seen in long succession, seldom favour even singly, our wave-**girt**① land. It was as if a band of Italian days had come from the South, like a flock of glorious passenger birds, and lighted to rest them on the cliffs of **Albion**②. The hay was all got in; the fields round Thornfield were green and **shorn**③; the roads white and baked; the trees were in their dark prime; hedge and wood, full-leaved and deeply **tinted**④, contrasted well with the sunny hue of the cleared meadows between.

On **Midsummer-eve**⑤, Adèle, weary with gathering wild strawberries in Hay Lane half the day, had gone to bed with the sun. I watched her drop asleep, and when I left her, I sought the garden.

It was now the sweetest hour of the twenty-four:—Day its **fervid**⑥ fires had wasted, and dew fell cool on panting plain and **scorched**⑦ summit. Where the sun had gone down in simple state—pure of the pomp of clouds—spread a solemn purple, burning with the light of red jewel and furnace flame at one point, on one hill-peak, and extending high and wide, soft and still softer, over half heaven. The east had its own charm or fine deep blue, and its own modest gem, a rising and solitary star: soon it would boast the moon; but she was yet beneath the horizon.

I walked a while on the pavement; but a subtle, well-known scent—that of a cigar—stole from some window; I saw the library casement open a handbreadth; I knew I might be watched thence; so I went apart into the orchard. No **nook**⑧ in the grounds more sheltered and more Eden-like; it was full of trees, it bloomed with flowers: a very high wall shut it out from the

---

① **girt**: *v.* **gird** (**girt**, **girt**), encircle, surround.
② **Albion**: an ancient name for Britain or England.
③ **shorn**: *v.* **shear** (**shore**, **shorn**), cut, trim.
④ **tinted**: *v.* **tint** (**tinted**, **tinted**), take on a shade of color.
⑤ **Midsummer-eve**: St John's Eve; the eve before St John's Day, June 24, which is designated as the feast day of the early Christian martyr St John the Baptist.
⑥ **fervid**: extremely hot.
⑦ **scorched**: baked, burned.
⑧ **nook**: a secluded or hidden place.

court, on one side; on the other, a **beech**① avenue screened it from the lawn. terminating Here one could wander unseen. While such honey-dew fell, such silence reigned, such **gloaming**② gathered, I felt as if I could haunt such shade for ever; but in **threading**③ the flower and fruit **parterres**④ at the upper part of the enclosure, enticed there by the light the now rising moon cast on this more open quarter, my step is stayed—not by sound, not by sight, but once more by a warning fragrance.

Sweet-briar⑤ and southernwood, jasmine, pink, and rose have long been yielding their evening sacrifice of incense: this new scent is neither of shrub nor flower; it is—I know it well—it is Mr. Rochester's cigar. I look round and I listen. I see trees laden with ripening fruit. I hear a nightingale **warbling**⑥ in a wood half a mile off; no moving form is visible, no coming step audible; but that perfume increases: I must flee. I make for the **wicket**⑦ leading to the shrubbery, and I see Mr. Rochester entering. I step aside into the ivy recess; he will not stay long: he will soon return whence he came, and if I sit still he will never see me.

But no—eventide is as pleasant to him as to me, and this antique garden as attractive; and he strolls on, now lifting the gooseberry-tree branches to look at the fruit, large as plums, with which they are laden; now taking a ripe cherry from the wall; now stooping towards a knot of flowers, either to inhale their fragrance or to admire the dew-beads on their petals. A great moth goes humming by me; it alights on a plant at Mr. Rochester's foot: he sees it, and bends to examine it.

Now, he has his back towards me, thought I, and he is occupied too; perhaps, if I walk softly, I can slip away unnoticed.

I **trode**⑧ on an edging of turf that the **crackle**⑨ of the pebbly **gravel**⑩ might not betray me: he was standing among the beds at a yard or two distant from where I had to pass; the moth apparently engaged him. I shall get by very well, I meditated. As I crossed his shadow, thrown long over the garden by the moon, not yet risen high, he said quietly, without turning—

Jane, come and look at this fellow.

I had made no noise: he had not eyes behind—could his shadow feel? I started at first, and then I approached him.

---

① **beech**: a tree with a smooth grey trunk and edible nuts.
② **gloaming**: twilight, dusk.
③ **threading**: *v*. **thread**, make one's way through.
④ **parterres**: flower beds.
⑤ **Sweet-briar**: Eurasian rose with white or deep rosy-pink single flowers
⑥ **warbling**: *v*. **warble**, sing in a quavering manner.
⑦ **wicket**: a small gate.
⑧ **trode**: *variant* of trod, *v*. tread (trod, trodden), walk on.
⑨ **crackle**: sharp snapping noise.
⑩ **gravel**: small stones.

Unit 14 Charlotte Brontë (1816–1855)

Look at his wings, said he, he reminds me rather of a West Indian insect; one does not often see so large and gay a night-**rover**① in England; there! he is flown.

The moth roamed away. I was sheepishly retreating also; but Mr. Rochester followed me, and when we reached the wicket, he said—

Turn back: on so lovely a night it is a shame to sit in the house; and surely no one can wish to go to bed while sunset is thus at meeting with moonrise.

It is one of my faults, that though my tongue is sometimes prompt enough at an answer, there are times when it sadly fails me in framing an excuse; and always the **lapse**② occurs at some crisis, when a **facile**③ word or **plausible**④ **pretext**⑤ is specially wanted to get me out of painful embarrassment. I did not like to walk at this hour alone with Mr. Rochester in the shadowy orchard; but I could not find a reason to **allege**⑥ for leaving him. I followed with lagging step, and thoughts busily bent on discovering a means of **extrication**⑦; but he himself looked so **composed**⑧ and so grave also, I became ashamed of feeling any confusion: the evil—if evil existent or prospective there was—seemed to lie with me only; his mind was unconscious and quiet.

Jane, he **recommenced**⑨, as we entered the laurel walk, and slowly strayed down in the direction of the sunk fence and the horse-chestnut, Thornfield is a pleasant place in summer, is it not?

Yes, sir.

You must have become in some degree attached to the house,—you, who have an eye for natural beauties, and a good deal of the organ of **Adhesiveness**⑩?

I am attached to it, indeed.

And though I don't comprehend how it is, I perceive you have acquired a degree of regard for that foolish little child Adèle, too; and even for simple dame Fairfax?

Yes, sir; in different ways, I have an affection for both.

And would be sorry to part with them?

Yes.

Pity! he said, and sighed and paused. It is always the way of events in this life, he

---

① **rover**: drifter, wanderer.
② **lapse**: a slight error.
③ **facile**: done with little effort.
④ **plausible**: seemingly acceptable.
⑤ **pretext**: ostensible reason, excuse.
⑥ **allege**: offer as a reason.
⑦ **extrication**: the act of releasing from a difficulty.
⑧ **composed**: calm.
⑨ **recommenced**: began.
⑩ **Adhesiveness**: the property of sticking together.

continued presently: no sooner have you got settled in a pleasant resting-place, than a voice calls out to you to rise and move on, for the hour of **repose**① is expired.

Must I move on, sir? I asked. Must I leave Thornfield?

I believe you must, Jane. I am sorry, Janet, but I believe indeed you must.

This was a blow: but I did not let it **prostrate**② me.

Well, sir, I shall be ready when the order to march comes.

It is come now—I must give it to-night.

Then you are going to be married, sir?

Ex-act-ly—pre-cise-ly: with your usual acuteness, you have **hit the nail straight on the head**③.

Soon, sir?

Very soon, my—that is, Miss Eyre: and you'll remember, Jane, the first time I, or Rumour, plainly intimated to you that it was my intention to put my old bachelor's neck into the sacred **noose**④, to enter into the holy estate of **matrimony**⑤—to take Miss Ingram to my bosom, in short (she's an extensive armful: but that's not to the point—one can't have too much of such a very excellent thing as my beautiful Blanche): well, as I was saying—listen to me, Jane! You're not turning your head to look after more moths, are you? That was only a lady-clock, child, 'flying away home.' I wish to remind you that it was you who first said to me, with that discretion I respect in you—with that foresight, prudence, and humility which befit your responsible and dependent position—that in case I married Miss Ingram, both you and little Adèle had better trot forthwith. I pass over the sort of **slur**⑥ conveyed in this suggestion on the character of my beloved; indeed, when you are far away, Janet, I'll try to forget it: I shall notice only its wisdom; which is such that I have made it my law of action. Adèle must go to school; and you, Miss Eyre, must get a new situation.

Yes, sir, I will advertise immediately: and meantime, I suppose—I was going to say, I suppose I may stay here, till I find another shelter to **betake**⑦ myself to: but I stopped, feeling it would not do to risk a long sentence, for my voice was not quite under command.

In about a month I hope to be a bridegroom, continued Mr. Rochester; and in the interim, I shall myself look out for employment and an **asylum**⑧ for you.

Thank you, sir; I am sorry to give—

---

① **repose**: the act of resting.

② **prostrate**: cast (oneself) down, as in submission.

③ **hit the nail straight on the head**: be precisely correct.

④ **noose**: a loop in the end of a rope.

⑤ **matrimony**: marriage.

⑥ **slur**: slander.

⑦ **betake**: cause (oneself) to go.

⑧ **asylum**: shelter.

Oh, no need to apologise! I consider that when a dependent does her duty as well as you have done yours, she has a sort of claim upon her employer for any little assistance he can conveniently render her; indeed I have already, through my future mother-in-law, heard of a place that I think will suit: it is to undertake the education of the five daughters of Mrs. Dionysius O'Gall of Bitternutt Lodge, Connaught, Ireland. You'll like Ireland, I think: they're such warm-hearted people there, they say.

It is a long way off, sir.

No matter—a girl of your sense will not object to the voyage or the distance.

Not the voyage, but the distance: and then the sea is a barrier—

From what, Jane?

From England and from Thornfield: and—

Well?

From you, sir.

I said this almost involuntarily, and, with as Little **sanction**① of free will, my tears gushed out. I did not cry so as to be heard, however; I avoided sobbing. The thought of Mrs. O'Gall and Bitternutt Lodge struck cold to my heart; and colder the thought of all the **brine**② and foam, destined, as it seemed, to rush between me and the master at whose side I now walked, and coldest the remembrance of the wider ocean—wealth, caste, custom intervened between me and what I naturally and inevitably loved.

It is a long way, I again said.

It is, to be sure; and when you get to Bitternutt Lodge, Connaught, Ireland, I shall never see you again, Jane: that's morally certain. I never go over to Ireland, not having myself much of a fancy for the country. We have been good friends, Jane; have we not?

Yes, sir.

And when friends are on the eve of separation, they like to spend the little time that remains to them close to each other. Come! we'll talk over the voyage and the parting quietly half-an-hour or so, while the stars enter into their shining life up in heaven yonder: here is the chestnut tree: here is the bench at its old roots. Come, we will sit there in peace to-night, though we should never more be destined to sit there together. He seated me and himself.

It is a long way to Ireland, Janet, and I am sorry to send my little friend on such weary travels: but if I can't do better, how is it to be helped? Are you anything **akin**③ to me, do you think, Jane?

I could risk no sort of answer by this time: my heart was still.

Because, he said, I sometimes have a queer feeling with regard to you—especially when

---

① **sanction**: approval for an action.
② **brine**: the water of a sea.
③ **akin**: similar.

you are near me, as now: it is as if I had a string somewhere under my left ribs, tightly and **inextricably**① knotted to a similar string situated in the corresponding quarter of your little frame. And if that **boisterous**② Channel, and two hundred miles or so of land come broad between us, I am afraid that cord of communion will be **snapt**③; and then I've a nervous notion I should take to bleeding inwardly. As for you,—you'd forget me.

That I never should, sir: you know—Impossible to proceed.

Jane, do you hear that nightingale singing in the wood? Listen!

In listening, I sobbed **convulsively**④; for I could repress what I endured no longer; I was obliged to yield, and I was shaken from head to foot with acute distress. When I did speak, it was only to express an **impetuous**⑤ wish that I had never been born, or never come to Thornfield.

Because you are sorry to leave it?

The **vehemence**⑥ of emotion, stirred by grief and love within me, was claiming mastery, and struggling for full sway, and asserting a right to predominate, to overcome, to live, rise, and reign at last: yes,—and to speak.

I grieve to leave Thornfield: I love Thornfield: —I love it, because I have lived in it a full and delightful life,—momentarily at least. I have not been trampled on. I have not been **petrified**⑦. I have not been buried with inferior minds, and excluded from every glimpse of communion with what is bright and energetic and high. I have talked, face to face, with what I **reverence**⑧, with what I delight in, —with an original, a vigorous, an expanded mind. I have known you, Mr. Rochester; and it strikes me with terror and anguish to feel I absolutely must be torn from you for ever. I see the necessity of departure; and it is like looking on the necessity of death.

Where do you see the necessity? he asked suddenly.

Where? You, sir, have placed it before me.

In what shape?

In the shape of Miss Ingram; a noble and beautiful woman, —your bride.

My bride! What bride? I have no bride!

But you will have.

Yes; —I will! —I will! He set his teeth.

---

① **inextricably**: inseparably.
② **boisterous**: stormy, violent.
③ **snapt**: *variant* of snapped, *v.* snap (snapped, snapped), break suddenly.
④ **convulsively**: in a sudden and uncontrolled way.
⑤ **impetuous**: marked by impulsive passion, forceful.
⑥ **vehemence**: the quality of being intensely emotional.
⑦ **petrified**: extremely frightened.
⑧ **reverence**: treat with profound awe and respect.

Unit 14 Charlotte Brontë (1816–1855)

Then I must go: —you have said it yourself.

No: you must stay! I swear it—and the oath shall be kept.

I tell you I must go! I retorted, roused to something like passion. Do you think I can stay to become nothing to you? Do you think I am an automaton? —a machine without feelings? and can bear to have my morsel of bread snatched from my lips, and my drop of living water dashed from my cup? Do you think, because I am poor, **obscure**①, plain, and little, I am soulless and heartless? You think wrong!—I have as much soul as you, —and full as much heart! And if God had gifted me with some beauty and much wealth, I should have made it as hard for you to leave me, as it is now for me to leave you. I am not talking to you now through the medium of custom, **conventionalities**②, nor even of mortal flesh; —it is my spirit that addresses your spirit; just as if both had passed through the grave, and we stood at God's feet, equal, —as we are!

As we are! repeated Mr. Rochester—so, he added, enclosing me in his arms, gathering me to his breast, pressing his lips on my lips: so, Jane!

Yes, so, sir, I **rejoined**③: and yet not so; for you are a married man—or as good as a married man, and wed to one inferior to you—to one with whom you have no sympathy—whom I do not believe you truly love; for I have seen and heard you sneer at her. I would scorn such a union: therefore I am better than you—let me go!

Where, Jane? To Ireland?

Yes—to Ireland. I have spoken my mind, and can go anywhere now.

Jane, be still; don't struggle so, like a wild frantic bird that is **rending**④ its own **plumage**⑤ in its desperation.

I am no bird; and no net **ensnares**⑥ me; I am a free human being with an independent will, which I now exert to leave you.

Another effort set me at liberty, and I stood erect before him.

And your will shall decide your destiny, he said: I offer you my hand, my heart, and a share of all my possessions.

You play a **farce**⑦, which I merely laugh at.

I ask you to pass through life at my side—to be my second self, and best earthly companion.

For that fate you have already made your choice, and must abide by it.

---

① **obscure**: of undistinguished or humble station; unknown.
② **conventionalities**: *pl.* of **conventionality**, a conventional practice.
③ **rejoined**: *v.* **rejoin (rejoined, rejoined)**, reply.
④ **rending**: *v.* rend, split or tear apart.
⑤ **plumage**: the feathers of a bird.
⑥ **ensnares**: *v.* ensnare, take in a trap.
⑦ **farce**: a humorous play in which complicated and unlikely situations are used, a ridiculous act.

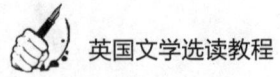

Jane, be still a few moments: you are over-excited: I will be still too.

A **waft**① of wind came sweeping down the laurel-walk, and trembled through the boughs of the chestnut: it wandered away—away—to an indefinite distance—it died. The nightingale's song was then the only voice of the hour: in listening to it, I again wept. Mr. Rochester sat quiet, looking at me gently and seriously. Some time passed before he spoke; he at last said—

Come to my side, Jane, and let us explain and understand one another.

I will never again come to your side: I am torn away now, and cannot return.

But, Jane, I summon you as my wife: it is you only I intend to marry.

I was silent: I thought he mocked me.

Come, Jane—come hither.

Your bride stands between us.

He rose, and with a stride reached me.

My bride is here, he said, again drawing me to him, because my equal is here, and my likeness. Jane, will you marry me?

Still I did not answer, and still I **writhed**② myself from his grasp: for I was still incredulous.

Do you doubt me, Jane?

Entirely.

You have no faith in me?

Not a **whit**③.

Am I a liar in your eyes? he asked passionately. Little sceptic, you shall be convinced. What love have I for Miss Ingram? None: and that you know. What love has she for me? None: as I have taken pains to prove: I caused a rumour to reach her that my fortune was not a third of what was supposed, and after that I presented myself to see the result; it was coldness both from her and her mother. I would not—I could not—marry Miss Ingram. You—you strange, you almost unearthly thing! —I love as my own flesh. You—poor and obscure, and small and plain as you are—I entreat to accept me as a husband.

What, me! I **ejaculated**④, beginning in his earnestness—and especially in his **incivility**⑤—to credit his sincerity: me who have not a friend in the world but you—if you are my friend: not a shilling but what you have given me?

You, Jane, I must have you for my own—entirely my own. Will you be mine? Say yes, quickly.

Mr. Rochester, let me look at your face: turn to the moonlight.

---

① **waft**: a slight breeze.

② **writhed**: *v.* **writhe** (writhed, writhed), twist the body in pain.

③ **whit**: a tiny amount.

④ **ejaculated**: uttered impulsively.

⑤ **incivility**: rude behaviour.

Unit 14 Charlotte Brontë (1816–1855)

Why?

Because I want to read your countenance—turn!

There! you will find it scarcely more **legible**① than a **crumpled**②, scratched page. Read on: only make haste, for I suffer.

His face was very much **agitated**③ and very much flushed, and there were strong workings in the features, and strange gleams in the eyes.

Oh, Jane, you torture me! he exclaimed. With that searching and yet faithful and generous look, you torture me!

How can I do that? If you are true, and your offer real, my only feelings to you must be gratitude and devotion—they cannot torture.

Gratitude! he ejaculated; and added wildly—Jane accept me quickly. Say, Edward—give me my name—Edward—I will marry you.

Are you in earnest? Do you truly love me? Do you sincerely wish me to be your wife?

I do; and if an oath is necessary to satisfy you, I swear it.

Then, sir, I will marry you.

Edward—my little wife!

Dear Edward!

Come to me—come to me entirely now, said he; and added, in his deepest tone, speaking in my ear as his cheek was laid on mine, Make my happiness—I will make yours.

God pardon me! he subjoined ere long; and man meddle not with me: I have her, and will hold her.

There is no one to meddle, sir. I have no kindred to interfere.

No—that is the best of it, he said. And if I had loved him less I should have thought his accent and look of **exultation**④ savage; but, sitting by him, roused from the nightmare of parting—called to the paradise of union—I thought only of the bliss given me to drink in so abundant a flow. Again and again he said, are you happy, Jane? And again and again I answered, Yes. After which he murmured, it will atone—it will atone. Have I not found her friendless, and cold, and comfortless? Will I not guard, and cherish, and **solace**⑤ her? Is there not love in my heart, and **constancy**⑥ in my resolves? It will **expiate**⑦ at God's **tribunal**⑧. I know my Maker sanctions what I do. For the world's judgment—I wash my hands thereof. For man's opinion—

---

① **legible**: able to be read.
② **crumpled**: *v.* crumple (**crumpled, crumpled**), crush together or press into wrinkles.
③ **agitated**: excited, unquiet.
④ **exultation**: a feeling of great joy.
⑤ **solace**: give comfort to a person in time of grief.
⑥ **constancy**: the quality of being faithful and loyal to a particular person.
⑦ **expiate**: atone for.
⑧ **tribunal**: a court or forum of justice.

I defy it.

But what had befallen the night? The moon was not yet set, and we were all in shadow: I could scarcely see my master's face, near as I was. And what ailed the chestnut tree? it writhed and groaned; while wind roared in the laurel walk, and came sweeping over us.

We must go in, said Mr. Rochester: the weather changes. I could have sat with thee till morning, Jane.

And so, thought I, could I with you. I should have said so, perhaps, but a **livid**①, vivid spark leapt out of a cloud at which I was looking, and there was a crack, a crash, and a close rattling peal; and I thought only of hiding my dazzled eyes against Mr. Rochester's shoulder.

The rain rushed down. He hurried me up the walk, through the grounds, and into the house; but we were quite wet before we could pass the threshold. He was taking off my shawl in the hall, and shaking the water out of my loosened hair, when Mrs. Fairfax emerged from her room. I did not observe her at first, nor did Mr. Rochester. The lamp was lit. The clock was on the stroke of twelve.

Hasten to take off your wet things, said he; and before you go, good-night—good-night, my darling!

He kissed me repeatedly. When I looked up, on leaving his arms, there stood the widow, pale, grave, and amazed. I only smiled at her, and ran upstairs. Explanation will do for another time, thought I. Still, when I reached my chamber, I felt a pang at the idea she should even temporarily **misconstrue**② what she had seen. But joy soon effaced every other feeling; and loud as the wind blew, near and deep as the thunder crashed, fierce and frequent as the lightning gleamed, **cataract**③-like as the rain fell during a storm of two hours' duration, I experienced no fear and little awe. Mr. Rochester came thrice to my door in the course of it, to ask if I was safe and tranquil: and that was comfort, that was strength for anything.

Before I left my bed in the morning, little Adèle came running in to tell me that the great horse-chestnut at the bottom of the orchard had been struck by lightning in the night, and half of it split away.

Exercise

I. Word Matching

Directions: Please choose the most appropriate ones from the given words to explain the original boldfaced words in the following lines.

  A. **odd**   B. **beaming**   C. **lure**   D. **expected**

---

① **livid**: a greyish colour.
② **misconstrue**: misinterpret the meaning.
③ **cataract**: waterfall.

E. **interfere**   F. **settle**   G. **speedy**   H. **carefulness**

1. A splendid Midsummer shone over England: skies so pure, suns so **radiant** as were then seen in long succession, seldom favour even singly, our wave-girt land.

2. **Enticed** there by the light the now rising moon cast on this more open quarter, my step is stayed—not by sound, not by sight, but once more by a warning fragrance.

3. A great moth goes humming by me; it **alight**s on a plant at Mr. Rochester's foot: he sees it, and bends to examine it.

4. It is one of my faults, that though my tongue is sometimes **prompt** enough at an answer, there are times when it sadly fails me in framing an excuse.

5. I became ashamed of feeling any confusion: the evil—if evil existent or **prospective** there was—seemed to lie with me only; his mind was unconscious and quiet.

6. I wish to remind you that it was you who first said to me, with that **discretion** I respect in you—with that foresight, prudence, and humility which befit your responsible and dependent position—that in case I married Miss Ingram, both you and little Adèle had better trot forthwith.

7. Because, he said, I sometimes have a **queer** feeling with regard to you—especially when you are near me, as now.

8. God pardon me! he subjoined ere long; and man **meddle** not with me: I have her, and will hold her.

II. English-Chinese Translation

Directions: Please translate the following classic dicta from English into Chinese.

1. It is one of my faults, that though my tongue is sometimes prompt enough at an answer, there are times when it sadly fails me in framing an excuse; and always the lapse occurs at some crisis, when a facile word or plausible pretext is specially wanted to get me out of painful embarrassment.

—Jane Eyre

2. Do you think, because I am poor, obscure, plain and little, I am soulless and heartless? You think wrong— have as much soul as you— and full as much heart! And if God had gifted me with some beauty and much wealth, I should have made it as hard for you to leave me, as it is now for me to leave you!

—Jane Eyre

3. Prejudices, it is well known, are most difficult to eradicate from the heart whose soil has never been loosened or fertilized by education; they grow firm there, firm as weeds among stones.

—Jane Eyre

4. To you I am neither man nor woman. I come before you as an author only.

—Jane Eyre

5. Life is so constructed, that the event does not, cannot, will not, match the expectation.

—*Villette*

III. Term Defining

Directions: *Please explain the following literary terms based on Jane Eyre.*

1. genre
2. metaphor
3. foreshadowing

IV. Content-Based Questions

Directions: *Please give a concise and adequate answer to the following questions based on the reading of Text B.*

1. Why did Jane voice such exclamation as "It was now the sweetest hour of the twenty-four" on a splendid midsummer eve at the beginning of the chapter?

2. Why did Rochester say that he had found a new employment of undertaking the education of the five daughters of a family in Ireland for Jane through his future mother-in-law?

3. Why did Jane respond with the words "I grieve to leave Thornfield: I love Thornfield" when Rochester told her Adèle must go to school and she must get a new situation.

V. Discussion Question

When we read the words "Jane accept me quickly. Say, Edward—give me my name—Edward—I will marry you.", all of us have come to understand that Rochester genuinely wants to marry Jane instead of Miss Ingram. Read through this chapter and list the reasons with other group members why Rochester made up his mind to marry Jane.

VI. Essay Question

We can notice from Chapter XXIII of *Jane Eyre* that Rochester and Jane secretly love each other, but it is extremely difficult for them to enter the marriage. Write a 200-word essay on the reasons why love cannot inevitably lead to marriage based on the speaker's narration and the reality of contemporary young people's lives.

Self-Improving Reading

Shirley: A Tale by Charlotte Brontë

Villette by Charlotte Brontë

Unit 15　Thomas Hardy (1840−1928)

Life and Works

  Thomas Hardy, one of the most celebrated English novelists and poets, was born in Higher Bockhampton, Dorset, England on June 2, 1840, the eldest son of Thomas Hardy, a stonemason and jobbing builder, and Jemima Hardy, an intellectual and talented woman. Hardy found inspiration for his fiction and poetry from the rural life in Dorset. Hardy received his first schooling in Lower Bockhampton at the age of eight and switched to non-conformist school in Greyhound Yard, Dorchester at the age of ten. He finished his formal education in 1856, when he undertook an apprenticeship with John Hicks, a reputable local architect. Hardy departed for London to pursue a career as a draftsman in Arthur Blomfield's office at the age of 22. Due to declining health, Hardy had to return to Dorchester in 1867, working for Hicks once again. While working as an apprentice architect, he wrote his debut novel, *The Poor Man and the Lady*, in 1868, which unfortunately faced repeated rejections from publishers. In 1870, Hardy was entrusted with the restoration of St. Juliot Church in Cornwall, where he encountered his first wife, Emma Lavinia Gifford. Hardy's next two novels, *Desperate Remedies* and *Under*

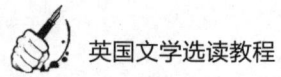

the Greenwood Tree were published successively in 1871 and 1872, which manifested his distinctive style gradually and also compelled him to dedicate himself to writing.

A Pair of Blue Eyes, a three-volume love story, was first serialised in *Tinsleys Magazine* in 1872 and published in May 1873. In 1874, serial publication of *Far from the Madding Crowd* in *The Cornhill Magazine* marked the initial success of Hardy's Wessex novels and Hardy married Emma in the same year. Hardy published a total of eleven novels from 1871 to 1897, including *The Return of the Native* in 1878 and *The Mayor of Casterbridge* in 1886. However, *Tess of the D'Urbervilles* in 1891 and *Jude the Obscure* in 1895 were met with unfavorable critiques, possibly prompting his later shift towards poetry. In 1885, Hardy and his beloved Emma moved into Max Gate, a dwelling for the rest of his life, designed by Hardy himself and constructed by his father and brother. *The Dynasts* in 1908, Hardy's epic-drama concerning the Napoleonic Wars consists of nineteen acts and 130 scenes. Two years following the death of Emma in 1912, Hardy wed Florence Emily Dugdale, who was 39 years his junior and esteemed him as one of the kindest, most humane men in the world. Hardy passed away in 1928 with his body buried at Westminster Abbey in Poet's Corner, and instead his heart interred in Stinson, England, adjacent to the graves of his parents and his first wife, Emma.

Text A

Tess of the d'Urbervilles
A Pure Woman
Chapter V

The **haggling**① business, which had mainly depended on the horse, became disorganized forthwith. Distress, if not **penury**②, loomed in the distance. Durbeyfield was what was locally called a **slack-twisted**③ fellow; he had good strength to work at times; but the times could not be relied on to coincide with the hours of requirement; and, having been unaccustomed to the regular toil of the day-labourer, he was not particularly persistent when they did so coincide.

Tess, meanwhile, as the one who had dragged her parents into this **quagmire**④, was silently wondering what she could do to help them out of it; and then her mother **broached**⑤

---

① **haggling**: bargaining over the price.
② **penury**: extreme poverty.
③ **slack-twisted**: lack of energy or due care.
④ **quagmire**: an embarrassing or difficult situation.
⑤ **broached**: *v.* **broach** (**broached, broached**), open up something for discussion, talk over.

her scheme.

We must take the ups wi' the downs, Tess, said she; and never could your high blood have been found out at a more called-for moment. You must try your friends. Do ye know that there is a very rich Mrs d'Urberville living on the outskirts o' The Chase, who must be our relation? You must go to her and claim kin, and ask for some help in our trouble.

I shouldn't care to do that, says Tess. If there is such a lady, 'twould be enough for us if she were friendly—not to expect her to give us help.

You could win her round to do anything, my dear. Besides, perhaps there's more in it than you know of. I've heard what I've heard, good-now.

The oppressive sense of the harm she had done led Tess to be more **deferential**① than she might otherwise have been to the maternal wish; but she could not understand why her mother should find such satisfaction in contemplating an enterprise of, to her, such doubtful profit. Her mother might have made inquiries, and have discovered that this Mrs d'Urberville was a lady of unequalled virtues and charity. But Tess's pride made the part of poor relation one of particular distaste to her.

I'd rather try to get work, she murmured.

Durbeyfield, you can settle it, said his wife, turning to where he sat in the background. If you say she ought to go, she will go.

I don't like my children going and making themselves **beholden**② to strange kin, murmured he. I'm the head of the noblest branch o' the family, and I ought to live up to it.

His reasons for staying away were worse to Tess than her own objections to going. Well, as I killed the horse, mother, she said mournfully, I suppose I ought to do something. I don't mind going and seeing her, but you must leave it to me about asking for help. And don't go thinking about her making a match for me—it is silly.

Very well said, Tess! observed her father **sententiously**③.

Who said I had such a thought? asked Joan.

I fancy it is in your mind, mother. But I'll go.

Rising early next day she walked to the hill-town called Shaston, and there took advantage of a van which twice in the week ran from Shaston eastward to Chaseborough, passing near Trantridge, the parish in which the vague and mysterious Mrs d'Urberville had her residence.

Tess Durbeyfield's route on this memorable morning lay amid the north-eastern **undulations**④ of the Vale in which she had been born, and in which her life had unfolded. The Vale of Blackmoor was to her the world, and its inhabitants the races thereof. From the gates

---

① **deferential**: showing respect.
② **beholden**: owing gratitude to someone else.
③ **sententiously**: moralistic in expression.
④ **undulations**: wavy forms.

and **stiles**① of Marlott she had looked down its length in the wondering days of infancy, and what had been mystery to her then was not much less than mystery to her now. She had seen daily from her chamber-window towers, villages, faint white mansions; above all, the town of Shaston standing majestically on its height; its windows shining like lamps in the evening sun. She had hardly ever visited the place, only a small tract even of the Vale and its environs being known to her by close inspection. Much less had she been far outside the valley. Every **contour**② of the surrounding hills was as personal to her as that of her relatives' faces; but for what lay beyond, her judgment was dependent on the teaching of the village school, where she had held a leading place at the time of her leaving, a year or two before this date.

In those early days she had been much loved by others of her own sex and age, and had used to be seen about the village as one of three—all nearly of the same year—walking home from school side by side; Tess the middle one—in a pink print **pinafore**③, of a finely **reticulated**④ pattern, worn over a stuff **frock**⑤ that had lost its original colour for a nondescript tertiary—marching on upon long **stalky**⑥ legs, in tight stockings which had little ladder-like holes at the knees, torn by kneeling in the roads and banks in search of vegetable and mineral treasures; her then earth-coloured hair hanging like pot-hooks; the arms of the two outside girls resting round the waist of Tess; her arms on the shoulders of the two supporters.

As Tess grew older, and began to see how matters stood, she felt quite a **Malthusian**⑦ towards her mother for thoughtlessly giving her so many little sisters and brothers, when it was such a trouble to nurse and provide for them. Her mother's intelligence was that of a happy child: Joan Durbeyfield was simply an additional one, and that not the eldest, to her own long family of waiters on Providence.

However, Tess became humanely beneficent towards the small ones, and to help them as much as possible she used, as soon as she left school, to lend a hand at haymaking or harvesting on neighbouring farms; or, by preference, at milking or butter-making processes, which she had learnt when her father had owned cows; and being deft-fingered it was a kind of work in which she excelled.

Every day seemed to throw upon her young shoulders more of the family burdens, and that Tess should be the representative of the Durbeyfields at the d'Urberville mansion came as a thing of course. In this instance it must be admitted that the Durbeyfields were putting their

---

① **stiles**: steps for people to pass over a fence.
② **contour**: outline of land or an irregular figure.
③ **pinafore**: a sleeveless garment worn as a dress or an apron.
④ **reticulated**: *v.* **reticulate (reticulated, reticulated)**, form a net or network.
⑤ **frock**: a girl's dress.
⑥ **stalky**: slender and tall.
⑦ **Malthusian**: of the theory of Malthus (British economist with his *An Essay on the Principle of Population*) arguing that population tends to be faster than food supply.

Unit 15 Thomas Hardy (1840–1928)

fairest side outward.

She **alighted**① from the van at Trantridge Cross, and ascended on foot a hill in the direction of the district known as The Chase, on the borders of which, as she had been informed, Mrs d'Urberville's seat, The Slopes, would be found. It was not a manorial home in the ordinary sense, with fields, and pastures, and a **grumbling**② farmer, out of whom the owner had to squeeze an income for himself and his family by hook or by crook. It was more, far more; a country-house built for enjoyment pure and simple, with not an acre of troublesome land attached to it beyond what was required for residential purposes, and for a little fancy farm kept in hand by the owner, and tended by a **bailiff**③.

The crimson brick lodge came first in sight, up to its eaves in dense evergreens. Tess thought this was the mansion itself till, passing through the side wicket with some **trepidation**④, and onward to a point at which the drive took a turn, the house proper stood in full view. It was of recent erection—indeed almost new—and of the same rich red colour that formed such a contrast with the evergreens of the lodge. Far behind the corner of the house—which rose like a **geranium**⑤ bloom against the **subdued**⑥ colours around—stretched the soft **azure**⑦ landscape of The Chase—a truly venerable tract of forest land, one of the few remaining woodlands in England of undoubted primaeval date, wherein **Druidical**⑧ **mistletoe**⑨ was still found on aged oaks, and where enormous yew-trees, not planted by the hand of man grew as they had grown when they were **pollarded**⑩ for bows. All this **sylvan**⑪ antiquity, however, though visible from The Slopes, was outside the immediate boundaries of the estate.

Everything on this **snug**⑫ property was bright, thriving, and well kept; acres of glass-houses stretched down the inclines to the **copses**⑬ at their feet. Everything looked like money—like the last coin issued from the **Mint**⑭. The stables, partly screened by Austrian pines and evergreen oaks, and fitted with every late appliance, were as dignified as Chapels-of-Ease. On the extensive lawn stood an ornamental tent, its door being towards her.

Simple Tess Durbeyfield stood at gaze, in a half-alarmed attitude, on the edge of the

---

① **alighted**: *v*. **alight** (**alighted**, **alighted**), get down from a vehicle.
② **grumbling**: complaining by muttering.
③ **bailiff**: steward of a landowner.
④ **trepidation**: a state of anxiety or fear.
⑤ **geranium**: a southern African plant with red, pink, purple, or white flowers
⑥ **subdued**: not bright in colours.
⑦ **azure**: the blue of a clear sky.
⑧ **Druidical**: related to the pre-Christian Celtic priests.
⑨ **mistletoe**: shrub of central and southeastern Europe usually parasitic on beeches, chestnuts and oaks.
⑩ **pollarded**: *v*. **pollard** (**pollarded**, **pollarded**), cut a tree back to the trunk so as to produce new shoots.
⑪ **sylvan**: relating to forests.
⑫ **snug**: enjoying comforting warmth and shelter.
⑬ **copses**: shrubs or bushes.
⑭ **Mint**: a place where money is manufactured under government authority.

gravel① sweep. Her feet had brought her onward to this point before she had quite realized where she was; and now all was contrary to her expectation.

I thought we were an old family; but this is all new! she said, in her artlessness. She wished that she had not fallen in so readily with her mother's plans for claiming kin, and had endeavoured to gain assistance nearer home.

The d'Urbervilles—or Stoke-d'Urbervilles, as they at first called themselves—who owned all this, were a somewhat unusual family to find in such an old-fashioned part of the country. Parson Tringham had spoken truly when he said that our **shambling**② John Durbeyfield was the only really lineal representative of the old d'Urberville family existing in the county, or near it; he might have added, what he knew very well, that the Stoke-d'Urbervilles were no more d'Urbervilles of the true tree then he was himself. Yet it must be admitted that this family formed a very good stock whereon to regraft a name which sadly wanted such renovation.

When old Mr Simon Stoke, latterly deceased, had made his fortune as an honest merchant (some said money-lender) in the North, he decided to settle as a county man in the South of England, out of hail of his business district; and in doing this he felt the necessity of recommencing with a name that would not too readily identify him with the smart tradesman of the past, and that would be less commonplace than the original bald, stark words. **Conning**③ for an hour in the British Museum the pages of works devoted to extinct, half-extinct, obscured, and ruined families **appertaining**④ to the quarter of England in which he proposed to settle, he considered that d'Urberville looked and sounded as well as any of them: and d'Urberville accordingly was annexed to his own name for himself and his heirs eternally. Yet he was not an extravagant-minded man in this, and in constructing his family tree on the new basis was duly reasonable in framing his inter-marriages and aristocratic links, never inserting a single title above a rank of strict moderation.

Of this work of imagination poor Tess and her parents were naturally in ignorance—much to their **discomfiture**⑤; indeed, the very possibility of such annexations was unknown to them; who supposed that, though to be well-favoured might be the gift of fortune, a family name came by nature.

Tess still stood hesitating like a bather about to make his plunge, hardly knowing whether to retreat or to persevere, when a figure came forth from the dark triangular door of the tent. It was that of a tall young man, smoking.

---

① **gravel**: rock fragments and pebbles.
② **shambling**: walking in an unsteady and slow manner.
③ **Conning**: examining carefully
④ **appertaining**: belonging as a right.
⑤ **discomfiture**: embarrassment, confusion.

Unit 15 Thomas Hardy (1840–1928)

He had an almost **swarthy**① complexion, with full lips, badly moulded, though red and smooth, above which was a well-groomed black moustache with curled points, though his age could not be more than three-or four-and-twenty. Despite the touches of barbarism in his **contours**②, there was a singular force in the gentleman's face, and in his bold rolling eye.

Well, my Beauty, what can I do for you? said he, coming forward. And perceiving that she stood quite confounded: Never mind me. I am Mr d'Urberville. Have you come to see me or my mother?

This embodiment of a d'Urberville and a namesake differed even more from what Tess had expected than the house and grounds had differed. She had dreamed of an aged and dignified face, the **sublimation**③ of all the d'Urberville **lineaments**④, furrowed with **incarnate**⑤ memories representing in hieroglyphic the centuries of her family's and England's history. But she screwed herself up to the work in hand, since she could not get out of it, and answered—

I came to see your mother, sir.

I am afraid you cannot see her—she is an **invalid**⑥, replied the present representative of the **spurious**⑦ house; for this was Mr Alec, the only son of the lately deceased gentleman. Cannot I answer your purpose? What is the business you wish to see her about?

It isn't business—it is—I can hardly say what!

Pleasure?

Oh no. Why, sir, if I tell you, it will seem—

Tess's sense of a certain **ludicrousness**⑧ in her errand was now so strong that, notwithstanding her awe of him, and her general discomfort at being here, her rosy lips curved towards a smile, much to the attraction of the swarthy Alexander.

It is so very foolish, she stammered; I fear I can't tell you!

Never mind; I like foolish things. Try again, my dear, said he kindly.

Mother asked me to come, Tess continued; and, indeed, I was in the mind to do so myself likewise. But I did not think it would be like this. I came, sir, to tell you that we are of the same family as you.

Ho! Poor relations?

Yes.

Stokes?

---

① **swarthy**: dark-skinned.
② **contours**: *pl.* of **contour**, shape or outline of an object.
③ **sublimation**: improving or refining.
④ **lineaments**: *pl.* of **lineament**, an outline of a face and body.
⑤ **incarnate**: embodied in form.
⑥ **invalid**: a person suffering from ill health.
⑦ **spurious**: not genuine.
⑧ **ludicrousness**: foolishness, eccentricity.

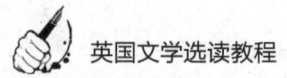

No; d'Urbervilles.

Ay, ay; I mean d'Urbervilles.

Our names are worn away to Durbeyfield; but we have several proofs that we are d'Urbervilles. Antiquarians hold we are,—and—and we have an old seal, marked with a **ramping**① lion on a shield, and a castle over him. And we have a very old silver spoon, round in the bowl like a little **ladle**②, and marked with the same castle. But it is so worn that mother uses it to stir the pea-soup.

A castle **argent**③ is certainly my **crest**④, said he **blandly**⑤. And my arms a lion rampant.

And so mother said we ought to make ourselves beknown to you—as we've lost our horse by a bad accident, and are the oldest branch o' the family.

Very kind of your mother, I'm sure. And I, for one, don't regret her step. Alec looked at Tess as he spoke, in a way that made her blush a little. And so, my pretty girl, you've come on a friendly visit to us, as relations?

I suppose I have, faltered Tess, looking uncomfortable again.

Well—there's no harm in it. Where do you live? What are you?

She gave him brief particulars; and responding to further inquiries told him that she was intending to go back by the same carrier who had brought her.

It is a long while before he returns past Trantridge Cross. Supposing we walk round the grounds to pass the time, my pretty Coz?

Tess wished to **abridge**⑥ her visit as much as possible; but the young man was pressing, and she consented to accompany him. He conducted her about the lawns, and flower-beds, and **conservatories**⑦; and thence to the fruit-garden and greenhouses, where he asked her if she liked strawberries.

Yes, said Tess, when they come.

They are already here. D'Urberville began gathering specimens of the fruit for her, handing them back to her as he stooped; and, presently, selecting a specially fine product of the British Queen variety, he stood up and held it by the stem to her mouth.

No—no! she said quickly, putting her fingers between his hand and her lips. I would rather take it in my own hand.

Nonsense! he insisted; and in a slight distress she parted her lips and took it in.

---

① **ramping**: rearing on left hind leg with forelegs elevated.
② **ladle**: a long-handled spoon.
③ **argent**: the metal silver.
④ **crest**: a device decorated above the shield on a coat of arms.
⑤ **blandly**: pleasantly in manner.
⑥ **abridge**: condense or shorten.
⑦ **conservatories**: greenhouses for growing and displaying plants.

Unit 15　Thomas Hardy (1840-1928)

They had spent some time wandering **desultorily**① thus, Tess eating in a half-pleased, half-reluctant state whatever d'Urberville offered her. When she could consume no more of the strawberries he filled her little basket with them; and then the two passed round to the rose-trees, whence he gathered blossoms and gave her to put in her bosom. She obeyed like one in a dream, and when she could affix no more he himself tucked a bud or two into her hat, and heaped her basket with others in the **prodigality**② of his **bounty**③. At last, looking at his watch, he said, Now, by the time you have had something to eat, it will be time for you to leave, if you want to catch the carrier to Shaston. Come here, and I'll see what grub I can find.

Stoke d'Urberville took her back to the lawn and into the tent, where he left her, soon reappearing with a basket of light luncheon, which he put before her himself. It was evidently the gentleman's wish not to be disturbed in this pleasant **tête-à-tête**④ by the servantry.

Do you mind my smoking? he asked.

Oh, not at all, sir.

He watched her pretty and unconscious **munching**⑤ through the **skeins**⑥ of smoke that pervaded the tent, and Tess Durbeyfield did not **divine**⑦, as she innocently looked down at the roses in her bosom, that there behind the blue **narcotic**⑧ haze was potentially the tragic mischief of her drama—one who stood fair to be the blood-red ray in the spectrum of her young life. She had an attribute which amounted to a disadvantage just now; and it was this that caused Alec d'Urberville's eyes to **rivet**⑨ themselves upon her. It was a luxuriance of aspect, a fulness of growth, which made her appear more of a woman than she really was. She had inherited the feature from her mother without the quality it denoted. It had troubled her mind occasionally, till her companions had said that it was a fault which time would cure.

She soon had finished her lunch. Now I am going home, sir, she said, rising.

And what do they call you? he asked, as he accompanied her along the drive till they were out of sight of the house.

Tess Durbeyfield, down at Marlott.

And you say your people have lost their horse?

I—killed him! she answered, her eyes filling with tears as she gave particulars of Prince's death. And I don't know what to do for father on account of it!

---

① **desultorily**: randomly or periodically.
② **prodigality**: excessive spending.
③ **bounty**: generosity in giving.
④ **tête-à-tête**: A French phrase meaning a private conversation between two persons.
⑤ **munching**: chewing with pleasure.
⑥ **skeins**: loose coils of something.
⑦ **divine**: guess or know by intuition.
⑧ **narcotic**: affecting one's mind in a harmful way or making him or her sleepy.
⑨ **rivet**: fasten or fix firmly.

I must think if I cannot do something. My mother must find a **berth**① for you. But, Tess, no nonsense about 'd'Urberville';—'Durbeyfield' only, you know—quite another name.

I wish for no better, sir, said she with something of dignity.

For a moment—only for a moment—when they were in the turning of the drive, between the tall **rhododendrons**② and **conifers**③, before the lodge became visible, he inclined his face towards her as if—but, no: he thought better of it, and let her go.

Thus the thing began. Had she perceived this meeting's import she might have asked why she was doomed to be seen and coveted that day by the wrong man, and not by some other man, the right and desired one in all respects—as nearly as humanity can supply the right and desired; yet to him who amongst her acquaintance might have approximated to this kind, she was but a transient impression, half forgotten.

In the ill-judged execution of the well-judged plan of things the call seldom produces the comer, the man to love rarely coincides with the hour for loving. Nature does not often say See! to her poor creature at a time when seeing can lead to happy doing; or reply Here! to a body's cry of Where? till the hide-and-seek has become an irksome, outworn game. We may wonder whether at the **acme**④ and summit of the human progress these **anachronisms**⑤ will be corrected by a finer intuition, a closer interaction of the social machinery than that which now **jolts**⑥ us round and along; but such completeness is not to be prophesied, or even conceived as possible. Enough that in the present case, as in millions, it was not the two halves of a perfect whole that confronted each other at the perfect moment; a missing counterpart wandered independently about the earth waiting in **crass**⑦ **obtuseness**⑧ till the late time came. Out of which **maladroit**⑨ delay sprang anxieties, disappointments, shocks, catastrophes, and passing-strange destinies.

When d'Urberville got back to the tent he sat down astride on a chair, reflecting, with a pleased gleam in his face. Then he broke into a loud laugh.

Well, I'm damned! What a funny thing! Ha-ha-ha! And what a crumby girl!

---

① **berth**: a job.
② **rhododendrons**: evergreen shrubs with leathery leaves and clusters of pink, red, or purple flowers.
③ **conifers**: evergreen trees of the pine and cypress families.
④ **acme**: the highest point of attainment or development.
⑤ **anachronisms**: errors in chronology.
⑥ **jolts**: *v.* **jolt**, move suddenly or roughly.
⑦ **crass**: stupid or insensitive.
⑧ **obtuseness**: lacking quickness of sensibility.
⑨ **maladroit**: clumsy or awkward.

Unit 15 Thomas Hardy (1840–1928)

Exercise

I. Word Matching

Directions: Please choose the most appropriate ones from the given words to explain the original boldfaced words in the following lines.

A. **lost**　　　　B. **desire**　　　　C. **direct**　　　　D. **emerge**
E. **injury**　　　F. **annoying**　　　E. **hesitate**

1. Distress, if not penury, **loom**ed in the distance.

2. John Durbeyfield was the only really **lineal** representative of the old d'Urberville family existing in the county, or near it.

3. And perceiving that she stood quite **confounded**: Never mind me. I am Mr d'Urberville. Have you come to see me or my mother?

4. I suppose I have, **falter**ed Tess, looking uncomfortable again.

5. There behind the blue narcotic haze was potentially the tragic **mischief** of her drama—one who stood fair to be the blood-red ray in the spectrum of her young life.

6. Had she perceived this meeting's import she might have asked why she was doomed to be seen and **covet**ed that day by the wrong man, and not by some other man.

7. Nature does not often say See! to her poor creature at a time when seeing can lead to happy doing; or reply Here! to a body's cry of Where? till the hide-and-seek has become an **irksome**, outworn game.

II. English-Chinese Translation

Directions: Please translate the following classic dicta from English into Chinese.

1. Never in her life—she could swear it from the bottom of her soul—had she ever intended to do wrong; yet these hard judgments had come. Whatever her sins, they were not sins of intention, but of inadvertence, and why should she have been punished so persistently?

—*Tess of the d'Urbervilles*

2. I have felt lately, more and more, that my present way of living is bad in every respect.

—*Far from the Madding Crowd*

3. That it would always be summer and autumn, and you always courting me, and always thinking as much of me as you have done through the past summertime!

—*Tess of the d'Urbervilles*

4. They spoke very little of their mutual feeling; pretty phrases and warm expressions being probably unnecessary between such tried friends.

—*Far from the Madding Crowd*

5. She hardly observed that a tear descended slowly upon his cheek, a tear so large that it

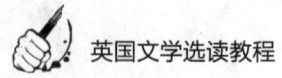

magnified the pores of skin over which it rolled, like the object lens of a microscope.

—*Tess of the d'Urbervilles*

III. Term Defining

Directions: *Please explain the following literary terms based on Tess of the d'Urbervilles.*

1. imagery
2. realism
3. foreboding mood

IV. Content-Based Questions

Directions: *Please give a concise and adequate answer to the following questions related to Text A.*

1. In what way was Tess's father, Mr. Durbeyfield locally called a "slack-twisted fellow"?

2. Why do you think Tess was regarded as the figure in the family who had dragged other parents into this quagmire based on your self-study of the plot before Chapter V?

3. How did Tess and his father immediately react to Mrs. Durbeyfield's scheme of persuading Tess to go to the rich Mrs d'Urberville living on the outskirts of The Chase, to claim kin, and even ask for her favor?

V. Discussion Question

Tess recounted her unforgettable past experience of the village school, where she had been much loved by others of her own sex and age in those early days. Retell the detailed points of what she recalled to your other group members and then share those good school memories of your own if possible.

VI. Essay Question

It is obvious that Mr. d'Urberville was unusually generous and hospitable on his first meeting with Tess from the descriptions in the text like "Well, my Beauty, what can I do for you?" and "he himself tucked a bud or two into her hat, and heaped her basket with others". Write a 200-word essay to predict the man's intentions and the woman's possible predicaments in the future.

Text B

Tess of the d'Urbervilles
A Pure Woman
Chapter LVIII

The night was strangely solemn and still. In the small hours she whispered to him the whole story of how he had walked in his sleep with her in his arms across the Froom stream, at the imminent risk of both their lives, and laid her down in the stone coffin at the ruined abbey. He had never known of that till now.

Why didn't you tell me next day? he said. It might have prevented much misunderstanding and woe.

Don't think of what's past! said she. I am not going to think outside of now. Why should we! Who knows what to-morrow has in store?

But it apparently had no sorrow. The morning was wet and foggy, and Clare, rightly informed that the caretaker only opened the windows on fine days, ventured to creep out of their chamber and explore the house, leaving Tess asleep. There was no food on the **premises**[①], but there was water, and he took advantage of the fog to emerge from the mansion and fetch tea, bread, and butter from a shop in a little place two miles beyond, as also a small tin kettle and spirit-lamp, that they might get fire without smoke. His re-entry awoke her; and they breakfasted on what he had brought.

They were **indisposed**[②] to stir abroad, and the day passed, and the night following, and the next, and next; till, almost without their being aware, five days had slipped by in absolute seclusion, not a sight or sound of a human being disturbing their peacefulness, such as it was. The changes of the weather were their only events, the birds of the New Forest their only company. By **tacit**[③] consent they hardly once spoke of any incident of the past subsequent to their wedding-day. The gloomy intervening time seemed to sink into chaos, over which the present and prior times closed as if it never had been. Whenever he suggested that they should leave their shelter, and go forwards towards Southampton or London, she showed a strange unwillingness to move.

Why should we put an end to all that's sweet and lovely! she **deprecated**[④]. What must

---

① **premises**: *pl.* of **premise**, a place or portion of a building.
② **indisposed**: averse or unwilling.
③ **tacit**: understood without direct expression, unspoken.
④ **deprecated**: v. **deprecate** (**deprecated**, **deprecated**) express disapproval of.

come will come. And, looking through the shutter-chink: All is trouble outside there; inside here content.

He peeped out also. It was quite true; within was affection, union, error forgiven: outside was the **inexorable**①.

And—and, she said, pressing her cheek against his, I fear that what you think of me now may not last. I do not wish to outlive your present feeling for me. I would rather not. I would rather be dead and buried when the time comes for you to despise me, so that it may never be known to me that you despised me.

I cannot ever despise you.

I also hope that. But considering what my life has been, I cannot see why any man should, sooner or later, be able to help despising me.... How wickedly mad I was! Yet formerly I never could bear to hurt a fly or a worm, and the sight of a bird in a cage used often to make me cry.

They remained yet another day. In the night the dull sky cleared, and the result was that the old caretaker at the cottage awoke early. The brilliant sunrise made her unusually brisk; she decided to open the **contiguous**② mansion immediately, and to air it thoroughly on such a day. Thus it occurred that, having arrived and opened the lower rooms before six o'clock, she ascended to the bedchambers, and was about to turn the handle of the one wherein they lay. At that moment she fancied she could hear the breathing of persons within. Her slippers and her antiquity had rendered her progress a noiseless one so far, and she made for instant retreat; then, deeming that her hearing might have deceived her, she turned anew to the door and softly tried the handle. The lock was out of order, but a piece of furniture had been moved forward on the inside, which prevented her opening the door more than an inch or two. A stream of morning light through the shutter-chink fell upon the faces of the pair, wrapped in profound slumber, Tess's lips being parted like a half-opened flower near his cheek. The caretaker was so struck with their innocent appearance, and with the elegance of Tess's gown hanging across a chair, her silk stockings beside it, the pretty **parasol**③, and the other habits in which she had arrived because she had none else, that her first **indignation**④ at the effrontery of **tramps**⑤ and **vagabonds**⑥ gave way to a momentary sentimentality over this genteel elopement, as it seemed. She closed the door, and withdrew as softly as she had come, to go and consult with her neighbours on the odd discovery.

Not more than a minute had elapsed after her withdrawal when Tess woke, and then Clare.

---

① **inexorable**: incapable of stopping or altering.
② **contiguous**: adjacent.
③ **parasol**: an umbrella for protection against the sun.
④ **indignation**: strong displeasure at something offensive.
⑤ **tramps**: *pl.* of **tramp**, prostitute.
⑥ **vagabonds**: *pl*, of vagabond, idle beggar or thief.

Unit 15 Thomas Hardy (1840–1928)

Both had a sense that something had disturbed them, though they could not say what; and the uneasy feeling which it engendered grew stronger. As soon as he was dressed he narrowly scanned the lawn through the two or three inches of shutter-chink.

I think we will leave at once, said he. It is a fine day. And I cannot help fancying somebody is about the house. At any rate, the woman will be sure to come to-day.

She passively assented, and putting the room in order, they took up the few articles that belonged to them, and departed noiselessly. When they had got into the Forest she turned to take a last look at the house.

Ah, happy house—goodbye! she said. My life can only be a question of a few weeks. Why should we not have stayed there?

Don't say it, Tess! We shall soon get out of this district altogether. We'll continue our course as we've begun it, and keep straight north. Nobody will think of looking for us there. We shall be looked for at the Wessex ports if we are sought at all. When we are in the north we will get to a port and away.

Having thus persuaded her, the plan was pursued, and they kept a bee-line northward. Their long **repose**① at the manor-house lent them walking power now; and towards mid-day they found that they were approaching the steepled city of Melchester, which lay directly in their way. He decided to rest her in a clump of trees during the afternoon, and push onward under cover of darkness. At dusk Clare purchased food as usual, and their night march began, the boundary between Upper and Mid-Wessex being crossed about eight o'clock.

To walk across country without much regard to roads was not new to Tess, and she showed her old **agility**② in the performance. The **intercepting**③ city, ancient Melchester, they were obliged to pass through in order to take advantage of the town bridge for crossing a large river that obstructed them. It was about midnight when they went along the deserted streets, lighted **fitfully**④ by the few lamps, keeping off the pavement that it might not echo their footsteps. The graceful pile of cathedral architecture rose dimly on their left hand, but it was lost upon them now. Once out of the town they followed the **turnpike-road**⑤, which after a few miles plunged across an open plain.

Though the sky was dense with cloud, a diffused light from some fragment of a moon had **hitherto**⑥ helped them a little. But the moon had now sunk, the clouds seemed to settle almost on their heads, and the night grew as dark as a cave. However, they found their way along,

---

① **repose**: the state of being at rest.
② **agility**: the ability to move quickly and actively.
③ **intercepting**: v. intercept, stop or interrupt on the way.
④ **fitfully**: off and on, irregularly.
⑤ **turnpike-road**: a road on which tolls are collected.
⑥ **hitherto**: until now.

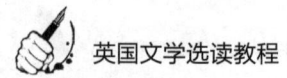

keeping as much on the turf as possible that their tread might not resound, which it was easy to do, there being no hedge or fence of any kind. All around was open loneliness and black solitude, over which a stiff breeze blew.

They had proceeded thus gropingly two or three miles further when on a sudden Clare became conscious of some vast erection close in his front, rising sheer from the grass. They had almost struck themselves against it.

What monstrous place is this? said Angel.

It hums, said she. Hearken!

He listened. The wind, playing upon the **edifice**①, produced a booming tune, like the note of some gigantic one-stringed harp. No other sound came from it, and lifting his hand and advancing a step or two, Clare felt the vertical surface of the structure. It seemed to be of solid stone, without joint or moulding. Carrying his fingers onward he found that what he had come in contact with was a colossal rectangular pillar; by stretching out his left hand he could feel a similar one adjoining. At an indefinite height overhead something made the black sky blacker, which had the **semblance**② of a vast **architrave**③ uniting the pillars horizontally. They carefully entered beneath and between; the surfaces echoed their soft rustle; but they seemed to be still out of doors. The place was roofless. Tess drew her breath fearfully, and Angel, perplexed, said—

What can it be?

Feeling sideways they encountered another tower-like pillar, square and uncompromising as the first; beyond it another and another. The place was all doors and pillars, some connected above by continuous architraves.

A very Temple of the Winds, he said.

The next pillar was isolated; others composed a **trilithon**④; others were **prostrate**⑤, their **flanks**⑥ forming a causeway wide enough for a carriage; and it was soon obvious that they made up a forest of **monoliths**⑦ grouped upon the grassy expanse of the plain. The couple advanced further into this pavilion of the night till they stood in its midst.

It is Stonehenge! said Clare.

The **heathen**⑧ temple, you mean?

Yes. Older than the centuries; older than the d'Urbervilles! Well, what shall we do,

---

① **edifice**: a large and impressive building.
② **semblance**: outward appearance.
③ **architrave**: the lowest part of a structure resting on the upper parts of the columns.
④ **trilithon**: a prehistoric structure consisting of two upright stones supporting a third horizontal one.
⑤ **prostrate**: lie flat.
⑥ **flanks**: lateral parts.
⑦ **monoliths**: large blocks of stone.
⑧ **heathen**: relating to the religious beliefs of the ancient Germanic peoples, pagan.

Unit 15　Thomas Hardy (1840-1928)

darling? We may find shelter further on.

But Tess, really tired by this time, flung herself upon an **oblong**① **slab**② that lay close at hand, and was sheltered from the wind by a pillar. Owing to the action of the sun during the preceding day, the stone was warm and dry, in comforting contrast to the rough and chill grass around, which had damped her skirts and shoes.

I don't want to go any further, Angel, she said, stretching out her hand for his. Can't we **bide**③ here?

I fear not. This spot is visible for miles by day, although it does not seem so now.

One of my mother's people was a shepherd hereabouts, now I think of it. And you used to say at Talbothays that I was a heathen. So now I am at home.

He knelt down beside her outstretched form, and put his lips upon hers.

Sleepy are you, dear? I think you are lying on an altar.

I like very much to be here, she murmured. It is so solemn and lonely—after my great happiness—with nothing but the sky above my face. It seems as if there were no folk in the world but we two; and I wish there were not—except 'Liza-Lu.

Clare thought she might as well rest here till it should get a little lighter, and he flung his overcoat upon her, and sat down by her side.

Angel, if anything happens to me, will you watch over 'Liza-Lu for my sake? she asked, when they had listened a long time to the wind among the pillars.

I will.

She is so good and simple and pure. O, Angel—I wish you would marry her if you lose me, as you will do shortly. O, if you would!

If I lose you I lose all! And she is my sister-in-law.

That's nothing, dearest. People marry sister-laws continually about Marlott; and 'Liza-Lu is so gentle and sweet, and she is growing so beautiful. O, I could share you with her willingly when we are spirits! If you would train her and teach her, Angel, and bring her up for your own self!... She had all the best of me without the bad of me; and if she were to become yours it would almost seem as if death had not divided us... Well, I have said it. I won't mention it again.

She ceased, and he fell into thought. In the far north-east sky he could see between the pillars a level **streak**④ of light. The uniform **concavity**⑤ of black cloud was lifting bodily like the lid of a pot, letting in at the earth's edge the coming day, against which the towering

---

① **oblong**: having the shape of a rectangle.
② **slab**: a broad flat piece of stone.
③ **bide**: dwell or stay.
④ **streak**: a ray of light.
⑤ **concave**: a curving-in surface.

monoliths and trilithons began to be blackly defined.

Did they sacrifice to God here? asked she.

No, said he.

Who to?

I believe to the sun. That lofty stone set away by itself is in the direction of the sun, which will presently rise behind it.

This reminds me, dear, she said. You remember you never would interfere with any belief of mine before we were married? But I knew your mind all the same, and I thought as you thought—not from any reasons of my own, but because you thought so. Tell me now, Angel, do you think we shall meet again after we are dead? I want to know.

He kissed her to avoid a reply at such a time.

O, Angel—I fear that means no! said she, with a suppressed sob. And I wanted so to see you again—so much, so much! What—not even you and I, Angel, who love each other so well?

Like a greater than himself, to the critical question at the critical time he did not answer; and they were again silent. In a minute or two her breathing became more regular, her clasp of his hand relaxed, and she fell asleep. The band of silver paleness along the east horizon made even the distant parts of the Great Plain appear dark and near; and the whole enormous landscape bore that impress of reserve, **taciturnity**[①], and hesitation which is usual just before day. The eastward pillars and their architraves stood up blackly against the light, and the great flame-shaped Sun-stone beyond them; and the Stone of Sacrifice midway. Presently the night wind died out, and the quivering little pools in the cup-like hollows of the stones lay still. At the same time something seemed to move on the verge of the dip eastward—a mere dot. It was the head of a man approaching them from the hollow beyond the Sun-stone. Clare wished they had gone onward, but in the circumstances decided to remain quiet. The figure came straight towards the circle of pillars in which they were.

He heard something behind him, the brush of feet. Turning, he saw over the prostrate columns another figure; then before he was aware, another was at hand on the right, under a trilithon, and another on the left. The dawn shone full on the front of the man westward, and Clare could discern from this that he was tall, and walked as if trained. They all closed in with evident purpose. Her story then was true! Springing to his feet, he looked around for a weapon, loose stone, means of escape, anything. By this time the nearest man was upon him.

It is no use, sir, he said. There are sixteen of us on the Plain, and the whole country is **reared**[②].

Let her finish her sleep! he implored in a whisper of the men as they gathered round.

---

① **taciturnity**: the quality of being untalkative.

② **reared**: *v.* **rear** (**reared, reared**), raise or start up.

Unit 15　Thomas Hardy (1840–1928)

When they saw where she lay, which they had not done till then, they showed no objection, and stood watching her, as still as the pillars around. He went to the stone and bent over her, holding one poor little hand; her breathing now was quick and small, like that of a lesser creature than a woman. All waited in the growing light, their faces and hands as if they were silvered, the remainder of their figures dark, the stones **glistening**① green-gray, the Plain still a mass of shade. Soon the light was strong, and a ray shone upon her unconscious form, peering under her eyelids and waking her.

What is it, Angel? she said, starting up. Have they come for me?

Yes, dearest, he said. They have come.

It is as it should be, she murmured. Angel, I am almost glad—yes, glad! This happiness could not have lasted. It was too much. I have had enough; and now I shall not live for you to despise me!

She stood up, shook herself, and went forward, neither of the men having moved.

I am ready, she said quietly.

Exercise

I. Word Matching

Directions: Please choose the most appropriate ones from the given words to explain the original boldfaced words in the following lines.

| A. **pass** | B. **produce** | C. **recognize** | D. **grief** |
| E. **gigantic** | F. **scorn** | G. **block** | H. **upright** |

1. Why didn't you tell me next day? he said. It might have prevented much misunderstanding and **woe**.

2. I would rather be dead and buried when the time comes for you to **despise** me, so that it may never be known to me that you despised me.

3. Not more than a minute had **elapse**d after her withdrawal when Tess woke, and then Clare.

4. Both had a sense that something had disturbed them, though they could not say what; and the uneasy feeling which it **engender**ed grew stronger.

5. The intercepting city, ancient Melchester, they were obliged to pass through in order to take advantage of the town bridge for crossing a large river that **obstruct**ed them.

6. No other sound came from it, and lifting his hand and advancing a step or two, Clare felt the **vertical** surface of the structure.

7. Carrying his fingers onward he found that what he had come in contact with was a

---

① **glistening**: *v.* **glisten**, gleam by reflecting light.

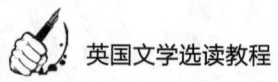

colossal rectangular pillar.

8. The dawn shone full on the front of the man westward, and Clare could **discern** from this that he was tall, and walked as if trained.

II. English-Chinese Translation

Directions: Please translate the following classic dicta from English into Chinese.

1. Why didn't you tell me there was danger? Why didn't you warn me? Ladies know what to guard against, because they read novels that tell them of these tricks; but I never had the chance of discovering in that way; and you did not help me!

—*Tess of the d'Urbervilles*

2. My life looks as if it had been wasted for want of chances! When I see what you know, what you have read, and seen, and thought, I feel what a nothing I am!

—*Tess of the d'Urbervilles*

3. Do not do an immoral thing for moral reasons.

—*Jude the Obscure*

4. All waited in the growing light, their faces and hands as if they were silvered, the remainder of their figures dark, the stones glistening green-gray, the Plain still a mass of shade. Soon the light was strong, and a ray shone upon her unconscious form, peering under her eyelids and waking her.

—*Tess of the d'Urbervilles*

5. It was the touch of the imperfect upon the would-be perfect that gave the sweetness, because it was that which gave the humanity.

—*Tess of the d'Urbervilles*

III. Term Defining

Directions: Please explain the following literary terms based on Tess of the d'Urbervilles.

1. motif

2. omniscient point of view

3. symbolism

IV. Content-Based Questions

Directions: Please give a concise and adequate answer to the following questions based on the reading of Text B.

1. How did the narrator depict the vast edifice "rising sheer from the grass" and "close in front" of Tess and Angel in this chapter?

2. Why did Tess simply fling herself upon an oblong slab of the Stonehenge and decline proceeding further instead of Angle's patient explanation and persuasion?

3. Why did Tess wish Angel to watch over 'Liza-Lu and even marry her if anything happens to her? What did this portend for the ending of the story?

V. Discussion Question

From Tess's words in the chapter like "Why should we put an end to all that's sweet and lovely! and All is trouble outside there; inside here content", we all know that she is very reluctant to let go of the five days she spent together with Clare day and night. Recollect and share the details of these days as much as possible with your partner after another in-depth reading of the related plot.

VI. Essay Question

There is a quote in *Tess of the D'Urbervilles* by Thomas Hardy, "The man to love rarely coincides with the hour for loving…till the hide-and-seek has become an irksome, outworn game". Write a 300-word hint fiction on an unfortunately missed love you have read from a classic work or personally experienced before.

Self-Improving Reading

Far from the Madding Crowd by Thomas Hardy
Jude the Obscure by Thomas Hardy

Unit 16 Oscar Wilde (1854–1900)

Life and Works

Oscar Wilde, a prominent Irish playwright, novelist and poet, was born to Sir William Wilde, Ireland's most distinguished eye surgeon and otology originator, and Lady Jane Wilde, the famous Irish writer Speranza, in Dublin, Ireland, on October 16, 1854. Oscar entered Trinity College after his study at the Portora Royal School in Enniskillen from 1864 to 1871 and then pursued an additional three-year program at Trinity College. In 1878 Oscar attained his Bachelor of Arts from the Magdalen College in Oxford. In April 1881, a main character of the play *Patience* was assumed to be inspired by Wilde and even American audiences appear to be fascinated with it. In the same year Wilde published *Poems*, his first book, at his own expense. The following year Oscar was invited to deliver a succession of lectures such as *The English Renaissance of Art*, *The House Beautiful*, and *Decorative Art* in America, Canada and Great Britain.

He encountered Constance Lloyd, an author and political activist, during his stay in London, with whom he married in 1884. In 1887 Wilde directed *The Woman's World* magazine,

Unit 16 Oscar Wilde (1854–1900)

previously titled *The Lady's World.* Oscar published his famous moral fantasy novel, *The portrait of Dorian Gray* in 1890. *Lady Windermere's Fan*, Oscar Wilde's first hit play was performed in 1892 and published the following year and meanwhile, his moral satire play, *A Woman of No Importance* published in 1892 and performed in 1893. Oscar's next society comedy, *An Ideal Husband* premiered at the Haymarket Theatre and *The importance of being Ernest*, his last play at St. James' Theatre in 1895. At the pinnacle of his writing career, Oscar found himself accused by the Marquess of Queensberry of an illicit romantic relationship with the latter's son and was sentenced to two-year compulsory labor and he wrote *The Ballad of Reading Gaol* during the incarceration. Oscar Wilde died of meningitis at the Hôtel d'Alsace in Paris on Nov. 30, 1900 at the age of 46.

Text A

The Importance of Being Earnest
A Trivial Comedy for Serious People
Act I (Excerpts)

[Enter Lane.]

LANE.
Mr. Ernest Worthing.

[Enter Jack.]
[Lane goes out.]

ALGERNON.
How are you, my dear Ernest? What brings you up to town?

JACK.
Oh, pleasure, pleasure! What else should bring one anywhere? Eating as usual, I see, Algy!

ALGERNON.
[Stiffly.] I believe it is customary in good society to take some slight refreshment at five o'clock. Where have you been since last Thursday?

JACK.

[Sitting down on the sofa.] In the country.

ALGERNON.

What on earth do you do there?

JACK.

[Pulling off his gloves.] When one is in town one amuses oneself. When one is in the country one amuses other people. It is excessively boring.

ALGERNON.

And who are the people you amuse?

JACK.

[Airily.] Oh, neighbours, neighbours.

ALGERNON.

Got nice neighbours in your part of Shropshire?

JACK.

Perfectly horrid! Never speak to one of them.

ALGERNON.

How immensely you must amuse them! [Goes over and takes sandwich.] By the way, Shropshire is your county, is it not?

JACK.

Eh? Shropshire? Yes, of course. Hallo! Why all these cups? Why cucumber sandwiches? Why such **reckless**① extravagance in one so young? Who is coming to tea?

ALGERNON.

Oh! merely Aunt Augusta and Gwendolen.

JACK.

---

① **reckless**: careless or rash.

Unit 16 Oscar Wilde (1854–1900)

How perfectly delightful!

ALGERNON.

Yes, that is all very well; but I am afraid Aunt Augusta won't quite approve of your being here.

JACK.

May I ask why?

ALGERNON.

My dear fellow, the way you flirt with Gwendolen is perfectly disgraceful. It is almost as bad as the way Gwendolen flirts with you.

JACK.

I am in love with Gwendolen. I have come up to town **expressly**① to propose to her.

ALGERNON.

I thought you had come up for pleasure?... I call that business.

JACK.

How utterly unromantic you are!

ALGERNON.

I really don't see anything romantic in proposing. It is very romantic to be in love. But there is nothing romantic about a definite proposal. Why, one may be accepted. One usually is, I believe. Then the excitement is all over. The very essence of romance is uncertainty. If ever I get married, I'll certainly try to forget the fact.

JACK.

I have no doubt about that, dear Algy. The Divorce Court was specially invented for people whose memories are so curiously constituted.

ALGERNON.

Oh! there is no use speculating on that subject. Divorces are made in Heaven—[Jack puts out his hand to take a sandwich. Algernon at once interferes.] Please don't touch the cucumber

---

① **expressly**: purposely, particularly.

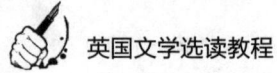

sandwiches. They are ordered specially for Aunt Augusta. [Takes one and eats it.]

JACK.

Well, you have been eating them all the time.

ALGERNON.

That is quite a different matter. She is my aunt. [Takes plate from below.] Have some bread and butter. The bread and butter is for Gwendolen. Gwendolen is devoted to bread and butter.

JACK.

[Advancing to table and helping himself.] And very good bread and butter it is too.

ALGERNON.

Well, my dear fellow, you need not eat as if you were going to eat it all. You behave as if you were married to her already. You are not married to her already, and I don't think you ever will be.

JACK.

Why on earth do you say that?

ALGERNON.

Well, in the first place girls never marry the men they flirt with. Girls don't think it right.

JACK.

Oh, that is nonsense!

ALGERNON.

It isn't. It is a great truth. It accounts for the extraordinary number of bachelors that one sees all over the place. In the second place, I don't give my consent.

JACK.

Your consent!

ALGERNON.

My dear fellow, Gwendolen is my first cousin. And before I allow you to marry her, you will have to clear up the whole question of Cecily. [Rings bell.]

Unit 16 Oscar Wilde (1854-1900)

JACK.

Cecily! What on earth do you mean? What do you mean, Algy, by Cecily! I don't know any one of the name of Cecily.

[Enter Lane.]

ALGERNON.

Bring me that cigarette case Mr. Worthing left in the smoking-room the last time he dined here.

LANE.

Yes, sir. [Lane goes out.]

JACK.

Do you mean to say you have had my cigarette case all this time? I wish to goodness you had let me know. I have been writing frantic letters to Scotland Yard about it. I was very nearly offering a large reward.

ALGERNON.

Well, I wish you would offer one. I happen to be more than usually hard up.

JACK.

There is no good offering a large reward now that the thing is found.
[Enter Lane with the cigarette case on a **salver**①. Algernon takes it at once. Lane goes out.]

ALGERNON.

I think that is rather mean of you, Ernest, I must say. [Opens case and examines it.] However, it makes no matter, for, now that I look at the inscription inside, I find that the thing isn't yours after all.

JACK.

Of course it's mine. [Moving to him.] You have seen me with it a hundred times, and you have no right whatsoever to read what is written inside. It is a very ungentlemanly thing to read a private cigarette case.

---

① **salver**: a silver plate for serving food or drinks.

ALGERNON.

Oh! it is absurd to have a hard and fast rule about what one should read and what one shouldn't. More than half of modern culture depends on what one shouldn't read.

JACK.

I am quite aware of the fact, and I don't propose to discuss modern culture. It isn't the sort of thing one should talk of in private. I simply want my cigarette case back.

ALGERNON.

Yes; but this isn't your cigarette case. This cigarette case is a present from some one of the name of Cecily, and you said you didn't know any one of that name.

JACK.

Well, if you want to know, Cecily happens to be my aunt.

ALGERNON.

Your aunt!

JACK.

Yes. Charming old lady she is, too. Lives at Tunbridge Wells. Just give it back to me, Algy.

ALGERNON.

[Retreating to back of sofa.] But why does she call herself little Cecily if she is your aunt and lives at Tunbridge Wells? [Reading.] 'From little Cecily with her fondest love.'

JACK.

[Moving to sofa and kneeling upon it.] My dear fellow, what on earth is there in that? Some aunts are tall, some aunts are not tall. That is a matter that surely an aunt may be allowed to decide for herself. You seem to think that every aunt should be exactly like your aunt! That is absurd! For Heaven's sake give me back my cigarette case. [Follows Algernon round the room.]

ALGERNON.

Yes. But why does your aunt call you her uncle? 'From little Cecily, with her fondest love to her dear Uncle Jack.' There is no objection, I admit, to an aunt being a small aunt, but why an aunt, no matter what her size may be, should call her own nephew her uncle, I can't quite make out. Besides, your name isn't Jack at all; it is Ernest.

Unit 16　Oscar Wilde (1854-1900)

JACK.

It isn't Ernest; it's Jack.

ALGERNON.

You have always told me it was Ernest. I have introduced you to every one as Ernest. You answer to the name of Ernest. You look as if your name was Ernest. You are the most earnest-looking person I ever saw in my life. It is perfectly absurd your saying that your name isn't Ernest. It's on your cards. Here is one of them. [Taking it from case.] 'Mr. Ernest Worthing, B. 4, The Albany.' I'll keep this as a proof that your name is Ernest if ever you attempt to deny it to me, or to Gwendolen, or to any one else. [Puts the card in his pocket.]

JACK.

Well, my name is Ernest in town and Jack in the country, and the cigarette case was given to me in the country.

ALGERNON.

Yes, but that does not account for the fact that your small Aunt Cecily, who lives at Tunbridge Wells, calls you her dear uncle. Come, old boy, you had much better have the thing out at once.

JACK.

My dear Algy, you talk exactly as if you were a dentist. It is very vulgar to talk like a dentist when one isn't a dentist. It produces a false impression.

ALGERNON.

Well, that is exactly what dentists always do. Now, go on! Tell me the whole thing. I may mention that I have always suspected you of being a confirmed and secret Bunburyist; and I am quite sure of it now.

JACK.

Bunburyist? What on earth do you mean by a Bunburyist?

ALGERNON.

I'll reveal to you the meaning of that incomparable expression as soon as you are kind enough to inform me why you are Ernest in town and Jack in the country.

JACK.

Well, produce my cigarette case first.

ALGERNON.

Here it is. [Hands cigarette case.] Now produce your explanation, and pray make it improbable. [Sits on sofa.]

JACK.

My dear fellow, there is nothing improbable about my explanation at all. In fact it's perfectly ordinary. Old Mr. Thomas Cardew, who adopted me when I was a little boy, made me in his will guardian to his grand-daughter, Miss Cecily Cardew. Cecily, who addresses me as her uncle from motives of respect that you could not possibly appreciate, lives at my place in the country under the charge of her admirable governess, Miss Prism.

ALGERNON.

Where is that place in the country, by the way?

JACK.

That is nothing to you, dear boy. You are not going to be invited... I may tell you candidly that the place is not in Shropshire.

ALGERNON.

I suspected that, my dear fellow! I have Bunburyed all over Shropshire on two separate occasions. Now, go on. Why are you Ernest in town and Jack in the country?

JACK.

My dear Algy, I don't know whether you will be able to understand my real motives. You are hardly serious enough. When one is placed in the position of guardian, one has to adopt a very high moral tone on all subjects. It's one's duty to do so. And as a high moral tone can hardly be said to conduce very much to either one's health or one's happiness, in order to get up to town I have always pretended to have a younger brother of the name of Ernest, who lives in the Albany, and **gets into the most dreadful scrapes**[①]. That, my dear Algy, is the whole truth pure and simple.

ALGERNON.

The truth is rarely pure and never simple. Modern life would be very tedious if it were

---

① **gets into the most dreadful scrapes**: gets in trouble.

Unit 16　Oscar Wilde (1854–1900)

either, and modern literature a complete impossibility!

JACK.

That wouldn't be at all a bad thing.

ALGERNON.

Literary criticism is not your **forte**①, my dear fellow. Don't try it. You should leave that to people who haven't been at a University. They do it so well in the daily papers. What you really are is a Bunburyist. I was quite right in saying you were a Bunburyist. You are one of the most advanced Bunburyists I know.

JACK.

What on earth do you mean?

ALGERNON.

You have invented a very useful younger brother called Ernest, in order that you may be able to come up to town as often as you like. I have invented an invaluable permanent invalid called Bunbury, in order that I may be able to go down into the country whenever I choose. Bunbury is perfectly invaluable. If it wasn't for Bunbury's extraordinary bad health, for instance, I wouldn't be able to dine with you at Willis's to-night, for I have been really engaged to Aunt Augusta for more than a week.

JACK.

I haven't asked you to dine with me anywhere to-night.

ALGERNON.

I know. You are absurdly careless about sending out invitations. It is very foolish of you. Nothing annoys people so much as not receiving invitations.

JACK.

You had much better dine with your Aunt Augusta.

ALGERNON.

I haven't the smallest intention of doing anything of the kind. To begin with, I dined there on Monday, and once a week is quite enough to dine with one's own relations. In the second

---

① **forte**: specialty, strong point.

place, whenever I do dine there I am always treated as a member of the family, and sent down with either no woman at all, or two. In the third place, I know perfectly well whom she will place me next to, to-night. She will place me next Mary Farquhar, who always flirts with her own husband across the dinner-table. That is not very pleasant. Indeed, it is not even decent... and that sort of thing is enormously on the increase. The amount of women in London who flirt with their own husbands is perfectly scandalous. It looks so bad. It is simply washing one's clean linen in public. Besides, now that I know you to be a confirmed Bunburyist I naturally want to talk to you about Bunburying. I want to tell you the rules.

JACK.

I'm not a Bunburyist at all. If Gwendolen accepts me, I am going to kill my brother, indeed I think I'll kill him in any case. Cecily is a little too much interested in him. It is rather a bore. So I am going to get rid of Ernest. And I strongly advise you to do the same with Mr.... with your invalid friend who has the absurd name.

ALGERNON.

Nothing will induce me to part with Bunbury, and if you ever get married, which seems to me extremely problematic, you will be very glad to know Bunbury. A man who marries without knowing Bunbury has a very tedious time of it.

JACK.

That is nonsense. If I marry a charming girl like Gwendolen, and she is the only girl I ever saw in my life that I would marry, I certainly won't want to know Bunbury.

ALGERNON.

Then your wife will. You don't seem to realise, that in married life three is company and two is none.

JACK.

[**Sententiously**①.] That, my dear young friend, is the theory that the corrupt French Drama has been **propounding**② for the last fifty years.

ALGERNON.

Yes; and that the happy English home has proved in half the time.

---

① **Sententiously**: in a concise manner.
② **propounding**: *v*. **propound**, put forward an idea for consideration.

Unit 16　Oscar Wilde (1854–1900)

JACK.

For heaven's sake, don't try to be cynical. It's perfectly easy to be cynical.

ALGERNON.

My dear fellow, it isn't easy to be anything nowadays. There's such a lot of beastly competition about. [The sound of an electric bell is heard.] Ah! that must be Aunt Augusta. Only relatives, or creditors, ever ring in that **Wagnerian**① manner. Now, if I get her out of the way for ten minutes, so that you can have an opportunity for proposing to Gwendolen, may I dine with you to-night at Willis's?

JACK.

I suppose so, if you want to.

ALGERNON.

Yes, but you must be serious about it. I hate people who are not serious about meals. It is so shallow of them.

[Enter Lane.]

Exercise

I. Word Matching

Directions: Please choose the most appropriate ones from the given words to explain the original boldfaced words in the following lines.

| A. **patient** | B. **prolix** | C. **disgraceful** | D. **implausible** |
| E. **ponder** | F. **promote** | G. **superficial** | H. **priceless** |

1. Oh! there is no use **speculat**ing on that subject.

2. My dear fellow, there is nothing **improbable** about my explanation at all.

3. As a high moral tone can hardly be said to **conduce** very much to either one's health or one's happiness, in order to get up to town I have always pretended to have a younger brother of the name of Ernest.

4. Modern life would be very **tedious** if it were either, and modern literature a complete impossibility!

5. I have invented an invaluable permanent **invalid** called Bunbury, in order that I may be

---

① **Wagnerian**: of the massive scale of the compositions by the musician Richard Wagner.

able to go down into the country whenever I choose.

6. The amount of women in London who flirt with their own husbands is perfectly **scandalous**.

7. I hate people who are not serious about meals. It is so **shallow** of them.

II. English-Chinese Translation

Directions: Please translate the following classic dicta from English into Chinese.

1. All women become like their mothers. That is their tragedy. No man does. That is his.

—*The Importance of Being Earnest*

2. I am sick to death of cleverness. Everybody is clever nowadays.

—*The Importance of Being Earnest*

3. It is a terrible thing for a man to find out suddenly that all his life he has been speaking nothing but the truth.

—*The Importance of Being Earnest*

4. We are all in the gutter, but some of us are looking at the stars.

—*Lady Windermere's Fan*

5. Morality is simply the attitude we adopt towards people we personally dislike.

—*An Ideal Husband*

III. Term Defining

Directions: Please explain the following literary terms based on The Importance of Being Earnest.

1. farce

2. sarcasm

3. pun

IV. Content-Based Questions

Directions: Please give a concise and adequate answer to the following questions related to Text A.

1. What is the question that Jack has to clear up before being allowed to marry Gwendolen, and how did Algenon find out about this question?

2. What is Jack's answer to Algernon's question "why you are Ernest in town and Jack in the country"?

3. According to Algernon, why didn't he have the smallest intention of dining with Aunt Augusta?

V. Discussion Question

What is in Algernon's mind when he defines Jack Worthing as a "Bunburyist"? And what does the word "Bunburyists" mean according to Algernon? Discuss this word and its implied meanings with your partners and share your opinions with the rest of your classmates in regard to how it is related to the plot and the theme of this play.

VI. Essay Question

Marriage, one of the most important themes of this play, is the main driving force behind the story as well as a topic for each of us to ponder over. Algernon showed a cynical attitude toward marriage, holding that Jack's proposal was business rather than pleasure, which was criticized by Jack, defining Algernon as utterly unromantic. What is your opinion with regard to this topic? Write a 200-word essay on your understanding and reflection on the two characters' lines.

Text B

The Importance of Being Earnest
A Trivial Comedy for Serious People
Act I (Excerpt)

[Lady Bracknell and Algernon go into the music-room, Gwendolen remains behind.]

JACK.
Charming day it has been, Miss Fairfax.

GWENDOLEN.
Pray don't talk to me about the weather, Mr. Worthing. Whenever people talk to me about the weather, I always feel quite certain that they mean something else. And that makes me so nervous.

JACK.
I do mean something else.

GWENDOLEN.
I thought so. In fact, I am never wrong.

JACK.
And I would like to be allowed to take advantage of Lady Bracknell's temporary absence...

GWENDOLEN.

I would certainly advise you to do so. Mamma has a way of coming back suddenly into a room that I have often had to speak to her about.

JACK.

[Nervously.] Miss Fairfax, ever since I met you I have admired you more than any girl... I have ever met since... I met you.

GWENDOLEN.

Yes, I am quite well aware of the fact. And I often wish that in public, at any rate, you had been more demonstrative. For me you have always had an irresistible fascination. Even before I met you I was far from indifferent to you. [Jack looks at her in amazement.] We live, as I hope you know, Mr. Worthing, in an age of ideals. The fact is constantly mentioned in the more expensive monthly magazines, and has reached the provincial **pulpits**①, I am told; and my ideal has always been to love some one of the name of Ernest. There is something in that name that inspires absolute confidence. The moment Algernon first mentioned to me that he had a friend called Ernest, I knew I was destined to love you.

JACK.

You really love me, Gwendolen?

GWENDOLEN.

Passionately!

JACK.

Darling! You don't know how happy you've made me.

GWENDOLEN.

My own Ernest!

JACK.

But you don't really mean to say that you couldn't love me if my name wasn't Ernest?

GWENDOLEN.

But your name is Ernest.

---

① **pulpits**: *pl.* of **pulpit**, a platform in a church used in preaching.

Unit 16 Oscar Wilde (1854-1900)

JACK.

Yes, I know it is. But supposing it was something else? Do you mean to say you couldn't love me then?

GWENDOLEN.

[**Glibly**①.] Ah! that is clearly a metaphysical speculation, and like most metaphysical speculations has very little reference at all to the actual facts of real life, as we know them.

JACK.

Personally, darling, to speak quite candidly, I don't much care about the name of Ernest... I don't think the name suits me at all.

GWENDOLEN.

It suits you perfectly. It is a divine name. It has a music of its own. It produces vibrations.

JACK.

Well, really, Gwendolen, I must say that I think there are lots of other much nicer names. I think Jack, for instance, a charming name.

GWENDOLEN.

Jack?... No, there is very little music in the name Jack, if any at all, indeed. It does not thrill. It produces absolutely no vibrations... I have known several Jacks, and they all, without exception, were more than usually plain. Besides, Jack is a notorious domesticity for John! And I pity any woman who is married to a man called John. She would probably never be allowed to know the **entrancing**② pleasure of a single moment's solitude. The only really safe name is Ernest.

JACK.

Gwendolen, I must get christened at once—I mean we must get married at once. There is no time to be lost.

GWENDOLEN.

Married, Mr. Worthing?

---

① **Glibly**: persuasively, but with little thought and sincerity.
② **entrancing**: fascinating, enchanting.

JACK.

[Astounded.] Well... surely. You know that I love you, and you led me to believe, Miss Fairfax, that you were not absolutely indifferent to me.

GWENDOLEN.

I adore you. But you haven't proposed to me yet. Nothing has been said at all about marriage. The subject has not even been touched on.

JACK.

Well... may I propose to you now?

GWENDOLEN.

I think it would be an admirable opportunity. And to spare you any possible disappointment, Mr. Worthing, I think it only fair to tell you quite frankly before-hand that I am fully determined to accept you.

JACK.

Gwendolen!

GWENDOLEN.

Yes, Mr. Worthing, what have you got to say to me?

JACK.

You know what I have got to say to you.

GWENDOLEN.

Yes, but you don't say it.

JACK.

Gwendolen, will you marry me? [Goes on his knees.]

GWENDOLEN.

Of course I will, darling. How long you have been about it! I am afraid you have had very little experience in how to propose.

JACK.

My own one, I have never loved any one in the world but you.

Unit 16 Oscar Wilde (1854-1900)

GWENDOLEN.

Yes, but men often propose for practice. I know my brother Gerald does. All my girl-friends tell me so. What wonderfully blue eyes you have, Ernest! They are quite, quite, blue. I hope you will always look at me just like that, especially when there are other people present. [Enter Lady Bracknell.]

LADY BRACKNELL.

Mr. Worthing! Rise, sir, from this **semi-recumbent**① posture. It is most **indecorous**②.

GWENDOLEN.

Mamma! [He tries to rise; she restrains him.] I must beg you to retire. This is no place for you. Besides, Mr. Worthing has not quite finished yet.

LADY BRACKNELL.

Finished what, may I ask?

GWENDOLEN.

I am engaged to Mr. Worthing, mamma. [They rise together.]

LADY BRACKNELL.

Pardon me, you are not engaged to any one. When you do become engaged to some one, I, or your father, should his health permit him, will inform you of the fact. An engagement should come on a young girl as a surprise, pleasant or unpleasant, as the case may be. It is hardly a matter that she could be allowed to arrange for herself... And now I have a few questions to put to you, Mr. Worthing. While I am making these inquiries, you, Gwendolen, will wait for me below in the carriage.

GWENDOLEN.

[Reproachfully.] Mamma!

LADY BRACKNELL.

In the carriage, Gwendolen! [Gwendolen goes to the door. She and Jack blow kisses to each other behind Lady Bracknell's back. Lady Bracknell looks vaguely about as if she could

---

① **semi-recumbent**: leaning against the ground.
② **indecorous**: socially unacceptable.

not understand what the noise was. Finally turns round.] Gwendolen, the carriage!

GWENDOLEN.
Yes, mamma. [Goes out, looking back at Jack.]

LADY BRACKNELL.
[Sitting down.] You can take a seat, Mr. Worthing.
[Looks in her pocket for note-book and pencil.]

JACK.
Thank you, Lady Bracknell, I prefer standing.

LADY BRACKNELL.
[Pencil and note-book in hand.] I feel bound to tell you that you are not down on my list of eligible young men, although I have the same list as the dear Duchess of Bolton has. We work together, in fact. However, I am quite ready to enter your name, should your answers be what a really affectionate mother requires. Do you smoke?

JACK.
Well, yes, I must admit I smoke.

LADY BRACKNELL.
I am glad to hear it. A man should always have an occupation of some kind. There are far too many idle men in London as it is. How old are you?

JACK.
Twenty-nine.

LADY BRACKNELL.
A very good age to be married at. I have always been of opinion that a man who desires to get married should know either everything or nothing. Which do you know?

JACK.
[After some hesitation.] I know nothing, Lady Bracknell.

LADY BRACKNELL.
I am pleased to hear it. I do not approve of anything that tampers with natural ignorance.

Unit 16 Oscar Wilde (1854-1900)

Ignorance is like a delicate exotic fruit; touch it and the bloom is gone. The whole theory of modern education is radically unsound. Fortunately in England, at any rate, education produces no effect whatsoever. If it did, it would prove a serious danger to the upper classes, and probably lead to acts of violence in **Grosvenor Square**①. What is your income?

JACK.

Between seven and eight thousand a year.

LADY BRACKNELL.

[Makes a note in her book.] In land, or in investments?

JACK.

In investments, chiefly.

LADY BRACKNELL.

That is satisfactory. What between the duties expected of one during one's lifetime, and the duties exacted from one after one's death, land has ceased to be either a profit or a pleasure. It gives one position, and prevents one from keeping it up. That's all that can be said about land.

JACK.

I have a country house with some land, of course, attached to it, about fifteen hundred acres, I believe; but I don't depend on that for my real income. In fact, as far as I can make out, the **poachers**② are the only people who make anything out of it.

LADY BRACKNELL.

A country house! How many bedrooms? Well, that point can be cleared up afterwards. You have a town house, I hope? A girl with a simple, unspoiled nature, like Gwendolen, could hardly be expected to reside in the country.

JACK.

Well, I own a house in Belgrave Square, but it is let by the year to Lady Bloxham. Of course, I can get it back whenever I like, at six months' notice.

---

① **Grosvenor Square**: a luxury and aristocratic square located at the heart of London.
② **poachers**: *pl.* of **poacher**, illegal hunter or fisher.

LADY BRACKNELL.
Lady Bloxham? I don't know her.

JACK.
Oh, she goes about very little. She is a lady considerably advanced in years.

LADY BRACKNELL.
Ah, nowadays that is no guarantee of respectability of character. What number in Belgrave Square?

JACK.
149.

LADY BRACKNELL.
[Shaking her head.] The unfashionable side. I thought there was something. However, that could easily be altered.

JACK.
Do you mean the fashion, or the side?

LADY BRACKNELL.
[Sternly.] Both, if necessary, I presume. What are your politics?

JACK.
Well, I am afraid I really have none. I am a **Liberal Unionist**[①].

LADY BRACKNELL.
Oh, they count as Tories. They dine with us. Or come in the evening, at any rate. Now to minor matters. Are your parents living?

JACK.
I have lost both my parents.
LADY BRACKNELL.
To lose one parent, Mr. Worthing, may be regarded as a misfortune; to lose both looks

---

① **Liberal Unionist**: member of a British political party which deviated from the liberal and later associated with the conservative.

like carelessness. Who was your father? He was evidently a man of some wealth. Was he born in what the Radical papers call the purple of commerce, or did he rise from the ranks of the aristocracy?

JACK.

I am afraid I really don't know. The fact is, Lady Bracknell, I said I had lost my parents. It would be nearer the truth to say that my parents seem to have lost me... I don't actually know who I am by birth. I was... well, I was found.

LADY BRACKNELL.

Found!

JACK.

The late Mr. Thomas Cardew, an old gentleman of a very charitable and kindly **disposition**①, found me, and gave me the name of Worthing, because he happened to have a first-class ticket for Worthing in his pocket at the time. Worthing is a place in Sussex. It is a seaside resort.

LADY BRACKNELL.

Where did the charitable gentleman who had a first-class ticket for this seaside resort find you?

JACK.

[Gravely.] In a hand-bag.

LADY BRACKNELL.

A hand-bag?

JACK.

[Very seriously.] Yes, Lady Bracknell. I was in a hand-bag—a somewhat large, black leather hand-bag, with handles to it—an ordinary hand-bag in fact.

LADY BRACKNELL.

In what locality did this Mr. James, or Thomas, Cardew come across this ordinary hand-bag?

---

① **disposition**: temperament, nature.

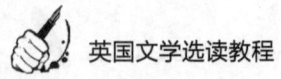

JACK.

In the cloak-room at Victoria Station. It was given to him in mistake for his own.

LADY BRACKNELL.

The cloak-room at Victoria Station?

JACK.

Yes. The Brighton line.

LADY BRACKNELL.

The line is **immaterial**①. Mr. Worthing, I confess I feel somewhat bewildered by what you have just told me. To be born, or at any rate bred, in a hand-bag, whether it had handles or not, seems to me to display a contempt for the ordinary decencies of family life that reminds one of the worst **excesses**② of the French Revolution. And I presume you know what that unfortunate movement led to? As for the particular locality in which the hand-bag was found, a cloak-room at a railway station might serve to conceal a social **indiscretion**③—has probably, indeed, been used for that purpose before now—but it could hardly be regarded as an assured basis for a recognised position in good society.

JACK.

May I ask you then what you would advise me to do? I need hardly say I would do anything in the world to ensure Gwendolen's happiness.

LADY BRACKNELL.

I would strongly advise you, Mr. Worthing, to try and acquire some relations as soon as possible, and to make a definite effort to produce at any rate one parent, of either sex, before the season is quite over.

JACK.

Well, I don't see how I could possibly manage to do that. I can produce the hand-bag at any moment. It is in my dressing-room at home. I really think that should satisfy you, Lady Bracknell.

---

① **immaterial**: irrelevant, unimportant.
② **excesses**: *pl.* of **excess**, immoderate, overdone behaviors.
③ **indiscretion**: misdeed, wrongdoing.

Unit 16 Oscar Wilde (1854-1900)

LADY BRACKNELL.

Me, sir! What has it to do with me? You can hardly imagine that I and Lord Bracknell would dream of allowing our only daughter—a girl brought up with the utmost care—to marry into a cloak-room, and form an alliance with a parcel? Good morning, Mr. Worthing!

[Lady Bracknell sweeps out in majestic indignation.]

Exercise

I. Word Matching

Directions: Please choose the most appropriate ones from the given words to explain the original boldfaced words in the following lines.

A. **blankly**	B. **decidedly**	C. **resonance**	D. **anger**
E. **flawed**	F. **infamous**	G. **entitled**	H. **uninterested**

1. For me you have always had an irresistible fascination. Even before I met you I was far from **indifferent** to you.

2. It suits you perfectly. It is a divine name. It has a music of its own. It produces **vibrations**.

3. Besides, Jack is a **notorious** domesticity for John! And I pity any woman who is married to a man called John.

4. Lady Bracknell looks **vaguely** about as if she could not understand what the noise was.

5. I feel bound to tell you that you are not down on my list of **eligible** young men.

6. The whole theory of modern education is radically **unsound**.

7. Lady Bracknell sweeps out in majestic **indignation**.

II. English-Chinese Translation

Directions: Please translate the following classic dicta from English into Chinese.

1. I do not approve of anything that tampers with natural ignorance. Ignorance is like a delicate exotic fruit; touch it and the bloom is gone.

—*The Importance of Being Earnest*

2. The truth is rarely pure and never simple.

—*The Importance of Being Earnest*

3. You will always be fond of me. I represent to you all the sins you never had the courage to commit.

—*The Picture of Dorian Gray*

4. There is only one thing in the world worse than being talked about, and that is not being talked about.

—*The Picture of Dorian Gray*

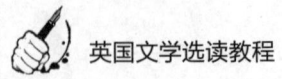

5. Death must be so beautiful. To lie in the soft brown earth, with the grasses waving above one's head, and listen to silence. To have no yesterday, and no tomorrow. To forget time, to forgive life, to be at peace.

—*The Canterville Ghost*

III. Term Defining

Directions: *Please explain the following literary terms based on The Importance of Being Earnest.*

1. comic effect
2. symbol
3. witticism

IV. Content-Based Questions

Directions: *Please give a concise and adequate answer to the following questions related to Text A.*

1. Why, according to Gwendolen, had Jack always had an irresistible fascination for her?
2. Lady Bracknell told Jack that "a man who desires to get married should know either everything or nothing", and asked him which one he was. What answer did Lady Bracknell prefer? Why?
3. What information from Jack made Lady Bracknell feel somewhat bewildered? And what advice did she give to Jack in return?

V. Discussion Question

The character Lady Bracknell in this excerpt manifests her witty personality and thereby creates a lot of humorous effects. How do you like this character? Discuss it with your partner and try to analyze how these effects are achieved in the conversation between Lady Bracknell and Jack.

VI. Essay Question

According to Lady Bracknell, Jack's family background seemed to "display a contempt for the ordinary decencies of family life", and she took a step further to suggest that "it could hardly be regarded as an assured basis for a recognized position in good society". Do you think the discrimination generated from people's family origin is a severe problem in today's society? Write a 200-word essay on your reflection on Lady Bracknell's attitude toward Jack in this regard and observation of some related social phenomena.

Self-Improving Reading

The Picture of Dorian Gray by Oscar Wilde
The Nightingale and the Rose by Oscar Wilde

图书在版编目(CIP)数据

英国文学选读教程 / 邵建宇主编；李烨辉副主编. -- 北京：中国传媒大学出版社, 2025. 3.
ISBN 978-7-5657-3828-9

Ⅰ. H319.37

中国国家版本馆CIP数据核字第2025DF2590号

英国文学选读教程
YINGGUO WENXUE XUANDU JIAOCHENG

主　　编	邵建宇
副 主 编	李烨辉
策划编辑	曾婧娴
责任编辑	曾婧娴
特约编辑	王玉凤
责任印制	李志鹏
封面设计	拓美设计
出版发行	中国传媒大学出版社
社　　址	北京市朝阳区定福庄东街1号　　邮　编 100024
电　　话	86-10-65450528　65450532　　传　真 65779405
网　　址	http://cucp.cuc.edu.cn
经　　销	全国新华书店
印　　刷	艺堂印刷（天津）有限公司
开　　本	787mm×1092mm　1/16
印　　张	15.5
字　　数	446千字
版　　次	2025年3月第1版
印　　次	2025年3月第1次印刷
书　　号	ISBN 978-7-5657-3828-9　　定　价 59.00元

本社法律顾问：北京嘉润律师事务所　　郭建平